# EUROPEAN INTEGRATION AND RURAL DEVELOPMENT

# Perspectives on Rural Policy and Planning

Series Editors:
**Andrew Gilg**, University of Exeter and University of Gloucestershire, UK
**Henry Buller**, University of Exeter, UK
**Owen Furuseth**, University of North Carolina, USA
**Mark Lapping**, University of South Maine, USA

*Other titles in the series*

**Rural Change in Australia**
**Population, Economy, Environment**
Edited by Rae Dufty-Jones and John Connell
ISBN 978 1 4094 5204 1

**Keeping it in the Family**
**International Perspectives on Succession and**
**Retirement on Family Farms**
Edited by Matt Lobley, John Baker and Ian Whitehead
ISBN 978 1 4094 0995 3

**Rural Revival?**
**Place Marketing, Tree Change and Regional Migration in Australia**
John Connell and Phil McManus
ISBN 978 1 4094 2471 0

**Rural Housing, Exurbanization, and Amenity-Driven Development**
**Contrasting the 'Haves' and the 'Have Nots'**
Edited by David Marcouiller, Mark Lapping and Owen Furuseth
ISBN 978 0 7546 7050 6

**Rural Policing and Policing the Rural**
**A Constable Countryside?**
Edited by Rob I. Mawby and Richard Yarwood
ISBN 978 0 7546 7473 3

# European Integration and Rural Development

## Actors, Institutions and Power

MICHAEL KULL
*MTT Agrifood Research Finland and*
*Tallinn University of Technology, Estonia*

Routledge
Taylor & Francis Group

LONDON AND NEW YORK

First published 2014 by Ashgate Publishing

2 Park Square, Milton Park, Abingdon, Oxfordshire OX14 4RN
711 Third Avenue, New York, NY 10017

*Routledge is an imprint of the Taylor & Francis Group, an informa business*

First issued in paperback 2018

**British Library Cataloguing in Publication Data**
A catalogue record for this book is available from the British Library

**The Library of Congress has cataloged the printed edition as follows:**
Kull, Michael.
    European integration and rural development : actors, institutions and power / by Michael Kull.
        pages cm. -- (Perspectives on rural policy and planning)
        Includes bibliographical references and index.
        ISBN 978-1-4094-6854-7 (hardback)
1. Rural development--European Union countries. 2. L.E.A.D.E.R. (Program)
3. Public-private sector cooperation--European Union countries. I. Title.
        HN380.Z9C6485 2014
        307.1'412094--dc23

                                                                                    2014006621


ISBN 978-1-4094-6854-7 (hbk)
ISBN 978-1-138-54655-4 (pbk)

# Contents

# List of Figures

# List of Tables

# Acknowledgements

Having grown up in the small village of Kaiserwinkel in rural Niedersachsen, and having experienced some of the recent structural transformations in rural areas when living at Echle Farm in the village of Prinzbach in Baden-Württemberg and working on this book – for me the problems, hopes and wishes of the people living in rural Europe have never been far away or marginal.

In addition to this socialisation and the 'village boy's' own observations of these rural trends, there are, of course, many people who played a fundamental role on my journey towards becoming a critical observer of transformations and power relations. This means a critical observer of the status of local level actors and the rural in the EU and in different parts of the globe. Above all, I am deeply indebted to Professor Dr Niilo Kauppi, who provided me with the necessary tools needed to start this journey as a young PhD student and also to continue after that. Furthermore, I would like to thank Niilo for his friendship and care.

Prof. Kauppi, Prof. Dr Ian Bache and Prof. Dr Aimo Ryynänen provided me with very valuable comments during the writing of this book. Likewise, my reviewer at Ashgate contributed to a further sharpening of the focus and storyline. I also very much appreciated collaborating on this project with Elaine, Katy, Margaret and Val from Ashgate.

Without my colleagues and friends at MTT Agrifood Research Finland, at the Centre and Network for European Studies, and the Department of Political Science of the University of Helsinki, as well as at the Ragnar Nurkse School of Tallinn University of Technology, surviving in academia would have been much, much harder, if not impossible. Critical discussions – which also slow down the pace – and looking into new adventures will be highly appreciated in the future too. Thank you for sharing the enthusiasm!

In relation to this, I would like to express my gratitude to Dr Stamatios Christopoulos, Prof. Dr Wolfgang Drechsler, Prof. Dr Rainer Kattel, Prof. Dr Pekka Kettunen, Prof. Dr Sulev Mäeltsemees, Prof. Dr Jyrki Niemi, Dr Jarkko Pyysiäinen, Prof. Dr Hilkka Vihinen, Prof. Dr Henri Vogt, Dr Olli Wuori, and Dr Teija Tiilikainen for creating a magnificent working environment and for their help in times when help was much appreciated.

In the lectures and seminars that I have given in Helsinki, Tallinn, Strasbourg and other parts of the EU and beyond, I have had the privilege to gain a great number of important new insights from brilliant young students.

Many, many thanks go to all the people in Finnish and German Local Action Groups and to the public authorities, who took the time to fill out my questionnaire and who gave me an interview. Prof. Dr Eero Uusitalo was one of them and with his critical and sharp analytical skills and tongue he continues to be an inspiration.

Diese Arbeit ist meiner geliebten Frau Lilli und meinen wunderbaren Kindern Moritz, Edit und Rasmus gewidmet. Dieses Projekt wäre ohne euch nicht denkbar gewesen. Ihr habt einerseits Freiräume geschaffen, andererseits, und noch viel wichtiger, einen perfekten Rückzugsort eröffnet, in dem ich neue Energie und Stärke sammeln kann. Ihr zeigt mir täglich und immer wieder, welche Dinge im Leben wirklich wesentlich und bedeutsam sind. Vielen Dank dafür.

Finally, I would like to express my gratitude to a number of institutions, who provided me with the necessary financial resources to realise this project. In addition to funding from MTT Agrifood Research Finland, this project was partially funded by grants from the Academy of Finland (grant number 1134103), the Estonian Targeted Funding Scheme (grant number 014006) and the Finnish Rural Policy Committee (grant number TEM/3344/09.01.03/2011).

# List of Abbreviations

| | |
|---|---|
| CAP | Common Agricultural Policy |
| CoR | Committee of the Regions and Local Authorities |
| CSF | Community Support Framework |
| DG | Directorate General of the European Commission |
| DStGB | *Deutscher Städte- und Gemeindebund* (German Association of Towns and Municipalities) |
| DVNS | *Deutsche Vernetzungsstelle (DVNS)* was the German national network unit responsible and aiming at fostering networking of German LEADER+ LAGs |
| EAGGF | European Agricultural Guidance and Guarantee Fund |
| EARDF | European Agriculture and Rural Development Fund |
| EC | European Community |
| ECJ | European Court of Justice |
| ECSC | European Coal and Steel Community |
| EIB | European Investment Bank |
| ELY-Keskus | *Elinkeino, Liikenne jaYmpäristö Keskus* (Centre for Economic Development, Transport and the Environment) |
| EP | European Parliament |
| ERDF | European Regional Development Fund |
| ESF | European Social Fund |
| ETUDE | Enlarging Theoretical Understanding of Rural Development |
| EU | European Union |
| EUREGIO | Cross-border Regions in the European Union funded by the European Commission |
| FIFG | Financial Instrument for Fisheries Guidance |
| GLL | *Behörden für Geoinformation, Landentwicklung und Liegenschaften*, was a *Land* agency which was responsible for dealing with LEADER+ applications in Niedersachsen. |
| INTERREG | Community Initiative to foster interregional cooperation in the EU |
| ISPA | Instrument for Structural Policies for Pre-accession |
| JDT | Joint Decision Trap |
| LAG | Local action group |
| LEADER | *Liaison entre actions de développement de l'économie rurale* (Links between the rural economy and development actions) |

| | |
|---|---|
| LEL | *Landesanstalt für die Entwicklung der Landwirtschaft und der ländlichen Räume.* The *LEL* was an agency that was responsible for the development of the rural areas and the farming sector in the *Land* Baden-Württemberg. |
| LK | *Landkreis* (county) |
| MEP | Member of the European Parliament |
| MLG | Multi-level governance |
| MMM | *Maa- ja metsätalousministeriö* (*Ministry of Agriculture and Forestry*) |
| NGO | Nongovernmental organisation |
| NPM | New Public Management |
| OECD | Organisation for Economic Co-operation and Development |
| OMC | Open Method of Coordination |
| POMO | *Paikallisen omaehtoisuuden maaseutuohjelma* (Rural Programme for Local Initiative) |
| RECHAR | Community initiative concerning the economic conversion of coalmining areas |
| REGIS | Community initiative concerning the most remote regions |
| RESIDER | Community programme to assist the conversion of steel areas |
| RETEX | Community initiative for regions heavily dependent on the textiles and clothing sector |
| SAPARD | Special Accession Programme for Agriculture and Rural Development |
| SEA | Single European Act |
| SEM | Single European Market |
| SG | *Samtgemeinde* (joint municipal district) |
| TEC | Treaty Establishing the European Community |
| TEU | Treaty on European Union |
| ToA | Treaty of Amsterdam |
| VG | *Verwaltungsgemeinschaft* (joint community) |

# Introduction

The rural has been largely absent from scholarly debates in the context of European integration and in EU Studies. Thus, the focus of this book is quite contrary to mainstream European integration theory but very suited to examination through a combination of multi-level governance theory and structural constructivist methodology. This combined approach is also a critique of conventional, mainstream approaches dealing with European integration.

As far as the local level is concerned in general, EU integration scholars only shifted their attention to those areas at the beginning of the 1990s with the concept of multi-level governance. Multi-level governance – the main theoretical approach applied in this book – has become a widely used concept to analyse processes of EU policy-making. It was initially meant to describe the interaction of multiple actors in EU Regional Policy and structural funding. In 1993, as one of the 'pioneers' in conceptualising multi-level governance in the EU, Gary Marks (1993: 392) described the EU as 'a system of continuous negotiation among nested governments at several territorial tiers – supranational, national, regional and local'.

With the exception of scholars such as Gary Marks, who perceive and describe the EU as a system of multi-level governance,[1] theories of European integration have for a long time neglected the study of sub-national and local actors. Several studies have demonstrated the empowerment of local levels through, for instance, increased institutional representation in Brussels, such as in the Committee of the Regions, or in liaison offices set up by regions or municipalities. In addition, sub-national actors are more commonly included in implementing different EU policies, such as EU Regional Policy. Furthermore, the private sector, non-governmental organisations and interest groups gain access to policy-making processes and increasingly interact with government institutions at all levels.

---

1   When proposing the term multi-level governance, Marks (1993) focussed on sub-national government and trans-national networks. Research on the involvement of private actors, social partners and interest organisations – essential actors for many to define governance – was focussed on at a later stage, when multi-level governance was further conceptualised. For subsequent conceptualisations, see for instance, Hooghe and Marks (2001; 2003); and Bache and Flinders (2005). Kohler-Koch (2003) links EU and national governance. For a historical analysis, see Piattoni (2009). Critical perspectives are provided in Benz (2003), Jachtenfuchs and Kohler-Koch (2003a, 2003b), Kauppi (2005) and Bache, Bartle and Flinders (2012).

In the multi-levelled EU, the sub-national and local levels are part of a polity that is characterised by a 'classical' multi-level structure of directly and indirectly legitimised institutions situated at the EU level, the member-state level and the sub-national level. In addition, new forms of governance, that is formal or informal networks or functional units of cooperation, have been set up to foster efficiency and democracy in policy-making. As will be seen in this book, the status of sub-national and local levels in those structures is very ambivalent, as are their strategies to cope with integration.

As to the academic debate in the two countries that are central to the empirical parts of this book, in 1996 the German political scientists Jachtenfuchs and Kohler-Koch (1996a and 1996b) provided a thorough analysis of the process of European integration and the ongoing arrival of new actors and their involvement in governance. What they termed *Regieren im Mehrebensystem* was in the years to follow to become a research topic of growing interest, as numerous publications demonstrate. In Finland, the multi-level governance approach needed another decade to make it into the academic debate on European integration. A translation of multi-level governance, which became a more generally used term in recent years, is '*monitasohallinta*'.

Scholars working with the concept of multi-level governance have adopted and influenced theoretical tools used in other disciplines. Of importance here are political science and administrative sciences. Furthermore, the terminology used is not unknown to scholars of local-government studies, public policies and international relations. Important is Lenschow's (2005: 56, cf. Kohler-Koch and Rittberger 2006: 38) claim that multi-level governance being introduced to the field of EU studies signified 'the end of the separate treatment of European and national politics'.

The concept of multi-level governance is dynamic, open for further theoretical debate and invites deeper conceptualisation. According to Benz, the concept is 'very imprecise and only gives a direction for analysis. Clear statements as to functionality and momentum within non-hierarchical structures are seldom found'.[2] Multi-level governance has also been characterised as remaining 'little more than a proto-concept in need of refinement' (Bache, Bartle and Flinders 2012: 1). Consequently, Grande (2000: 13) argues to further advance it 'from a descriptive metaphor to a theoretical concept' and to 'answer three questions: firstly, how do we precisely comprehend a system of multi-level governance; secondly, what distinguishes the European system of multi-level governance from other institutional forms of governance, and thirdly, what specific requirements on governance in Europe result from the multi-level structure'.[3] Approaching those three questions the researcher may, as Jachtenfuchs (2000) suggests, shift the

---

2　Benz, cf. E. Grande (2000: 13). The text is in German, and the translation done by the author of this book.

3　The text is in German, and the translation done by the author of this book.

research focus onto micro-analyses in order to foster a better understanding of the European multi-level governance system.

For this book this means that the research focus is not only on certain policy fields but also on sub-fields. More precisely the book not only looks at EU Structural Funds or the Common Agricultural Policy but also at the LEADER+[4] Community Initiative as being part of the EU's cohesion strategy and financed by the structural funds. Of particular interest is the status of local-level actors in policy-making and the implementation of these policies that aim at improving the economic situation in Europe's countryside. The integration of Europe's rural areas and its local and sub-national levels into the EU seen through the eyes of Europeans lies at the heart of this study.

Rural areas and the local level are very heterogeneous. Part of the multi-levelled EU, they include the public sector in addition to private and social actors. Both the impact of European integration and local-level response are ambivalent. There are a number of questions and observations that are worth considering in this context:

1. The public sector develops and takes part in new inter-institutional relations. Public administration seeks the involvement of private and social partners in policy-making and implementation. What is the status of these new actors in multi-level governance?
2. Horizontal cooperation between the public and private sector as well as the inclusion of social partners has been fostered by different EU policies, such as Regional Policy, structural funding, or LEADER. What is the position of higher levels of government within new governance units, especially *vis-à-vis* the local level?
3. The institutional structures of each member state determine the degree of involvement of non-public actors. Furthermore, looking at individuals positioned in the different institutions makes much sense in order to explain the distribution of power in multi-level governance and rural policy.

To deal with these questions and observations, studies on multi-level governance have to focus both on the impacts on the public sector and additionally on the ability of new actors, such as local residents, social actors and interest groups, to participate in new units of governance. But there are several problems that occur in this respect:

---

4 LEADER stands for '*Liaison Entre Actions de Développement de l'Économie Rurale*', which means 'Links between the rural economy and development actions'. LEADER stands at the core of the empirical studies outlined in this book. LEADER was a Community initiative sponsored by the EU's structural funds and was financed by the Guidance Section of the European Agricultural Guidance and Guarantee Fund (EAGGF) (see Chapter 4).

- The sub-national and local levels differ in function and degree of participation, with differences even within one member state.
- While multi-level governance is one of the few theoretical approaches to analyse the processes of EU integration by focussing on the sub-national and local level, it has some methodological shortcomings. It underestimates the role of the public sector and government institutions located at higher levels and their ability to preserve their powerful positions in the EU multi-level game. These actors continue to shape, construct and reconstruct policy fields, particularly those that effect rural areas.
- The scholarly discourse is changing its focus from government to governance, focussing on new forms of network-type interactions but tending to neglect the impact on directly legitimised institutions.

In other words, while multi-level governance was the first concept to scrutinise the position of local levels of public administration and other local actors within the EU polity, it is too optimistic in the degree of influence it ascribes to local levels, particularly as far as the rural is concerned. Thus, combining multi-level governance with other concepts, such as structural constructivism, an approach inspired by the work of French political sociologist Pierre Bourdieu, makes sense and reveals some of the hidden aspects of EU integration. This combination is particularly useful if one perceives the EU as a 'more or less structured multipolar political field where supranational, intergovernmental, national, and regional public, semi-public, and private institutions share power' and are engaged in processes to manifest or improve their position in the struggle for influence and power (Kauppi 2002: 19). Decision-making and implementation of the Community Initiative LEADER+ – within the empirical focus of the book – is multi-levelled in nature. A variety of public and private actors situated at several levels are potentially included in governing this policy. LEADER is embedded in the institutional structures of the member states and, implemented by different actors positioned in those institutions, is subject to different interest constellations and strategies and driven by the will to receive optimal outcomes and to manifest the influence and power of individuals.

**Structure of the Book**

The book contains 11 chapters along with an Introduction and Conclusion. Chapter 1 reflects on different European integration theories that have contributed to the development of current approaches for analysing European integration. The concept of multi-level governance as the conceptual framework of this book is one of them.

Early theories of European integration, such as federalism, functionalism and transactionalism, all had a normative implication and were seeking answers as to how post-WWII Europe should be governed and what position the nation states should occupy in the politico-administrative architecture of Europe. From the 1960s onwards European integration theories tried to explain the outcomes of integration and why integration takes place (e.g. Wiener and Diez 2004, 2009). Neofunctionalists, for instance, perceived (European) integration as a process and a continuum in which supranational institutions are set up to realise the demands of different societal actors and for an increasing number of policy-fields. Opposed to other theories, state-centrist approaches to European integration, such as liberal intergovernmentalism, see the state dominating the institutional structures and decision-making procedures in the EC and EU. From the 1980s onwards, the focus shifted to the analysis of governance and fundamental questions such as 'what kind of political system is the EU?', 'how can political processes within the EU be described?' or they touched on technical issues, such as 'how does the EU's regulatory policy work?' (Wiener and Diez 2004: 7).

There were a number of important trends that developed during the 1990s and continue to the present day. One example is the emerging share of competence not only between nation states and the EU but also between sub-national levels and the EU or within the member states as such. At the same time and since the 1990s, older 'grand theories' such as federalism, functionalism or neofunctionalism have had to compete with new mid-range theories and concepts, such as social constructivism or multi-level governance and structural constructivism which are discussed in the following chapter.

Chapter 2 discusses multi-level governance and structural constructivism. It also critiques mainstream European integration theory and proposes its replacement with multi-level governance theory and structural constructivist methodology. Chapter 2 also sets the scene for the discussion of empirical findings in the subsequent chapters of the book.

The concept which mainly inspired this book, multi-level governance, appeared under this label in 1993/1994. Scholars of multi-level governance (e.g. Benz and Eberlein 1999; Blank, Hooghe and Marks 1996; Enderlein, Wälti and Zürn 2010; Grande and Jachtenfuchs 2000; Hooghe and Marks 2003; Jachtenfuchs and Kohler-Koch 2003a; Marks 1993, 1996; Piattoni 2009) argue that some decisive factors that determine sub-national involvement – but also the shifting-back of tasks to the supranational level – are policy fields as such, the advancement of the project in question as well as the institutional setting and administrative structure of the member states.

Structural constructivism, an approach inspired by the work of Bourdieu, reveals some of the hidden aspects of EU integration. Structural constructivist approaches, such as the one developed by Kauppi (2005) are concerned with 'hard' facts in analysing the distribution of political power and inequalities in the availability of social resources. Part of the sociological turn in EU studies, structural constructivism is well known in France, but not so much in Anglo-Saxon political science. In their work, structural constructivists study how and through what mechanisms and players the EU is made and shaped in every-day interactions. Of central concern is the status and potential power of actors – embedded in different policy-making structures – in the construction of the European political space. The power potential of actors is, according to structural constructivists, conditioned and constrained by material and symbolic structures and their access to resources such as economic (e.g. EU funding) or social ones (e.g. education, access to networks). The 'motives, schemes of perception and action with which actors interpret and shape their social environment' (Mérand 2011: 180) are within the focus of structural constructivist research and of this book. Due to some shortcomings in the multi-level governance approach, research methods applied in structural constructivist research are applied in the empirical analysis.[5]

A perspective combining concepts and methodologies from both structural constructivism and multi-level governance, as applied in this book, aims at contributing to a more accurate picture of multi-level interaction in rural policy. Through this combined approach, one can identify problems and mistakes that have been made and which should be avoided in the future in rural 'multi-level governance as practice' (Bache, Bartle and Flinders 2012: 1). At the same time, empirical findings gained through a combined research strategy can contribute to theorising about European integration and additionally also feed back to our 'conventional knowledge and wisdom' about 'multi-level governance as theory'.

Chapter 3 briefly reviews earlier studies of LEADER. It also introduces actors, institutions and power structures through a discussion of the historical and institutional transformations of the EU's structural funds in general and the Community Initiative LEADER+ in particular. Chapter 3 provides the reader with relevant information about the emergence of LEADER and country specific information from all EU member states. It is based on an intensive study of policy documents and also contains interview material. Policy makers and stakeholders critically follow the reader through the construction and transformation of LEADER.

The focus on Finland and Germany allows for an assessment of the relative importance of unitary versus federal structures in shaping the governance of rural policy. Furthermore, Finland is the most rural member state in the EU and one that is also perceived as conducting a very successful rural policy through the involvement and space for intervention given to local residents and civil society. While LEADER+ offered considerable influence at local levels and according to the Commission was to 'play (an) important role in improving governance and mobilising the endogenous development potential of rural areas',[6] and to that end required the inclusion of non-public actors from multiple levels of governance, a closer look reveals that much power remained with administrative units located at higher levels. As far as Finland is concerned, the central state level was engaged in

---

5    On the research methods applied in this book, such as structured and unstructured interviews, surveys or analyses of mid-term evaluations, see Kauppi (2005: 195–196). On research methods applied and concepts used in structural constructivist research, see Kauppi (2005: 56–57).

6    See Commission of the European Communities (2005: 7).

bargaining over the overall financial framework of the EU's budget as well as the proportions for the Common Agricultural Policy, Regional Policy, the Structural Funds and LEADER. Furthermore, the Ministry of Agriculture and Forestry was the administrative and financing authority in the Finnish LEADER+ programme. In the Federal Republic of Germany, there was not a single national LEADER+ programme. Instead, all the *Länder*[7] had set up their own programmes. This does not mean that the federal level was de-coupled from this policy field. In negotiating the overall budget for the Structural Funds and the Common Agricultural Policy, the federal level continues to be in a very powerful position.

Chapter 4 presents the research approach and methodology applied for the study of the status of local actors in the Community Initiative LEADER+. Empirical data was first gathered through exploratory, unstructured interviews and by visiting projects financed and implemented by so-called local action groups (LAGs). After that a survey among Finnish and German LAGs was carried out. The survey was supplemented and completed by interviewing LAG members, LAG managers, Finnish and German civil servants from decision-making and managing authorities and from the EU Commission.

Chapters 5–11 are a detailed, or 'thick', analysis critically discussing specific characteristics, advantages and shortcomings of rural policy. In the field of rural policy, the Community Initiative LEADER was supposed to become a true bottom-up approach for endogenous rural development and a model for new governance in the EU. LEADER is – by intention and design – a test ground for a policy that engages all potential actors in a given field to utilise their knowledge and expertise. In order to comprehend the challenges and opportunities of rural-development policy, it is necessary to focus on the different layers of governance and identify good practices as well as malfunctions. The challenges and opportunities are context dependent and the future of rural-development policies, their shape and institutional configuration depend on reforms put in place at all levels of governance. Chapters 5–11 demonstrate how actors are embedded in the institutions and power structures in place in rural Europe and that emerged through the implementation of the EU's Community Initiative LEADER+.

Patterns of interaction among different actors from all the levels involved in the EU's Community Initiative LEADER+ are discussed. The empirical chapters show how these actors construct and shape EU co-financed rural policy, especially local actors organised in the LAGs. This includes a reflection on who these actors are in terms of functional background, education or gender. Intra-institutional relations within LAGs are examined, in order to find out who the most influential and powerful actors within them are and why. It will be seen that network-type relations (both open and closed) are characteristics of this policy field. It is shown how local actors organised in the LAGs cooperated with other administrative units within the LEADER+ administrative chain. Another crucial point of investigation was the interaction of public and private actors not taking part in the LAG or the

---

7    This is with the exception of the city-states Berlin, Hamburg and Bremen.

LEADER+ programme, especially local residents. Do LAGs have the potential to attract and mobilise these actors or even bring the EU closer to them?

Overall, the mobilisation of local residents and the 'bringing together' of actors from the local area with different social and institutional backgrounds to become an active part of rural policy has been more successful in Finland than in Germany and other EU member states. Despite the fact that the governments of the member states agreed on the empowerment of EU institutions and conceded more influence to the local level, they continue to control even those policy fields which provide easy access for new actors. Top-down approaches are not uncommon in EU rural-development policy. Yet, solutions imposed from above, without relying on contextual knowledge to be transposed into area-based solutions, are ill-suited to improve the socio-economic situation of rural Europe. These results and arguments are only possible and convincingly made when approaching this field seen 'through the eyes of the local actors' and by giving space to actors from all administrative levels engaged in LEADER to outline their perception of this policy.

By and large, EU integration has changed the formal and informal inter-institutional relations linking different levels of government. The third sector including non-governmental institutions and interest groups has gained access to policy-making processes and has increasingly interacted with government institutions at all levels of public administration. These developments have not necessarily resulted in the empowering of the local level. We can still observe differences among the member states and even within them. Access to decision-making centres and participation in the framing of the rules of the game are conditioned by the local actors' resources and subject to an unequal distribution of power.

As far as the Community Initiative LEADER+ is concerned, this policy has created a space for multi-level interaction and local-level involvement in rural Europe. This space enabled highly motivated people to actively contribute to the improvement of the quality of life and economy in Europe's countryside. However, their actions have also been dependent on national and local power structures and restricted by national administrative practices, implementation approaches and cultures.

# Chapter 1

# Theories and Concepts of European Integration

To understand EU policies from a multi-level governance perspective one needs to understand the context in which these policies were shaped. As Jordan (2001: 196–197) put it,

> the big, constitutive decisions (Pollack 1994) studied by state-centric theorists are important because they determine the EU's operating framework of laws, policies and norms within which multi-level governance takes place. Consequently, multi-level governance needs to be viewed in the context of older, 'macro' theories of the EU.

Therefore, and as a first step, this book briefly reviews some of those theories that also contributed – in one way or another – to the emergence of multi-level governance.

Analysing European integration theory, four phenomena stand out. First, since the 1990s older 'grand theories' such as federalism, functionalism or neofunctionalism have had to compete with new mid-range theories and concepts, such as multi-level governance, social constructivism or structural constructivism. These are no longer necessarily focussed on questions such as why member states integrate, what role supranational institutions play or what form the 'end-product' will or should have. Instead scholars seek to answer questions such as how integration is realised, e.g. in terms of implementing EU policies, what impact European integration had on the identity of Europeans, who is empowered to participate in supranational-national-sub-national interaction and what consequences this has on the status of the actors involved.

Secondly, and related to the first phenomenon, there is a trend from prediction to description. Scholars shift their focus onto particular policy processes within the EU polity instead of trying to anticipate the overall result of a successful integration process.

Thirdly, the descriptive approach narrows the focus of analysis and fosters specialisation. Increasingly, policy sectors and programmes can only be assessed after first having accumulated a great deal of technical expertise. This might pose problems in terms of communicating with other 'schools' of thought. However, due to these scholars' more or less distinct ability to reflect on their own theoretical impasse, positions are no longer as conflicting as they used to be. As Jachtenfuchs and Kohler-Koch (2003b: 11) argue, the fierce competition of the 1960s is over.

The fourth phenomenon is important for the empirical focus of this book. The conventional theories, such as neofunctionalism and liberal intergovernmentalism, have neglected to include the sub-national level and especially local-level actors in their analytical frames. Those approaches can be characterised as being unable or unwilling to cover developments that are not central to their theoretical focus but which have nevertheless emerged in reality – developments that increased the role of the local level in EU public policies and governance. While these approaches have quite sophisticated theoretical foundations but have had and continue to have problems in explaining real-life developments, especially after the Maastricht and Lisbon Treaties empowered sub-national actors. In this connection, these mainstream theories of European integration can be reproached for neglecting one key systemic function within the present EU polity: cooperation and its most prominent form, networks (Jachtenfuchs and Kohler-Koch 2003b: 11).

The concept of multi-level governance is different in this respect. It is one of the few theoretical approaches to analyse the processes of EU integration by considering these neglected issues and by focussing on the sub-national and local levels. However, it has some methodological shortcomings. It underestimates or misperceives the role of higher levels of the public-sector and government institutions above the local level and their strategies to preserve their position in the EU multi-level polity. It also overestimates the empowerment of sub-national actors. For some scholars it is a middle-range theory others perceive it as no more than a description of contemporary change in the EU and accuse it of being too descriptive in nature and of being built on or still remaining on a weak theoretical footing (Jordan 2001; Bache et al. 2012). Thus, looking at other approaches, such as structural constructivism, in order to provide a more nuanced picture of the status of local levels of governance in the EU's multi-levelled polity, makes much sense.

Before going more deeply into the conceptualisation of multi-level governance and structural constructivism, a short overview of EU integration theories that are important for the understanding of both the historical development of EU integration and the involvement of local-level actors in the integration process is provided.

## Federalism, Functionalism and Transactionalism

Federalism, functionalism and transactionalism are theories that Chryssochoou (2001: 37–63) once called 'the formative theories' of European integration. These 'early' theories of European integration – which are most prominently linked with the names of Altiero Spinelli, David Mitrany and Karl Deutsch – have several issues in common but they also differ in a number of important positions. This section gives a short overview of all three theories.

## Federalism

One aspect that makes the evaluation and critique of federalist theory somewhat difficult is that not only is there no school of federalist theory but there is not even a 'single, coherent body of European federalist theory', as Rosamond (2000: 29) noted. Chryssochoou (2001) observed that by 1988 no less than 267 different definitions of federalism had been recorded.

One important name to be mentioned in the discussion of federalism *vis-à-vis* EU integration theory is that of Altiero Spinelli. Spinelli, born in 1907 in Rome, was one of the co-founders of the European Federalist Movement, founded in August 1943. In 1941, during their imprisonment on the island of Ventotene, Spinelli, Ernesto Rossi and Eugenio Colori (1941) wrote the *Ventotene Manifesto* on cigarette paper. Having seen the destructive nature of the Second World War, it was important for Spinelli that any restoration of the old nation-states in building the post-WWII order in Europe was resisted. Spinelli's federalism was very critical of the function and even existence of the state in post-WWII Europe. In his view (1957: 48–49), the sovereign national state 'could no longer guarantee a minimum of security and independence to their people'; it had become 'discredited and obsolete'. In Spinelli's view, national independence paired with capitalist imperialism results in fascism. His alternative for a free and united Europe was a European Federation. Similarly to Mitranian functionalism, the member states within this Federation would have to renounce their sovereignty.

Spinelli's mistrust if not rejection of the nation state, was only one among many positions. Other federalists theorising on European Integration saw statehood as either inevitable or even hoped for a federal state as the 'end-product' of integration. There is also a disagreement among federalist scholars on how to federalise the EU. Rosamond (2000: 27) distinguishes between those in favour of the construction of a federal polity at a certain point in time in an 'act of constitutional immediacy', referring to what Héraud (1968) described as a revolutionary settlement, and those in favour of a gradualist approach of federalising the EU, such as Brugmans (1948, 1969). Henri Brugmans saw the necessity of federalisation being based on a popular movement.

Carl Joachim Friedrich was a leading scholar in the field of federalism. In his view (1964), scholars researching federalism in the EC context, instead of focussing on the end-product or the constitutional design, should analyse the federalising tendencies. One example of the focus on federalising tendencies in the EU and an attempt to seek answers to the question of what a future federation might look like by comparing federal systems is Börzel and Risse's response to former German Foreign Minister Fischer's speech on the finality of European Integration.[1]

---

1 Both Fischer's speech 'From Confederacy to Federation: Thoughts on the Finality of European Integration', speech at the Humboldt University in Berlin, 12 May 2000 and Börzel and Risse (2000) have been published in Joerges, Mény and Weiler (eds) (2000).

Overall, the epistemology of federalist theory was transformed during the first two decades of the EC and beyond and was characterised by questions about the sociological interaction of people and the careful, incremental as well as rationalist institutional design. It both followed and propelled the real-life events of the integration process. Yet, there was no clear-cut school of federalists similar to those of transactionalism or functionalism.

## Functionalism

The key figure in the conceptual development of functionalism and the functionalist theory of politics was David Mitrany.[2] What Mitrany shared with Spinelli, was his very critical perception of the nation-states. He doubted that the state, its leaders and key politicians could fulfil the functional needs of its citizens. Political leaders, Mitrany argued, were motivated by holding onto and increasing their power while nationalism in the international environment is a key causal factor in the fragmentation of the world community. The 'political track', according to Mitrany (1975: 71), does not lead to 'possible universality'. Thus, the result of integration must not be a political union, since this 'by its nature and tendency ... must be nationalistic; and that as such must impede and may defeat, the great historic quest for a general system of peace and development' (Mitrany 1975: 71).

In functionalist logic, supra- and international agencies and transnational institutions will be the bodies best organised to realise public welfare and create the continuum for (economic) functional integration. According to Mitrany, these institutions need to recruit international staff who foster economic development and satisfy the functional and public welfare needs of the people. Once the results become visible, people will shift their loyalties towards the new emerging institutions and entities that have been constructed and are now shared by former enemies. At this stage of social learning conditioned by a change of attitudes, conflicts are less likely to occur than in the anarchic environment of hostile nation-states.

Although this ontology has much in common with some adherents of federalist theory, there is at least one key difference between functionalism and federalism. While federalism sees a federal state as the end-product of integration, functionalists, like Mitrany, argue that integration is a process with no end-point. Institutions are constructed, reshaped and deconstructed according to functional needs and necessities. The logic is that form follows function and function determines structure. According to functionalists, there should be no restrictions of a geographical nature. They opposed regional schemes of integration since they impose unnecessary limits upon membership and thus induce conflict.

---

2 Mitrany was born in Bucharest in Romania in 1888 and died in 1975, the same year his influential *The Functional Theory of Politics* was published. He was an influential figure in the international peace-movement-influenced social democracy and English pluralism.

*Transactionalism*

The key scholar on transactionalism, another prominent, early integration theory, which is also known as communication theory, was Karl W. Deutsch.[3] In contrast to federalism and functionalism Deutsch was not searching for a system that might overcome the nation-state but was looking for methods to tame its destructive nature. Despite his personal experiences, Deutsch had a positive image of men and believed in the possibility that war will be overcome. According to Deutsch (1972: 123) 'so many people in so many countries are becoming aware of the problem, and of the need for increasing intellectual, moral, and political efforts to deal with' war and conflict. Both increasing awareness and motivation to deal with war make it more likely to be prevented. The key in this is, according to Deutsch, communication and a change in people's attitudes. People 'learn to act together and eliminate war as a social institution'.[4] Political science, in Deutsch's view, has to help here. Deutsch considered political science a 'branch of medicine' (ibid.). According to Deutsch 'understanding and doing politics well was to prevent death and relieve suffering' (ibid.). His analyses were not restricted only to Europe or the integration of European states. Rather Deutsch was interested in the political integration of security communities and set out four 'tasks of integration':

- maintaining peace;
- attaining greater multipurpose capabilities;
- accomplishing some special tasks;
- gaining a new self-image and role identity.

In contrast to early federalists and functionalists, the national state is not an obstacle to integration. According to Deutsch, states need to be stabilised and integrated into the international state system. International integration was needed to achieve security. During the integration process, there is the potential for developing a 'no war community', where war among its partners becomes illegitimate (Deutsch 1972: 115). Social mobilisation – a concept developed by Deutsch – and communication can foster integration. According to Deutsch, state governments have an important function here. They have the potential to foster social learning, and social and economic development.

---

3   Deutsch was born in 1912 as a Sudeten German in Prague. In his thesis 'Nationalism and Social Communication' (1953) he tried to seek an answer to why the world of his youth had been destroyed by war and racism and, similar to those scholars working with the other two theories discussed above, how war and conflict can be eliminated.

4   Karl W. Deutsch: International Political Scientist 1912–1992 – Memorial Minute Adopted by The Faculty of Arts and Sciences, Harvard University available at http://www.harvardsquarelibrary.org/unitarians/deutsch.html.

*Similarities and Differences*

What federalism, functionalism and transactionalism all had in common was that they offered an alternative to the then dominant realist approaches. All were in search of ways and means to avoid conflict and war. If one looks at what the scholars of these three approaches were and are interested in, the differences are striking.

While federalists are interested in the end-product of integration and how to institutionalise it, functionalists are interested in the process of integration. Transactionalists were mostly interested in international community-building, with the EC being one case among many. While federalists were and are mainly interested in the political implications and conditions of integration, functionalists saw transformation propelled by economic forces and necessities as opposed to transactionalists who believed that sociological change, i.e. the mentality of the people, is a sufficient condition for change and integration.

Probably most important for those scholars working at the time when the theories were being developed, was the search for a theoretical explanation for aspects of European integration that could provide an alternative to the dominant, state-centric approaches originating from international relations theory.

It is also important to try to see the close connection between theory and practice. All three theories have even been criticised for their advocacy of certain causes, be it a particular institutional configuration or policy style.

However, despite all these commonalities, especially all three theories' searches for ways to render conflict between European states impossible, their basic interest in the integration process was very different. While functionalism was interested in the process of replacing territorial units with functional ones (e.g. agencies), federalism, at least a large number of its proponents, was interested in the end-product of the integration process. Transactionalism was concerned with international community building.

All three theories were influential and even served as the basis for the conceptual developments of subsequent theories of European integration. One example is neofunctionalism, which was one of the most influential integration theories.

## Neofunctionalism

Neofunctionalism was 'developed explicitly' as a challenge to the two theories of international relations that were dominant in the 1950s, namely classical state-centric realism in order 'to show that the fetishizing of power ... was far less of a law of politics' and Kantian idealism 'that saw in more international law the road to world peace' and that was, according to Ernst Haas, as 'unnecessary as it was (and is) naïve' (Haas 2004: xiv). Being 'heavily influenced' by functionalists, such as David Mitrany, neofunctionalists such as Ernst Haas or Philippe Schmitter reacted to unpredicted trends in the integration process by introducing new concepts to explain and correct the shortcomings in functionalist theory.

Neofunctionalists share with functionalists the perception of integration as a process and a continuum in which institutions were constructed to realise the demands of different societal actors. Once those relations are established and institutionalised, policy measures can 'spill-over' into other areas or policy-fields under specific conditions. The spill-over into new functions is incremental in nature. This means that functions are accumulated, and new supporters might be attracted until functions formerly in the sphere of European governments have clearly moved 'beyond the nation-state'. This is the title of a very influential book by Ernst Haas (1964) that analyses this development.

Haas's (1966: 96) definition of supranationalism is a combination of intergovernmental interaction (e.g. negotiation) with other stakeholders with different backgrounds, such as interest groups, parliaments, political parties or independent experts. In analysing the process of European integration, the core area of interest for functionalists and neofunctionalists was issues and functions, not primarily actors and institutions. In their perception, the integration process starts with the less controversial, easy-to-agree-upon policy fields and then spills over and paves the way for action in more sensitive areas. The EC and other international organisations are – in the view of neofunctionalists – institutions for the co-ordination of their nation-states' interests, in which their sovereignty is not going to be weakened, but jointly exercised together (Jachtenfuchs and Kohler-Koch 1996a: 18). These institutions propel the way towards unity in a 'pro-community direction' to ever more and new 'functional contexts' (Haas 1966: 98).

For Haas (1966: 98), the 'upgrading of common interests' is a key step in integration, or as he put it, 'their (nation-states) true contribution to the art of political integration'.

What neofunctionalists often underestimated was the fact that even when nation-states delegate certain powers to an international institution, they may also renegotiate bargains. Intergovernmentalists criticised neofunctionalists for neglecting to give sufficient consideration to the fact that national governments might invest considerable efforts in resisting further integration by assumed functional logic.

One attempt to react to this intergovernmentalist critique, to rethink and revive neofunctionalism and to conceptualise it further was made by Haas's pupil Philippe Schmitter (2004) under the heading 'neo-neofunctionalism'. But also Haas himself took a stance in this discussion. In the introduction to the 2004 re-print of *The Uniting of Europe* Haas asked and answered the question whether neofunctionalism was still relevant. According to Haas, neofunctionalism was the forerunner of constructivist theories of the study of integration processes. Haas also develops a pragmatic-constructivist ontology, part of which is an amended neofunctionalism. The ontological development from neofunctionalism via its merger with constructivism to 'neoconstructivism' is based, on the one hand, on lessons drawn from the ontologies of theories that have developed over the past two decades, such as constructivisms interested in institutions, networks or discourse, but also on reflecting the multi-level governance approach and on criticism by the rival of the old version of neofunctionalism, liberal intergovernmentalism.

Concluding the critical reflection on the theory of neofunctionalism, there are a number of positive aspects that need to be highlighted. First of all, at the time neofunctionalist ontology was developed it became a very viable alternative, even a challenge, to state-centric realism and idealism, the two dominant schools engaged with the epistemology and ontology of international relations. Second, looking at the historical development of neofunctionalism, its readiness to critically self-reflect was exceptional. Haas himself once declared the theory obsolete. Nevertheless, right up until his death he critically reflected on neofunctionalism's achievements and pitfalls by placing 'his' theory in a wider theoretical context and incorporating new concepts into neofunctionalist ontology.

Finally, neofunctionalism not only paved the way and inspired a large number of scholars to study regional integration in Europe and beyond by testing neofunctionalist methodology, it also resulted in the conceptualisation of new approaches, partly through the lessons learnt from neofunctionalism. One of these being, as Haas (2004: xii) argued, constructivism.

## State-Centric Approaches and Liberal Intergovernmentalism

Unlike functionalists and neofunctionalists, intergovernmentalists present a state-centric, rational approach to European integration. In their perception, states are key actors despite the fact that important aspects of decision-making have been shifted to the EU level. Stanley Hoffmann, Alan Milward, and Andrew Moravcsik are three influential scholars who saw the integration process from a state-centric perspective.

Hoffmann's most valuable contribution to the debate on European integration was probably his article 'Obstinate or Obsolete? The Fate of the Nation-State and the Case of Western Europe', published in 1966. Hoffmann analysed the tensions between those who resisted a supranational Europe, and who opposed moving too quickly and taking too much substance away from the nation state, and the member states of the EC 6 (Belgium, the Federal Republic of Germany, France, Italy, Luxembourg, Netherlands). There were different reasons why individual states and their leaders either resisted integration or approved, or were indifferent to it. While the central contexts were similar for all European states, one has to look, as Hoffmann suggested, at individual cases more carefully. While federalists like Spinelli had high hopes for the demise of nationalism and the replacement of the nation state by a supranational one, Hoffmann (1966: 870–872) pointed out the temporary nature of this demise and the differences between the states in post-World War II Europe.

Despite changes at the regional level with integrating further policies and further empowering supranational institutions, the nation state in Hoffmann's view was not obsolete at that time. In his view, states were the objects of integration, not the subjects. According to Hoffmann (1966: 909) a state was 'initiator, pace-setter, supervisor, and often destroyer of the larger entity, the highest possessor of power'. In his view, and in contrast to the main, rival theories of integration popular during the 1950s and 1960s, before a 'genuine' integration could be achieved in Europe, the conditions for the move beyond the nation-state still had to be created.[5]

About three decades after Hoffmann's contribution to state-centric approaches towards the study of European integration, Alan Milward in cooperation with Vibeke Sørensen (1994) presented a historical analysis of the integration process arguing that 'virtually all power remained with the nation-states and their bureaucracy' and that the European Community (EC) was an 'international framework constructed by the nation-state for the completion of its own domestic policy objectives'. As far as supranational institutions had been empowered, this was very limited and only affected a few areas. In the authors' view, the member states were able to realise their interests within the supranational institutions as well as against interest groups and even against their populations. The old members had certain mechanisms to control the process for outsiders to join the exclusive club. The authors conclude that the 'driving force' for enlargement was 'discrimination and the exclusive power to define agendas'.

Andrew Moravcsik (1993), who, like Milward, is a historian, perceived the EU as a successful 'intergovernmental regime', which has developed 'through a series of celebrated intergovernmental bargains'. In developing his theory of liberal intergovernmentalism, Moravcsik presents a rational choice-approach in theorising on the making of the EU. Liberal intergovernmentalists argue that the EU's institutions will only be as strong as the EU's central actors, in their view the member states, are prepared to allow. International organisations like the EU are meant to co-ordinate the interests of nation-states. The development of integration starts from and is based on negotiations among nation-states (Moravcsik 1991 and 1993). States have the ultimate power to make key decisions. Their executives control the overall direction of policy-making in the EU, whilst civil servants in the supranational institutions have gained only minimal powers.

In sum, according to state-centrists, European integration does not challenge the autonomy of the member states. Member states integrate only to the extent they are prepared to accept. According to some state-centrists, this is possible since the domestic realm can be separated from the international realm.

Liberal intergovernmentalism has been criticised for a number of other reasons as well. Burgess (2004: 34) criticised Moravcsik's liberal intergovernmentalism for having failed to explain why and how the EU developed strong characteristics of a federal state. In their review of Moravcsik's (1998) *The Choice for Europe*, Wallace et al. (1999) criticised Moravcsik's lack of precision in how state preferences are formed. This is in addition to a number of other critical remarks and

---

5 For the critique of the competing theories as well as Hoffmann's view on the conditions and prospects for political integration, see Hoffmann (1966: 909–912).

positive evaluations of the book, such as Moravcsik's success in mainstreaming EU studies and regional integration theory.

Another strand of argumentation has been against state-centrism as such. Koslowski (1999: 575) provided one powerful argument against this restricted focus. In short, he criticised state-centrists for not seeing that increasingly 'subnational political processes bypass the member states'. Those processes, which are either transgovernmental or involve civil society, are directed at supranational institutions and led, for instance, to the emergence of the discourse on 'Europe of the Regions'. Focussing on these 'new processes' and discussing the status of new actors in EU governance is the terrain of new, mid-range theories, such as multi-level governance, structural or social constructivism, discussed in the next section.

## Social Constructivism

> Social constructivism ... certainly does contribute to the study of the EU as a multilevel governance system.[6]

After the 'constructivist turn' in international relations theory (Checkel 1998), Thomas Christiansen, Knud Erik Jørgensen and Antje Wiener (1999), introduced constructivist approaches to the study of European integration. In their article 'The Social Construction of Europe', they formulated powerful arguments for a constructivist turn in analysing European integration. Christiansen, Jørgensen and Wiener were not trying to develop a grand theory of European integration but wanted to find tools to analyse the impact of intersubjectivity and social context in order to get better answers than those provided by other theories as to why and how the integration process had developed as it had. In their view (1999: 530), in addition to the material reality there was a socially constructed reality existing by human agreement, which makes social realities 'fragile', 'changeable' and 'contestable'.

Similarly, Checkel (1998: 326) has argued that 'material structures are given meaning only by the social context through which they are interpreted'. This interpretation and the focus on social ontologies is the concern of social constructivists. Risse (2009: 145) reminds us that social constructivism is based on a 'social ontology which insists that human agents do not exist independently from their social environment and its collectively shared systems of meaning'. Reflecting on the short section on intergovernmentalism, the difference between intergovernmentalism and social constructivism becomes noticeable; the former is based on a rationalist ontology taking 'actors' preferences as given' (Risse 2009: 147).

Social constructivists, in turn, analyse such diverse phenomena as, for example, discourse, norms, rules, institutions, symbolic politics, communicative action

---

6   This quote is from T. Risse (2009: 144–145).

or epistemic communities. As Christiansen, Jørgensen and Wiener (1999: 532) claim, one of the major contributions of constructivist approaches is 'to include the impact of norms and ideas on the construction of identities and behaviour'. The research focus was and is either on the impact of European norms and ideas on the domestic/national setting or on the impact of domestic/national norms on the European polity or even the international system.

In addition to moving the focus to a meta-theoretical level by analysing the structure of integration theory and its role in working out the weak points of other approaches' ontologies and epistemologies, Christiansen, Jørgensen and Wiener saw two other important contributions constructivists could make to the study of European integration. First, a combination of constructivist theories might help to develop a middle-range theory on European integration. Second, to identify important elements that formed the EU polity, constructivists could develop strategies and frameworks to study social ontologies that contributed to its construction, for instance via language, norms or political discourse. Related to this are separations of constructed in-groups as opposed to outsiders, which have been fostered by such phenomena as elite communication and the use of a technocratic and unique language.

*Critique and Self-Critique*

Smith (1999: 690), despite his conclusion that social constructivism has 'enormous potential' for studying the EU, reminded us that one core epistemological problem has not been solved by its adherents. According to him, 'the current literature is more united on what is rejected than on what is being proposed'. This means that there is no single social constructivism but many variants of social constructivisms, such as critical, naturalistic, neo-classical, or modernist (Smith 1999: 689).

Checkel (2006: 2) critically remarked that a number of important issues have been neglected by social constructivists. He voiced concern about meta-theoretical reflection, especially as concerns 'conventional constructivists' and their unclear epistemology as well as about conceptual limitation such as the underspecified role of power. Risse (2009: 158) in turn, argues that social constructivism represents a meta-theory, albeit and similar to Checkel's view, rather an ontological perspective. Checkel (2006: 8) argued that there is 'no common epistemological ground for constructivists', but a lack of 'meta-theoretical clarity' about epistemology or 'how we come to know'. In this connection, one of Christiansen, Jørgensen and Wiener's most important contributions to developing European integration theory was to lift the discourse on European integration onto a meta-theoretical level and in so doing structured and mapped the field and provided an overview of how the different approaches stood after the field witnessed a trend whereby scholars focussed on ever more specificities and details of the integration process. Furthermore, they linked the field of European studies to other disciplines by using concepts and tools familiar to scholars of other disciplines, such as international relations theory or comparative politics.

Both Checkel (2006) and Risse (2009) reason that social constructivism, rather than developing into a specific or 'full-fledged' theory of European or regional integration, a theory that possibly even competed with integration theories such as intergovernmentalism or neofunctionalism, should contribute to providing insights and answers to a variety of issues that concern the EU. Regarding this latter point, Risse (2009) sees three main contributions of social constructivism to theorising about European integration: A 'deeper understanding of Europeanization and its impact on statehood in Europe'; The ability to study the shaping of social identities through processes of European integration; The ability to study how 'Europe and the EU are constructed discursively' and how actors interpret the meaning of such processes and how actors develop a 'European public sphere'.

However, regarding the first point and if we believe Checkel (2006: 4), social constructivists need to provide deeper insights and reflection on the process of the 'integration of domestic politics into their arguments'.

To understand the process of European integration, an understanding of European integration theories is valuable. Different concepts and theories of European integration, such as social constructivism, are and have been useful in filling gaps left by many scholars of (the process of) European integration, especially those of rationalist approaches, such as liberal intergovernmentalism and neofunctionalism. However, Checkel (2006: 22) sees that a focus on 'hard-edged and multi-faceted' power is missing in many contributions to this debate on European integration. What is more, mainstream integration theories, as discussed in this chapter, did not reflect on the processes in which the local and the rural are embedded in. Yet, for a better understanding of the European integration process, a much clearer and more nuanced conception of how the local level is situated in these processes and power structures is needed. Multi-level governance and structural constructivism, discussed in the next chapter, fill this gap.

# Chapter 2
# Multi-Level Governance and Structural Constructivism – Understanding Multilevel Politics in the European Union

The term governance is widely used in different academic disciplines and is also part of the language of public institutions, civil society organisations and private companies. Governance is also high on the agenda of scholars of the process of European integration and rural policy. According to Bache, Bartle and Flinders (2012: 1) multi-level governance (MLG) in particular has evolved 'as almost the über-concept of the two decades spanning the millennium'. Different meanings have been attached to governance. Consequently, different governance definitions are introduced in this chapter. A discussion of MLG as a concept of European integration follows and some of the concept's shortcomings in conceptual terms are highlighted. This discussion relates to and includes problems in coming to terms with real-life developments, such as the overestimation of the local level in multi-level systems but also questions related to legitimacy and democracy, such as accountability or participation.

Regarding European integration and the MLG of public policy in the EU (Marks 1993; Enderlein, Wälti and Zürn 2010; John 2001; Jessop 2005; Hooghe and Marks 2003; Piattoni 2009), nation states have empowered EU institutions and conceded more influence to sub-national and local levels. Increased institutional representation, inter-institutional cooperation and a more intense inclusion of local actors in different policy fields are characteristic of the current EU polity. The involvement of civil-society and sub-national actors, thereby bringing the project of European Integration closer to the people, is a huge step forward compared to the predominant intergovernmental mode of cooperation of early EC years. However, systems of governance have their shortcomings and need be further developed, especially as local actors in rural governance are concerned.

MLG is appropriate in mapping and analysing the general structure of the EU polity, that is EU, member states and sub-national levels as well as functional units and networks of problem-solving. Structural constructivism as discussed in the final section of this chapter, places those structures under the microscope to zoom in on individuals, the principals and agents of a given field in order to provide a better understanding of how the structures are constructed, and by whom and where power is situated and specifically with whom. The process of European integration lead to the construction of the European political field, that is a symbolic and material entity which is composed of the supranational level in addition to national and regional units as well as Europe's civil societies. In this perception, structural constructivism comes close to the ontology of MLG. Kauppi (2003: 785) defined the model as a 'variation of the multi-level governance model'.

However, one important difference between MLG and structural constructivism is the critical element employed in structural constructivism. The structural constructivist perception of integration is that of a process which is driven and propelled by agents who are constrained by 'material and symbolic structures' and who 'struggle to accumulate social resources' (Kauppi 2003: 777). This ontology is based on the structural constructivists' interest in the detail, the specificities of the fields, their structures and agents, not only their general characteristics, or the obvious.

**Defining Governance**

Reflecting on the intellectual context in which the term governance is used, we encounter it in different disciplines such as administrative science, economics, European Studies, international relations, law, political science, sociology and philosophy. Semantically, governance can be traced back to the Greek verb *kubernân,* which means to navigate or steer a ship or chariot.

The Oxford English Dictionary defines governance as:

1. The action or manner of governing; the fact that (a person, etc.) governs.
2. The office, function, or power of governing; authority or permission to govern; the command (of a body of men, a ship).
3. The manner in which something is governed or regulated; method of management, system of regulations.
4. Conduct of life or business; mode of living, behaviour, demeanour.

A French definition of the term *gouvernance* is provided in *Le grand dictionnaire*: '*Manière d'orienter, de guider, de coordonner les activités d'un pays, d'une région, d'un groupe social ou d'une organisation privée ou publique*'. *Gouvernance* is here defined as a particular method of orienting, steering or coordinating the activities of a country, a region, a social group or a private or public organisation.

Focussing on the terminology used in different EU member states, it is interesting to take a look at the Danish and Swedish translations of the term governance. The Danish translation of governance in the White Paper on European Governance is *nye styreformer i EU*. The Swedish translation is similar to the Danish, *styrelseformerna i EU*. In both languages, forms of steering in the EU are highlighted, in the Danish case with the additional qualification of the new.

While in the Finnish case the term *hallinta* is mainly used, the official translation employed in the White Paper on European Governance included the term *hallintotapa*.[1] A third translation is *hallitustapa*. While *hallinto* means administration, *hallitus* is the government. To highlight the inclusion of CSOs and the cooperation between public, non-public and social actors, the term *yhteishallinta* has been introduced. As to European MLG, the term *monitaso hallinta* is appropriate, with *monitaso* meaning multi-level or multi-levelled.

Taking a look at Germany, both in the white paper and in academic discourses, the term *Regieren* is widely used. Beate Kohler-Koch and Markus Jachtenfuchs, for instance, used *Regieren im dynamischen Mehrebenensystem* and highlighted the EU's multi-levelled character but also the dynamics within this system of governance. Consulting the dictionary DUDEN for a definition of *regieren,* a reminder of the old-French (*reger*) and its Latin roots (*regere*) is provided. The meaning is to reign, control, steer or navigate and to adjust. As regards the timeline this could last a short time or cover a very long period. As to the way in which power is executed, this ranges from wise and lawful to the despotic and dictatorial.

Reflecting on the translations above, there are some aspects worth considering. On the one hand, there is a reference to an action, namely, the way of orienting, steering and coordinating activities. On the other hand, in addition to the public sector, be it a country, a region or a public organisation, the definition also includes private organisations and social groups. The French translation comes quite close to the definition of the World Bank and the Organisation for Economic Co-operation and Development (OECD). Their underlying motivation to introduce the term at the beginning of the 1990s was to distinguish between the act of governing and the institutions involved, and to highlight the involvement of civil society in multi-tiered structures in which governance is organised and coordinated.

In political science, it was the political theorists James Rosenau and Ernst-Otto Czempiel who contributed to the revival of the term governance in academic discourse. In *Governance without government: order and change in world politics*, Rosenau (1992: 4) differentiates between governance and government:

> Governance is not synonymous with government. Governance is a more encompassing phenomenon than government. It embraces governmental institutions but it also subsumes informal, non-governmental mechanisms whereby those persons and organisations within its purview move ahead, satisfy their needs, and fulfil their wants. Governance is a system of rule that works only if it is accepted by the majority (or, at least, by the most powerful of those it affects), whereas governments can function even in the face of widespread opposition to their policies.

---

1   See KOM (2001). Other translations of the White Paper on European Governance are as follows: in Spanish *la gobernanza europea*; in Greek *ευρωπαϊκή διακυβέρνση*; in Italian *la governance europea*; in Dutch *europese governance*; and in Portuguese *governança europeia*.

Answering the question of how governance differs from government, Bevir (2010: 1) argues that:

> The concept of governance evokes a more pluralistic pattern of rule than does government: governance is less focussed on state institutions, and more focussed on the processes and interactions that tie the state to civil society.

Rhodes (2000: 62) also pointed out one key difference between governance and government, namely that governance is broader, covering non-state actors as well. Pollitt and Bouckaert (2011: 21) are right when they say that governance is no 'alternative' to government since government remains as one of the principal constituent elements of governance. Studies on governance then might not only identify key changes in government but pose distinctive and new questions about government, for instance on the forms of interaction with non-public actors (Rhodes 2000: 84). March and Olson (1995) stressed the importance of the interaction of citizens and officials as the 'affects of governance'. In March and Olson's view this not only concerns political institutions but has much broader implications and includes the shaping of the identities of civil society as well.

In the EU 'new' actors find new forms of interaction and tend to utilise them by bypassing traditional levels of hierarchy. Sub-national and local levels of government, for instance, have taken the opportunity to deal directly with and within EU institutions, bypassing national levels. This might be formally institutionalised, for instance, in the form of liaison offices or by being members of the Committee of the Regions and Local Authorities (Kettunen and Kull 2009). In addition, as is shown in Chapter 5, informal relations are of paramount importance. While new opportunities exist to interact with EU institutions, the access to and utilisation of those new forms of interaction are not equally available to all potential actors but are dependent on the actors' possession of various capitals, such as economic capital or social capital. Structural constructivists are particularly interested in these hidden and informal relations in shedding light on them.

Governance scholars focus also on different forms of interaction between private actors, civil society, the public sector and different government institutions. While some scholars emphasise the inclusion of new actors as such, others are more interested in the forms of interaction between government institutions from and between all levels of government and non-state actors, for instance formal or informal networks. Some are most interested in how these interactions might be managed, steered or coordinated a) most effectively, b) most efficiently, c) most democratically or d) including all from a) to c).

Scholars also identified different uses or versions of governance. Already in the early 2000s, Rhodes (2000: 54) identified at least seven uses of governance employed in studies of public administration. Table 2.1 lists five versions of governance as suggested by Hirst (2000).

**Table 2.1    Five Versions of Governance According to Hirst**

| Governance version | Definition |
|---|---|
| Good Governance | In the field of economic development, to create 'an effective political framework conducive to private economic action. This is not only reduced to the state but for its development also civil society and rule of law are essential'. |
| Governance in the context of international institutions and regimes | To focus on the role of international agencies, inter-state agreements and potential problems that might emerge when those are operating such as accountability, democratic control and exclusivity through elitist technocracy. |
| Corporate Governance | To improve accountability and transparency of the board's management of a corporation *vis-à-vis* the shareholder. |
| New Public Management | Privatisation of publicly owned firms and public services, management-type action in public administration, agencification etc. |
| Networks, partnerships and deliberative forums | This 'negotiated social governance' is typically for the micro- and meso-levels of governance. The problem is its exclusivity, which means it is difficult to find an entry option. Members that manage to be part of networks, partnerships or deliberative forums have exclusive benefits. |

The latter point is crucial for the functioning of new governance units in rural policy, such as for the LEADER groups analysed in Chapters 5 to 11.

According to Kooiman, these new governance structures have the potential to prevent the accumulation of power by single actors. According to Kooiman (1993: 4), this is because 'no single actor, public or private, has all knowledge and information required to solve complex, dynamic and diversified problems; no actor has sufficient overview to make the application of particular instruments effective; no single actor has sufficient action potential to dominate unilaterally in a particular governing model'. Hirst (2000: 24) goes even further and sees power as being shared between the 'nation state, sub-national governments, quasi-public and private organizations, with NGOs, and with international agencies and other forms of supra-national governance'.

However, as this book will show as regards new functional units of cooperation in rural governance, there are accumulations of resources and political capitals with public administration, especially as far as levels at 'the top' of the bottom-up stream are concerned. Pierre (2000b: 241) argued in that sense that governments can be either the 'key [actors], co-ordinating actor or simply one of several powerful players' in governance. However, Kooiman is quite right that the underlying motive for including actors with different institutional backgrounds is the complexity and diversity of the problems to be solved and policies to be implemented. The utilisation of expertise from different strands and levels of society is not only to increase legitimacy – especially if local-level implementation is concerned – but very importantly to foster efficiency in problem-solving. This is vital for implementing policies in governance systems such as the EU that are multi-levelled in character and lack a proper government at the supranational level. How cooperation and partnerships function in the EU's multi-levelled polity is the concern of scholars of MLG; and the following section is an analysis of key aspects of MLG. It highlights MLG's valuable contributions to the study of the EU and the process of integration and critically looks at its problems and shortcomings. In so doing, it also looks beyond MLG and into related concepts, such as structural constructivism.

## Multi-Level Governance and European Integration

The historical and theoretical contexts in which MLG was developed were of paramount importance. Over the course of European integration 'grand theories' had problems to leave the beaten tracks and to try to explain new developments in integration, such as the growing importance of sub-national actors in EU policy-making (Chapter 1). While this empowerment has not been expected or even downplayed by intergovernmentalists, new forms of interaction, such as the partnership principle in Regional Policy, between an increasing number of actors emerged during the 1990s, giving decision-making in the EU a new face.

There are various opinions with some scholars arguing that the nation-state dominates the integration process, and the institutional structures and decision-making procedures of the EU, while others highlight the emergence of a new system of governance enabling actors from multiple levels to get involved. Decisive factors here are the concerned policy field as such, the advancement of the project in question and the institutional setting of the country in question, such as whether the state is federally structured or a unitary one. The first view is that of state-centric approaches to European integration, such as liberal intergovernmentalism. The latter position is that of those who see the EU as a dynamic system of MLG.

Member states continue to be very important actors in the multi-level game but power has been divided. On the one hand, the EU level has become a more important actor especially after Maastricht, Amsterdam and particularly Lisbon. On the other hand, the sub-national level has been empowered as a result of these treaty amendments, too.

As these examples show, the concept of MLG did not come out of the blue but has been the result both of real world changes, such as restructured forms of participation in the EU, especially after the ratification of the Maastricht treaty, and the theoretical impasse mainstream theories had to cope with. Consequently, Gary Marks suggested the term MLG. In 1993, as one of the 'pioneers' in conceptualising MLG in the EU, Marks (1993: 392) described the EU as 'a system of continuous negotiation among nested governments at several territorial tiers – supranational, national, regional and local'. Initially meant to analyse the interaction of multiple actors in EU Regional Policy and structural funding, research on MLG covers a great number of additional policy fields today. Economic policy, environmental policy and rural-development policy as discussed in this book are but a few examples of new policy sectors covered by MLG scholars. For some analysts, MLG is more an analytical framework for understanding the nature of policy-making in the EU than an integration theory. Referring to Marks, Jordan (2001: 200) highlights five key aspects of European Union integration that the MLG approach is concerned with:

- 'Big decisions dominated by member states are just the beginning' of a policy cycle;
- state power has been diluted upwards to supranational institutions and downwards to the sub-national level;
- states are 'losing their grip', that is they are having difficulties in controlling the whole policy process;
- even at the intergovernmental level of bargaining, states find it difficult to predict the outcome;
- MLG is a phenomenon 'very likely to evolve into something else'.

As to the academic debate in Finland, the MLG approach started to be in the focus of academic work since the early 2000s (e.g. Aarrevaara 2003, Aarrevaara and Seppälä 2001, Haveri 2005). As regards Germany, it was in 1996 that Jachtenfuchs and Kohler-Koch (1996a, 1996b, 2003a) provided a thorough analysis of the process of European integration, which they characterised by the increasing inclusion of new actors in governance. What they termed as *Regieren im Mehrebenensystem* was, in the years to follow, to become a research topic of growing interest in Germany and beyond.

Scholars applying the concept of MLG see the European Union structured at different levels bound together and cooperating in contexts that are quite similar to those that Fritz Scharpf characterised as early as 1976 as *Politikverflechtung*.[2] There are a number of parallels to theories of federalism, too. Federalist approaches and the concept of MLG both focus on certain characteristics, such as the principle of subsidiarity, the bottom-up principle and above all the inclusion of the sub-national level. Furthermore, type-I MLG as discussed below, *resembles* the structure of federal states. Scholars are interested in similar aspects such as the relations between regional and national levels of government and governance.

---

2   Scharpf proposed the term in his analysis of German co-operative federalism. See F. Scharpf, W. Reissert and F. Schnabel (1976). Some scholars (Benz 1998, Peters 1997) have claimed that the so-called Joint-Decision-Trap described by Scharpf is not necessarily as likely to emerge in the EU context as in the German federal state.

Federalism has been blamed for being too normative in propagating the construction of a federal *state* as the end-product of integration (Rosamond 2000). MLG by contrast focusses on policy-making *processes* and *interaction* between EU institutions, member states and their sub-national levels and institutions and does not speculate about a future *finalité*. In comparison to other 'grand theories' of European integration such as neofunctionalism, the concept of MLG, despite having some strong antecedents in that theory (George and Bache 2001: 30), is more flexible for not being focussed on one level only. Scholars of MLG assume that all three levels of the EU – the supranational, national and sub-national levels – may be in a powerful position in the policy-making process as they may have different levels of access to policy formulation and implementation. Of paramount importance is the fact that all levels tend to be bound together and interconnected in formal or informal networks. Furthermore, actors can circumvent each other. Sub-national levels for instance have established liaison offices to communicate directly with staff in the EU Commission and other institutions in Brussels. As a result, sub-national actors no longer necessarily channel their interests via the central state level.

Former, predominant problem-solving approaches are replaced with new ones. As a result the relationship between the state, interest groups and political parties is transformed, too. As an example one might look at regionalisation in Finland where, with the constitution of Regional Councils, a new administrative level has been created for managing EU structural funds (Kull 2008). Zürn (1996: 36) describes the European Union in this context as being constructed of national and community institutions, which can only be constituted in relation to each other. Since they are highly interwoven, it is no longer possible to treat them as separate political systems.

## Different Types of Multi-level Governance and their Interconnectedness

In order to deal with these growing complexities of EU policy-making, Gary Marks made noticeable contributions to improve 'his' concept. In the article 'Unraveling the Central State, But How? Types of Multi-Level Governance' Marks and his colleague Liesbet Hooghe (2003) further conceptualised earlier observations on systems of EU MLG. They differentiate between two types of MLG. Whilst the EU's institution at the supranational level, member-state and all sub-national levels are comprised of reasonably stable and solid forms of governance structures, the EU is also characterised by an increase in functional structures created in order to solve specific policy-problems. The latter are embedded within the former, and both types co-exist. Hooghe and Marks discussed this as type-I MLG and type-II MLG.

This further conceptualisation proved fruitful for several reasons. Firstly, the researcher may choose to reflect on type-I MLG, that is the framework which is composed of EU, member-state, sub-national and local-level institutions and structures (or the 'classical' type-I MLG structure). Alternatively, one might focus on selected cases to test how functional problems are solved, what the structures created for that purpose look like and how they are managed (type-II MLG).

According to Marks and Hooghe, the key systemic characteristics of type-I MLG are:

- a limited number of jurisdictional levels, and
- a system-wide, durable architecture; that is, reforms do not change the basic structure of the jurisdiction.

Key systemic characteristics of type-II MLG are:

- the presence of many jurisdictional levels, and
- a flexible design.

To exemplify general-purpose jurisdiction in type-I MLG, one might take a look at German municipalities, which are responsible for a variety of different tasks, such as social policy, building inspection, local planning, or environmental protection. An example of a task-specific jurisdiction, a characteristic of type-II MLG, would be institutions that implement EU Community initiatives, such as LEADER+, discussed in the empirical chapters of this book.

While the structure of municipalities in the EU is rather stable, a local action group (LAG) engaged in LEADER+ at the local level is set up specifically for that purpose. Its functions are task-specific. These groups include a variety of public, private and social actors, and membership is open. In contrast, a municipality stretches over a certain geographical area and is non-intersecting as regards other levels of governance. Another important difference is the constitutional structure. In contrast to type-I MLG, type II has neither a legislative nor a judicative body.

The concept of MLG focuses on two different problems. On the one hand a multiple system of governance can be economically more effective with problem-solving taking place at the very level concerned and effected. Furthermore, it is closer to the people and, at least theoretically, offers space to them to participate. That means legitimacy can potentially be increased and the policy-process might become more transparent. Hooghe and Marks (2003) characterised MLG systems as providing 'more complete information of constituents' preferences, it is more adaptive in response to changing preferences, is more open to experimentation and innovation, facilitates credible commitments'.

While according to Bache et al. (2012: 2) the distinction into Type I and Type II has been widely accepted, the authors suggest that it would be high time to move the focus onto the interconnectedness of the two types and challenge the maintenance of this binary divide. In conducting precise micro-analyses focussing on the interconnectedness of type I and type-II MLG, one may be closer to the core problems that occur in systems of MLG. These problems include incomplete information, inter-jurisdictional coordination, interest-group capture and corruption, coordination of networks on decision-making and policy-formulation as well as decision-blocking by higher-level administrations and last but not least problems related to accountability.

In that sense, it is also the interlinkages between different sets of actors – public, private and third-sector – within LEADER+ that is in the focus of the empirical study presented in Chapters 5 to 11. Studies of this kind can show that the EU's MLG system is faced with a number of steering and co-ordination deficits. Some of those deficits have negative effects on legitimacy and democracy. For instance, in some policy fields information is not equally distributed. Not all actors, such as municipalities in EU Regional Policy, who should have the same starting position according to the legal-institutional logic of this policy field, are equally enabled to take part. This is not only due to information deficits generated in the national field but also due to their lack of financial and human resources (e.g. Lorvi 2013). Bache et al. (2012: 9) pose the important question of choice in this context, particularly in relation to Type-II jurisdictions; 'how much choice is there and who has it?'

Overall, if one looks at the issue of inclusion, new actors have the opportunity to get involved and contribute their technical expertise. Importantly, though seldom discussed, others in similar positions are excluded. An example discussed in this book is the dissection of municipal boundaries for the creation of LEADER+ LAGs. While scholars applying the concept of MLG hypothesise that actors from different levels are expected to participate in policy-making, questions such as who dominates and why, or what are the outcomes and for whom, and are the results satisfactory and for whom were not addressed specifically and intensively enough. While protagonists of the concept of MLG argue that a growing number of local- or regional level actors seek participation, this happens – as is shown in the empirical chapters of this book – with varying degrees of success and is subject to a number of constellations and restrictions. One problem, according to some respondents of a survey utilised here, is that the construction of functional MLG-II entities (the LEADER+ LAGs) took place without information being equally accessible to all the potential groups. The analysis of the internal structures of German LEADER+ LAGs, for instance, makes visible another noteworthy issue, namely, that despite an overall positive evaluation of how the executive committees took the ideas of other members into consideration, members with a professional background in public administration are the most influential (Chapter 5). While throughout the history of LEADER there was a quantitative increase in actors able to participate, not all of them are included in the actual decision-making process (Chapter 5). This number is kept small (see also Benz 1998).

These internal and external realities of an MLG II entity cannot be identified if one does not look at the interlinkages of MLG II and MLG I. It is also a problem that can be meaningfully addressed through a combination of MLG and structural constructivism. Structural constructivists found that 'individuals and groups institute structured power relations regularising certain types of interactions at the expense of others' (Kauppi 2005: 47). Whilst this is the case of LEADER in Germany, the Finnish case shows that covering the whole country with a network of LAGs is possible.

The institutional context of the member state in question and, as far as LAGs are concerned, their resources and ability to communicate with higher-level actors, are of paramount importance, too. Jachtenfuchs and Kohler-Koch (1996a: 22) argued that balances of power among different actors, developed over time, are transformed and offer new channels for new actors to participate. The transformative nature of MLG II networks, their links to hierarchical (modes of) governance and the legitimacy of new governance structures are the subject of the next section.

## Networks, Legitimacy and Hierarchy in Systems of Governance

*Networks and Legitimacy*

According to MLG scholars, in addition to the 'classical' multi-level structure of directly and indirectly legitimised institutions and organs situated at the EU level, the member-state level and the sub-national level, 'new forms' of governance, that is, formal and informal networks or functional units of horizontal cooperation have been created to foster efficiency and democracy. Looking at the debates in disciplines that are related to EU MLG, such as public administration or governance theory, useful knowledge about the institutional logic of networks can be gained for MLG processes in the making, too. Table 2.2 summarises the work and main arguments of some of the key scholars dealing with multi-level problems in networks.

While new actors – both public and private – have indeed been offered the chance to participate in networks, partnerships and deliberative forums, one needs to ask how open these forms of governance are for new actors to be able to participate. This also includes the question as to who may participate in these network-type modes of interaction; that is are they exclusive and shut or inclusive and open? The governance-type inclusion of individuals at the local level is the key to enhancing legitimacy and furthering the democratisation of the EU – not only on the research agenda of MLG scholars but among the reform targets of the different EU institutions, such as the European Commission or the Committee of the Regions, thus democratising and legitimising European Governance and emerging formal and informal networks.[3] One problem in governance systems, with multiple actor constellations that are multi-levelled in character is, as Rhodes (2000: 84) discussed, the large democratic deficit. According to Rhodes, the

---

3   For the Commission's conception of European Governance, see the White Paper on European Governance, above all the 5 principles of 'Good Governance', namely openness, participation, accountability, effectiveness and coherence. After consultations and public debate, which focussed on and included public and private actors as well as civil society, the Commission's focus seemingly, more than before, shifted on to problems related to subsidiarity and proportionality.

**Table 2.2        Networks and Multi-level Governance**

| Scholar | Concept or Claim | Role of the State | Problems in Networks and Preconditions |
|---|---|---|---|
| Börzel (1997) | Policy networks are a new form of governance (market and hierarchy are traditional forms). Power is shared. Governments can mobilise political resources in fields that are widely dispersed between public and private actors. | The state shares power with 'sub-national governments, quasi-public and private organisations, with NGO's, and with international agencies and other forms of supra-national governance'. | Governance requires a relatively stable institutional architecture. |
| Hirst (2000) | Networks are typical for the micro- and meso-levels of governance. | | Exclusivity, it is difficult to find an entry option Members that manage to be part of networks, partnerships or deliberative forums have exclusive benefits. |
| Jachtenfuchs & Kohler-Koch (1996a) | Networks strengthen citizen participation. | | Networks tend to have negative effects on transparency. |
| Rhodes (1996, 2000) | Governance as 'self-organizing, interorganisational networks'. Network-governance has a clear advantage over traditional government as it combines and brings together the expertise of policy-makers and implementing agencies and involves private and voluntary actors. | Networks have a significant degree of autonomy from the state but the State can steer networks, albeit 'indirectly and imperfectly'. | Closed nature; accountability deficits; often unrepresentative; tend to serve private interests; 'often inefficient, difficult to steer, immobilised by internal conflicts and difficult to combine with other governing structures'. |
| Scharpf (1997) | Actor-centred-institutionalism. Networks as new 'structural arrangement (s)' dealing with specific 'policy problems'. | Networks are a significant change in the structure of government. | |
| Taylor (1996) | Supportive networks can contain 'cooperative hierarchies', are more 'responsive and consensual and ... more legitimate'. | | |

Commission and others are aware of democratic deficits but one 'does know little how to democratize functional domains'.

As to the multi-level nature of the European polity, the problems of the democratic deficit and how to tackle it in a governance system and the role that representative government institutions should play are highly important questions for scholars and policy practitioners. One characteristic of decision-making and policy formulation in the current EU polity is the bypassing of directly legitimised institutions. Parliaments are sidestepped by the executive, which interacts with technical experts or invites different representatives of civil society, both at the supranational and national levels (e.g. Kull 2008). Furthermore, it is of great importance to find answers to the question of how to hold these new forms of public-private cooperation accountable. The public sector at the local and regional levels has established and takes part in new channels and institutions that do not necessarily follow the hierarchical logic of politics and administration we know from the classical liberal democratic state. In his analysis of environmental policy in Britain, Jordan (2008) argued that the ability to fine-tune policy instruments to make them fit to local needs – a freedom and opportunity enjoyed by local and technical officials – increased through the more intensive setting of standards by the EU. At the same time, we can also and according to Jordan, witness greater public involvement in certain domains of environmental policy. The high complexity and related problems of involving cooperative actors, such as sectoral associations, research funding organisations and 'pressure groups', in European MLG systems through the example of European research and development and regional policies and their inter linkages is analysed by Lang (2010).

Overall, one may have doubts that new channels of influencing public policy are open and accessible for all equally. One line of criticism is that the representative system is at risk of being eroded with the mushrooming of technocratic expert networks. At times it is not completely clear how one is to safeguard citizens' representation. The European Commission was supposed to tackle some of these problems. After it adopted the White Paper on European Governance in July 2001, which dealt with problems regarding openness, participation, accountability, effectiveness and coherence, it started public consultations. The consultations were completed by 31 March 2002. Among other institutions, the Association of Finnish Local and Regional Authorities, the German Association of Towns and Municipalities, the German Association of Cities and Towns and Eurocities welcomed the initiative and the five principles on 'Good Governance' mentioned earlier. However, they criticised the White Paper for being too focussed on transnational aspects instead of problems concerning the multi-level nature of the European polity. For instance, the problem of the democratic deficit and how to tackle it in a governance system. Some criticised the paper for being too focussed on efficiency and effectiveness and only marginally concerned with problems related to democracy and legitimacy.[4] The associations also called for the inclusion of subsidiarity and democratic legitimacy in addition to the openness, participation, accountability, effectiveness and coherence proposed. Furthermore, these associations reminded the Commission not to erode the representative system by increasing the inclusion of civil society, especially as it is not completely clear how to safeguard representation and responsibility. They also demanded more clarification about how the mechanisms of local-level involvement suggested by the Commission, such as tripartite contracts, are put into practice more effectively.

In the 'White Paper on Multilevel Governance', the Committee of the Regions (2009) raised a number of points that are worth critically considering in this context, especially with view to Europe's rural areas and rural policy. However, from a rural policy perspective, the authors could have been more courageous. Table 2.3 summarises some relevant issues for rural areas.

What is the role of networks in the EU's multi-level system of governance, then? Are networks suitable for overcoming the democratic deficit in the EU or do they exacerbate it? Some scholars (Héritier 1999) argued that representative democracy cannot be the only 'measuring rod' for analysing the EU's democratic substance. Other forms of participation have been discussed in terms of the EU's democratic deficit, such as networks or public-private partnerships. Given that they are implemented at the local level, they might have more potential to enhance legitimacy in the EU than a reform of the overall institutional structure at the supranational level, at least for the time being. Banchoff and Smith (1999), who did not see much of a legitimacy problem, tried to challenge the thesis of a legitimacy crisis arguing that 'new patterns of political activity' contribute to legitimacy. Instead of concentrating on EU institutions such as the EP, Banchoff and Smith (1999: 9) suggested looking at issues such as mobilisation of interest groups and parties 'around EU policies and at various institutional sites'. This is a step in the right direction but in addition to focussing on the 'empowerment of civil society', one should not neglect the study of government in governance. This is particularly important when reflecting on one of the arguments Bevir raised in his interpretation of governance and as one of the reasons for spreading the concept. According to Bevir (2010: 1), 'new theories of politics and public sector reform inspired by these theories have led to a crisis of the faith in the state'. In other words, theories downplaying the role of the public sector in their envisaged reform scenarios – such as the New Public Management (NPM) paradigm[5] – fuelled the believe in alternative forms of state-society relations

---

4   See the Position Papers of the Association of Finnish Local and Regional Authorities; the German Association of Towns and Municipalities; and Eurocities. For a summary of the responses and the Commission's comments on them, see European Commission (2003).

5   For a comparative, cross-country analysis, see Pollitt and Bouckaert (2000, 2004, 2011). According to Drechsler (2004), the decline of the NPM paradigm started in 1994 when 'it was still possible to believe in NPM, although there were first strong and substantial critiques'. He goes on saying that in 1999 this concept 'was on the defensive, empirical findings spoke clearly against it'. Pollitt and Bouckaert (2011) show that the concept was not suitable in some

**Table 2.3    The Rural and the 'White Paper on Multilevel Governance'**

| Suggestions by the CoR | Critique |
|---|---|
| 'Submit proposals to support the use of experimentation at local and regional level in certain areas of intervention of the European Union, such as the strategy for growth and jobs, the social agenda, integration policy, innovation policy, cohesion policy, sustainable development and civil defence' (CoR 2009: 32). | A more specific reference to *rural and regional development policies* would have been useful and reasonable. The latter is the policy field where MLG has been conceptualised for the first time. The former knows a number of good examples of MLG in practice, for instance, the principle of tri-partition in Finland, Finland and contractibility, or the implementation of LEADER enabling self-sufficient structures to emerge. The LEADER method is a good example of experimentation at the local level. The White Book could have referred to LEADER, also to further enhance the LEADER method.* |
| 'Integrated strategies should be drawn up for rural areas which are based on multi-level governance and are designed to boost sustainable development and competitiveness' (CoR 2009: 24). | This crucial point implies a more territorial approach with a spatial dimension at its core. It has been repeatedly questioned in research why considerable shares of funds for rural development are used to sponsor agricultural industries (see Voutilainen 2012). |
| Administrative culture in the EU must be 'encouraged and stimulated' (CoR 2009: 5). | An important asset in EU MLG is that there are different administrative cultures throughout the EU. However, in some member states local and regional actors are – in policy praxis – not empowered to the degree that they are on paper. Good practices from member states, where relevant stakeholders are part of policy-making and networks, for instance in public-private partnerships, may encourage other member states to follow suit. |

*Note:* * High and Nemes (2007) suggest in this context that LEADER evaluation practice does not sufficiently foster social learning also because programmatic evaluation is centralised and not travelling sufficiently to the delivery organisations. According to the authors, evaluation is almost entirely concerned with economic performance and financial accountability and appears as an apparatus of control rather than as a mechanism to support policy-learning.

such as governance without government. What is more, and continuing with Bevir (2010: 1), the crisis of faith in the state 'also make[s] our image of representative democracy implausible' which, paired with 'faith in policy expertise' constrains a due response to challenges of modern governance.

As the empirical chapters of this book discuss, people are also engaged in functional units, such as LAGs, that implement EU policies. These 'direct' elements of participation (paired with institutional reforms) are the most suitable

countries such as France, Germany and the Mediterranean states due to the (missing) cultural, political and ethical dimensions and its 'Anglo-Saxon ideas'. The re-emergence of NPM is critically discussed by Drechsler (2013) in relation to coercive municipal amalgamation.

for enhancing the EU's legitimacy. The inclusion of individuals at the local level takes place both during the input phase of policy-making, that is the formulation of certain programmes, and even more so during the implementation phase. This is when the EU becomes most visible to its citizens. In the creation of something concrete, that is the realisation of certain projects by functional units that are open to individuals' participation, the EU can be most easily and directly experienced by its citizens. This is not only for participatory forms of democracy but also, and probably more importantly for the individual at the local level, in the visibility of concrete results of the (cooperative) work of the EU.

If one takes a closer look at local levels within the European context, one has to consider that both elements of representative democracy and participatory democracy are of importance in terms of legitimising the functions of EU institutions and public-private interaction. Alternative forms of democracy, such as deliberative democracy, associative democracy or responsive democracy have considerable potential when it comes to legitimising the Union's actions from below. Chapter 5 looks at the work of a LAG set up by private individuals, social partners, trade unions and representatives of local governments/executives to foster rural development by implementing the LEADER+ Community Initiative. In a survey, respondents painted a rather positive picture of cooperation with public administration and accessibility for new members. This type of inclusion of individuals in new governance arrangements at the local level is an important step in enhancing legitimacy and in further democratising the EU. However, while this is the case in some member states, the administrative cultures in other member states prevent a more thorough utilisation of the opportunities already available. Individuals that represent hierarchical governance modes are not willing to allow or implement a style change and the hierarchical mode of governance continues to be the dominant one (Meuleman 2013).

*Hierarchy*

The empirical chapters of this book demonstrate that hierarchies are a feature of MLG in the EU. Yet, the question of hierarchy in systems of MLG is by no means equally perceived. This is one of the conceptual problems or challenges of the MLG approach.

According to Börzel (1997), hierarchy is one of the traditional forms of governance and a network is a new form of governance. At the other extreme, there are scholars arguing that the EU as a system of governance is 'multi-level, non-hierarchical, deliberative and apolitical', and that governance takes place in a 'complex web of public/private networks and quasi-autonomous executive agencies'.[6] Some scholars can be placed in the middle ground such as Peters and Pierre (2001: 133), who argue that the relations between different actors are characterised more by 'dialogue and negotiation than command and control'.

---

6   S. Hix cf. Sbragia, A. (2000), p. 220.

As the analysis of LAGs within the policy-making and administrative chain of LEADER+ shows, hierarchies exist in rural governance, too. More precisely, one can distinguish between internal and external hierarchies. Internal hierarchies focus on functional networks as such, whereas external hierarchies focus on the degree of steering capacity of government. Thus, one comes quite close to Peters' distinction (2000: 36) between 'old' and 'new' governance. Peters' 'new governance' is on the coordination and various forms of formal and informal forms of public-private interaction, most prominently on networks. Researchers interested in 'new governance' try to see for instance whether the public sector seeks interaction with and the inclusion of civil society or whether societies can be independent and implement policies by self-steering. 'Old governance' is focussed on the 'capacity of the center of government to exert control over the rest of government and over the economy and society' (Peters 2000: 36).

In line with Peters' and Börzel's definitions, hierarchy and the way government institutions or the state can steer or influence decisions and processes in governance are the most important issues that motivated this study on LEADER. How members of Finnish and German LEADER+ LAGs perceive their position in EU-supported rural-development policy not only shows that local-level actors play an important role in this multi-levelled policy field. While hierarchies exist, many respondents to a survey questionnaire perceived this as a necessity. Whether it was perceived as domination also depended on how actors in more influential positions communicated their influence. The results of the analysis also reveal that 'good relations' with higher-level authorities in terms of informal contacts are very important, too (Chapter 5).

## Multi-level Politics in the EU and Structural Constructivism

MLG is an alternative to more mainstream approaches in the study of policy making in the EU and one of the very few concepts that consider sub-national and local levels of governance in their ontology of the EU. Many scholars seem to agree that during the process of European integration both the EU institutions and sub-national levels, such as regions and local-level actors, have been empowered. Public, private and social actors, for instance, participate in policy initiation, decision-making and implementation. Regarding decision-making, it is assumed that power monopolies of single institutions are harder to construct and maintain in systems of MLG, since a variety of actors with different backgrounds, and originating from different levels, share competencies and are dependent on each other. In other words, political arenas become increasingly interconnected instead of remaining nested and loosely coupled. Intertwinements stretch beyond local, regional and national jurisdictions. However, MLG has a number of weaknesses, which this book seeks to tackle. It sets out to consider claims such as the overstating of the autonomy of sub-national actors as well as questions of hierarchy and agency.

The differentiation between two types of MLG (Hooghe and Marks 2003) allows us to deal with structures, functions or both and enables us specifically to address potential policy problems in relation to a units' operation. One example for a type-II functional unit of governance from rural Europe is the LEADER LAG and its position in the multi-tiered fabric of rural governance. Type II is embedded in Type I, and both types co-exist. However, having said this, a number of problems occur, which have been voiced in a number of powerful counter-arguments against MLG's ontology and epistemology. Critical objections consider, for instance, the characterisations of structures in MLG as 'non-hierarchical' and the degree of empowerment of local actors (e.g. Bache 1999; Bache and Flinders 2005; Bache et al. 2012; Carter and Smith 2008; Jordan 2001).

The power dimension and the status of the agents in multi-levelled structures of policy-making is often absent from studies on MLG. In this context of a lacking power dimension and reflection on individual actors, the concept of the political field proves useful. Kauppi's early conceptualisation of the political field also serves as a good bridge builder from MLG to structural constructivism. According to Kauppi (2002: 1), the EU is a 'multileveled and polycentric emerging political field' and allows for an analysis of the power relations within the EU polity and between its various layers. The conceptualisation of a field by Favell and Guiraudon (2011b: 21) as an 'unclearly defined and ever-shifting political space' points to the relationships between different political actors and their 'struggle over dominance and influence over each other'. During these conflictual processes, characterised by competition for political influence and prestige (Mérand 2011: 178), new European political fields are emerging also as a result of the integration of several national political fields.

MLG has also been criticised for being little more than 'compelling description' and for being too focussed on highly technical policy fields (Fairbrass and Jordan 2005). This means that in order to be able to approach the problem of EU integration and with a specific focus on rural Europe by using a MLG methodology, extensive expertise on complex policy fields, such as Regional Policy, Social Policy or the Common Agricultural Policy, is an important pre-condition. In addition, others have criticised the fact that the focus is mainly on redistributive policies, such as those implementing structural funds. While broad and holistic statements on the nature of EU integration based on studies focussing on these specific policy fields are hardly possible, their findings do add important knowledge to the functions of the EU polity. This means that here is a dilemma in that there are on the one hand numerous and very distinct analyses of policy fields with an intense coverage of all policy cycles, from initiation to implementation, but on the other hand there hardly any answers to questions like who is acting, and why?

In the field of rural policy the further involvement of local-level actors was designed to both enhance democracy and effectiveness but, as is demonstrated in Chapters 5 to 11, effectiveness weighs heavier in rural policy. A clear decentralisation of decision-making power did not always take place. Ultimately, governmental institutions have the final word. While a number of countries have decentralised authority to a regional tier, the empirical findings below suggest that in the field of rural policy and in some member states decentralisation need to bear the 'quasi' attribute. The central state and its institutions continue to preserve their influence and shape outcomes.

*Bringing Structural Constructivism in*

While MLG is the first concept to scrutinise the position of local levels of public administration and other actors within the EU polity, it is too optimistic in the degree of influence it ascribes to local levels, particularly as far as the rural is concerned. Thus, combining MLG with other concepts, such as structural constructivism, an approach inspired by the work of Pierre Bourdieu and brought to a wider international audience by Niilo Kauppi, helps to reveal some of the hidden aspects of policy making in the EU and European integration.[7] A combined approach as carried out in this book contributes to a more realistic picture of multi-level interaction in rural policy.

Structural constructivism seeks to answer how and through what mechanisms and players the EU is made and shaped in every-day interactions. Structural constructivists are interested in the status and potential power of actors in the construction of the European political space. For collecting data, structural constructivists engage in quantitative analyses of biographies, combine statistical analyses with in-depth interviews and participant observation, and link habitus to the structure of the fields (Kauppi 2002: 16) not least by reflecting on how individuals perceive and interpret their position in a given field. This approach thus avoids the mistake of detaching institutions from individuals and groups working in them, which would be a problematic disconnection leading to a distorted understanding of how institutions function (Kauppi 2011: 157).

High on the research agenda of structural constructivists has been the social characteristics of the agents, their cultural, economic, social and symbolic capital. Structural constructivists see the EU as a 'multileveled and polycentric emerging political field' (Kauppi 2002: 1) and focus on the power relations within this polity

---

7    The structural constructivist approach to the study of European integration is quite popular in France, probably more than elsewhere. However, Kauppi's book *Democracy, Social Resources and Political Power in the European Union* was an important contribution to introducing the concept to a broader audience. Favell and Guiraudon's (2011a) *Sociology of the European Union* is another important contribution to introducing structural constructivist concepts, research and methodologies together with other sociological approaches to a larger audience. In developing and testing Pierre Bourdieu's theoretical concepts such as habitus and political field for the study of the European political field, structural constructivists of the 'Strasbourg school' such as Beauvallet and Michon (2006), Georgakakis and de Lasalle (2008) or Kauppi have provided important analyses of different policy areas and social phenomena.

and between its various layers to try and answer the fundamental question of 'who gets what, when and how?' (Kauppi 2002: 24). Similar questions that are of importance in EU policy-making and for the analysis of the rural policy field are questions such as 'who gets to define what a problem is' and do 'only officials get to influence the policy process' (Mérand 2011: 172). With this focus, one comes very close to what Guzzini termed the performative aspect of the concept of power which asks the question 'what does power do?'[8]

The structural-constructivist perception of European integration is that of a process which is driven and propelled by agents who are constrained by material and symbolic structures and who struggle to accumulate social resources (Kauppi 2003: 777). The power position of actors and institutions – such as in LEADER+ LAGs analysed in this book – is of central importance here. As Bourdieu (2006: 58) has argued, an institution is 'complete and fully viable only if it is durably objectified not only in things ... but also in bodies, in durable dispositions to recognise and comply with the demands immanent in the field'.[9] This perception of institutional characteristics makes one sensitive for identifying the elements that are dominant over others and the reasons that lead to domination and unequal power relations.

The considerable dimension of the individual must not be neglected in the analysis of rural policy-making (Chapter 5). Uusitalo (2009) looks at the role of individual politicians and civil servants and demonstrates how skilful *social entrepreneurs* can succeed in policy design and implementation but also how a few individuals as *representatives of partial interests* were able to have a clear impact on, if not to dominate, fundamental decisions in Finnish rural policy. Uusitalo shows how, why and under whose individual opposition the chance of further reacting to the needs of the people in Finnish rural areas has been partially missed in the 2007–2013 programming period for the sake of sectoral interests.

In addition to actors or individuals within institutions, the study of groups, procedures of will-formation and policy making as well as knowledge structures within and across levels are fundamental for our understanding of each field of political action (Kauppi 2011: 154).

One useful approach in relation to this power dimension, which is an under-researched conceptual component in MLG, is the one developed by Imre Kovách and colleagues. In the field of rural governance, scholars such as Kovách and Kučerová (2006) found that rural-development projects in some member states are

---

8   On a constructivist analysis of the concept of power, in particular the performative aspect of power, see Guzzini (2005).

9   According to Bourdieu (2006: 71), the body and its characteristics are 'constituted as an analogical operator establishing all kinds of practical equivalences among the different divisions of the social world – divisions between the sexes, between the age groups and between the social classes among the meanings and the values associated with the individuals occupying practically equivalent positions in the spaces defined by these divisions'.

often implemented by a new powerful class, the project class. Related dimensions, such as knowledge and interest are discussed in Csurgó et al. (2008). The powerful status of this class is based on the possession and accumulation of fundamental capitals, such as language (EU speak), education and knowledge – all related to the execution of EU projects. The possession of these capitals puts these new elites in an advanced position *vis-à-vis* the older elites, who are often employed in municipal administration. Whilst the project class may also encompass individuals from old local elites, it potentially competes with them. With their insights on the project class, Kovách et al. have contributed to the creation of a more realistic picture of local and rural governance and multi-level interaction in European policy-making and processes of European integration.[10] These processes can be seen as conditioned by a 'myriad of field level struggles for power and influence' (Kauppi 2011: 152).

At this level of abstraction, structural constructivism can make a contribution to the MLG approach. While MLG is appropriate in mapping and analysing the general structure of the EU polity, that is EU, member states and sub-national levels as well as functional units and networks of problem-solving, structural constructivism places those structures under the microscope to zoom in on the agents in order to provide a better understanding of how the structures are constructed, and by whom and where power is situated and specifically with whom. Important variables in this context are education, gender, political experience or nationality (Kauppi 2002: 25–26). In the field of rural policy and in line with the work of Kovách et al., more attention should be paid to the political activist who can take over a relevant role in multi-levelled rural governance. Bourdieu (2005b: 29) reminds us that the political activist must be someone who is empowered to be in a position that what he says, what he does and what one lets him do lies in his own hands.

Reflecting on these issues and their inclusion in analyses of multi-level systems of governance is important and necessary if one perceives power not only as visible, institutionalised and officialised but also as something hidden and secret. As the empirical chapters of this book show, the delegation and decentralisation of power was often no more than symbolic and did not necessarily lead to more influence for the local level and local residents. In his analysis of Bourdieu's theory of the political field, Kauppi (2002: 15) comes to a similar conclusion, in so far as the 'delegation of power and political representation logically lead to usurpation and manipulation, not to real democracy' in the sense of direct democracy.

Overall, structural constructivism comes close to the ontology of MLG. However, one important difference between MLG and structural constructivism is the critical element employed in the latter as well as the interest in the detail and in the 'bodies' that are engaged in the constructing and reconstruction of institutions and policy-making structures. For structural constructivists European integration is a process which is driven and propelled by agents who are

---

10    For an analysis of Estonia, see Aunapuu-Lents (2013).

constrained by 'material and symbolic structures' and who 'struggle to accumulate social resources' (Kauppi 2003: 777). This ontology is based on the structural constructivists' interest in the detail, the specificities of the fields, their structures and agents, not only their general characteristics, or the obvious. MLG, in turn, has been blamed for being rather vague, too technocratic in its selection and coverage of policy fields and for doing no more than describing recent developments. Another line of criticism is that the MLG approach is too optimistic as to the institutional logics of networks. This can be readily understood when presented with definitions of MLG in the EU as 'multi-level, non-hierarchical, deliberative and apolitical', being realised in 'a complex web of public/private networks and quasi-autonomous executive agencies' (Hix 1998: 39).

Structural constructivism proves valuable in dealing with such methodological shortcomings in MLG. It is a rather holistic approach and not restricted to analyses of the multi-level structure of the EU, or to analyses of supranational and intergovernmental actors and forms of policy-making. As its proponents use analytical tools such as field and social resource or capital, they are not restricted to specific policies or national contexts (Kauppi 2011: 158). Last but not least, while both MLG and structural constructivist scholars contribute important bottom views of European integration and policy-making in the EU, the latter, as well as other sociological approaches dealing with the EU, add important questions regarding the 'social bases of European integration', questions that are neglected by mainstream approaches (Guiraudon and Favell 2007, 2011). MLG helped to build bridges to other academic fields or as Jordan (2001: 201) put it, 'successfully carries European studies into other subdisciplines of politics and public administration'. The bridge-building function carries us into the field of rural development policy. This field has remained largely outside the focus of MLG scholars so far. Through providing new empirical evidence from these policy fields, one aim is also to contribute to methodological and theoretical weaknesses of European integration theory. The picture the reader will receive on the position of sub-national actors in the multi-levelled EU polity is rather ambivalent. The European Union has developed into a multi-level system of governance. New actors did and do benefit from the dynamic process of integration and new opportunities to participate. For others – especially at the local level and as this book demonstrates – the situation is often unsatisfactory. Mainstream approaches of European integration are ill-suited to understand and study these complexities of (rural) governance. For European integration theory and as far as local phenomena are concerned, this means that a replacement with a combined approach, as applied in this book, is needed for a better and more accurate understanding of the impacts and consequences of European integration for Europe's societies.

# Chapter 3

# Governing the Rural – Actors, Institutions and Power Structures

In order to comprehend the challenges and opportunities of rural-development policy, it is necessary to focus on the different layers of governance to identify good practices as well as malfunctions. The challenges and opportunities are often context dependent and the future of rural-development policies, their shape and institutional configuration will depend on reforms put in place at all levels of governance.

In his pioneering study on Structural Funds implementation, Gary Marks (1993) has demonstrated that a variety of different levels are involved in structural funding and that there is no uniformity among the member states. While Marks and others have shown that the strength of the level involved depends, above all, on the phase of policy-making, others have pointed out the interaction of the supranational and the national levels. For instance, Allen (2000: 243), in his analysis of the historical development of the Structural Funds, argues that especially with the 1993 reforms, but also in terms of the Agenda 2000 bargains among the member state governments, 'much of the control of policy (has shifted) back to national governments'.

As many scholars have shown, new governance approaches in the field of rural-development policy continue to be tied to or are embedded in strong hierarchical environments (e.g. Bruckmeier 2000, Buller 2000, Shucksmith 2010, Thuesen 2010). In his analysis of LEADER+ in six German regions, Böcher (2008: 372) comes to the conclusion, that 'regional governance still needs some forms of hierarchical co-ordination by higher levels of state'. In his case study of the Alpujarra Leader Programme (Spain), Remmers comes to a conclusion quite similar to the one made in this book about some managing authorities in Germany. While a new space for negotiation between provincial and community authorities has been constructed and a smooth payment of subsidies took place, the problem is that higher levels of administration have either a lack of understanding or a 'biased understanding, of local reality'.[1]

In this context, the debate among policy makers, academics and practitioners of whether participatory rural-development approaches should be reformed and genuinely opened up to a wide array of actors is of importance (van der Ploeg et al.

---

[1]  See Remmers (1996: 11), who also argues that EU subsidies potentially diminish local sustainability instead of enhancing it.

2008). The ETUDE[2] project developed and applied the rural web model. The web was defined as a conglomerate of actor networks being multi-level and multi-actor. The web covers local and regional levels of governance and is also linked to higher levels. Rural webs involve a variety of different actors, institutions, enterprises, state agencies and social movements (van der Ploeg et al. 2008: 7). Identified problems in these new governance arrangements are openness and the organisation of participation. The ETUDE project analysed differences among EU member states and recognised a number of shortcomings in rural governance. The analysis of case studies revealed, for instance, that in the Netherlands and in Finland, participatory rural-development approaches are certainly at the centre of rural-development discourses, whilst in other countries, such as Italy, they play a fairly marginal role (see also Milone and Ventura 2010). According to researchers from the ETUDE project, the mobilisation of new resources and actors in multi-level and multi-stakeholder arenas is essential in triggering sustainable development in rural Europe.

The idea to enable new actors to gain better access to participatory rural-development arrangements has also been acknowledged in the 2008 SCAR[3] report (Brunori et al. 2008: 57). The SCAR demanded the utilisation and advancement of alternative approaches in rural development such as multi-level governance and the need to work across sectors. The authors of the SCAR report argue that 'a new distribution of roles between State, markets, and civil society is needed in relation to access to and distribution of food, land, relevant knowledge and decision-making' (Brunori et al. 2008: 71).

Whilst the argument that the multi-level governance of rural development policy needs a more prominent role for civil society in policy initiation and policy implementation is widely accepted by policy-makers and academics alike (e.g. OECD 2006), the opening up of decision-making and implementation of bottom-up approaches implies self-evaluation and learning processes. Importantly, it also requires the public sector to rethink current practices. The public sector should support capacity building and strengthening of social capital, and provide both the spaces and incentives for third-sector activities. This is because the political experience as a social resource (Kauppi 2011: 169) continues to be unequally distributed, and specific individuals and groups tend to utilise these inequalities for political domination. This is what studies by Bell and Newby (1971), Shucksmith (2000) Kovách (2000) and Kovách and Kučerová (2006, 2009) have shown as well.

In order to unmask this unequal distribution of social resources and to make visible political struggles around ideas and meanings, particularly in policies where will-formation (Habermas 1989) and policy-making takes place across

---

2    ETUDE stands for Enlarging Theoretical Understanding of Rural Development. The project was financed by the EU's Sixth Framework Programme.

3    SCAR is the EU Commission's Standing Committee on Agricultural Research.

multiple scales, approaches that move beyond multi-level governance, such as structural constructivism, are needed.

This is what this book is aiming at by its institutional analysis of the Community Initiative LEADER+. The book focuses on the status of sub-national levels of member states and answers a number of questions:

1. To what extent are sub-national actors able to influence the process of designing and implementing rural policy?
2. What does the cooperation between sub-national actors, national governments and the Commission look like?
3. How influential is the community level?

The argument – backed by empirical findings – is that in both Germany and Finland, LEADER offers a space for multi-level interaction and local-level involvement, a space that consists of highly motivated people actively contributing to the improvement of the quality of life and economy in Europe's countryside. Local residents, for instance, are included in networks that are created to foster rural development throughout the EU. However, this space is dependent on, and also restricted by, national administrative practices, implementation approaches and cultures.

This chapter is meant to review the history and institutionalisation of the Community Initiative LEADER+ and thus set the scene for the empirical chapters that follow. It also looks into the development of the EU's structural funds, specifically that of the Community Initiatives. This chapter first looks into the emergence and transformation of the EU's structural funds. The subsequent section deals with structural funds and the community initiatives and analyses aspects of multi-level governance. The third section on LEADER provides the reader with relevant information about the emergence of LEADER and country specific information from all EU member states. It is based on an intensive study of policy documents and also contains the author's interview material and other quantitative data. Policy makers and stakeholders critically comment on the construction and transformation of LEADER. LEADER is – by intention and design – a test ground for a policy that engages all potential actors in a given field to utilise their knowledge and expertise. At the same time, actors are dependent on national and local power structures and restricted by national administrative practices, implementation approaches and cultures.

## The Emergence and Transformation of the EU's Structural Funds

The Treaty of Rome signed on 25 March 1957 by the leaders of Belgium, France, Italy, Luxemburg, the Netherlands, and West Germany mentioned the problem of less favoured regions in its preamble. Its signatories were encouraged 'to strengthen the unity of their economies and to ensure their harmonious development by reducing the differences existing between the various regions and the backwardness of the less favoured regions'.[4] However, during the first two and a half decades, the poorest regions of the EC 6 'looked almost entirely to their own member-state governments for regional policy assistance'.[5]

In spite of this weight of the member states, two funds were already set up in the context of the EC in 1958. In addition to the European Social Fund (ESF), the EC financed a few measures aimed at regional development with the help of the European Agricultural Guidance and Guarantee Fund (EAGGF). The EAGGF was used to promote rural development within the context of the LEADER community initiatives from 1991 onwards. The initiators of this EC-sponsored cohesion policy were to find solutions for the widening gap between core and periphery. Cohesion policy in the early stages can be understood as an 'instrument of compensation' to counterbalance the concentration of 'economic power in the core of the EC'.[6]

Reforms of EC structural funding carried out until the mid-1980s mainly caused alterations and changes in terms of programming and implementation. In addition, new funds were introduced. Responsibilities and power in terms of financing and realising policies were shifted, too. The process of creating the Single European Market (SEM), triggered by the 1986 SEA, led to one of the most thoroughgoing reforms of structural funding. With the SEA, regional policy has been embodied in a treaty for the first time. Regional policy reform was implemented via a series of new EC regulations. The poorest member states gained a doubling of the financial resources available for structural funding.[7] This was one of the most noteworthy aspects of the 1986 reform. Of great importance in the context of reforming the structural funds was the fact that the maps of areas eligible for aid drawn up by the member states were abandoned and replaced by maps defining areas eligible for help drawn up by the Commission. The major category of problem regions in the EC at that time were the so-called Objective-1 regions, which were economically the most backward regions in the EC with a GDP per capita at less than 75% of the community average. These included a large number of economically very weak regions in the Mediterranean and Ireland. Funding for the Objective-2 regions – the so-called declining industrial areas – was less extensive and was targeted at many regions witnessing the decline and collapse of their traditional

---

4    The quote is from the 'Treaty establishing The European Economic Community', p. 11.

5    See, among others, Armstrong (1995: 34). Financial support was also provided by early institutions of the Communities, such as, for instance, the EAGGF or the European Investment Bank.

6    Keating (1995) reflects on the 'core-periphery'-problem and argues that the periphery suffers from a lack of economic concentration which is aggravated in a free-trade area.

7    While in 1988, 7.7 billion ECUs were made available, 15 billion ECUs were planned for 1993. The three structural funds at that time were the European Regional Development Fund (ERDF), ESF and the EAGGF.

manufacturing industries as the result of EC competition and globalisation. The rural areas formed the group of Objective-5b regions, a very minor category of problem regions in terms of their size, although structural-fund expenditures per capita in these regions were quite large. In addition to these three remarkable alterations – embodying of regional policy in a community treaty, doubling of the financial resources for the poorest member states and new definitions and mapping of eligibility – the concept of programming has been laid down as a rule for all structural funds, which is, from a multi-level governance perspective, interesting to look at.[8]

With the Commission's four principles for the implementation of the structural funds – additionality, concentration, partnership and programming – that were central to the 1988 reforms, the Commission wanted to play a more prominent role in this policy field and sought to involve actors from regional and local levels as partners. According to the partnership principle, which according to Bache (2010: 72) was created by the Commission with the 'aim of promoting greater participation between government levels and across public, private and voluntary sectors', the structural funds are administered by local, regional, multi-regional or national partnerships. The partnership principle 'involves close collaboration between the Commission and all relevant authorities at national, regional or local level appointed by each member state in the Programme'.[9] According to the concentration principle, funding will be concentrated around priority objectives. The funds made available from the EU are paid in addition to a national share (principle of additionality). According to the programming principle, 'multi-annual, multi-task, and occasionally multi-regional programmes, rather than uncoordinated individual national projects, are funded' (Allan 2000: 254).

Some scholars (e.g. Bache 1998) came to the conclusion that national governments succeeded in re-nationalising power and acting as the gate-keepers in this policy field. What is more, in his recent political history of the partnership principle, Bache (2010: 69) summarises the democratic implications of partnership and makes out two main views. One is that partnership promotes technocratic efficiency ('drawing on the knowledge and skills of various partners'), which happens at the expense of political control. According to Bache (2010: 70), while partnership may even 'disempower oppositionist local political elites' it also

---

8   According to the programming principle, the member states were to formulate regional plans. The next step after a process of consultation and negotiation with the Commission was to draw up a set of Community Support Frameworks (CSF). The CSFs were drafted by the Commission after consultation with the responsible authorities of the member states, utilising the member states' regional plans. The CSFs applied to all structural funds. The CSFs represent forms of multi-level cooperation empowering regional and local levels, and offering them an early opportunity to take part in the planning and execution of regional policy initiatives. Armstrong (1995, 1996), Bursig (1990) and Tömmel (1992) came to similar conclusions.

9   See Article 4 of the Council Regulation (EEC) No 4255/88.

serves to include previously excluded groups in public policy and thus positively contributes to enhance pluralist democracy.

## Structural Funds and the Community Initiatives – Analysing Aspects of Multi-Level Governance

Since 1988, the Commission has drawn on an 'integrated' cohesion policy that combines the use of the Structural Funds. In the programming period 2000–2006, there were four Structural Funds:

1. The European Regional Development Fund to promote measures fostering the development of infrastructure and economic development.
2. The European Social Fund to 'combat unemployment, prevent people from dropping out of the labour market, and promote training to make Europe's workforce and companies better equipped to face new, global challenges'.[10]
3. The Financial Instrument for Fisheries Guidance provided structural assistance in the fisheries sector.
4. The European Agricultural Guidance and Guarantee Fund aimed at modernising farming, organising agricultural markets and promoting rural activities.

Figure 3.1 (below) provides an overview of the structural funds that have been set up for the period 2000–2006. The figure is meant to inform on their usage, financial configurations and goals.

While the lion's share of the money available for supporting structural measures, that is, 94% or € 182.45 billion, was used to promote regions that fell into the Objective-1, Objective-2 or Objective-3 categories, 5.35% or € 10.44 billion of the Structural Funds were concentrated on the four community initiatives URBAN II, INTERREG III, EQUAL and LEADER+.[11] The budget for LEADER+ for the period 2000–2006 was € 2,020 billion. This sum was substantially higher than that used in earlier programming periods.[12]

The use of structural policy funds and resources varied considerably from country to country and within countries. There are also differences among the member states when it comes to planning, negotiating, implementing and evaluating regional programmes.

---

10   This quote is from the Commission's website on introducing the ESF.

11   During the 1991–1994 and 1994–1999 programming round of the structural funds, the following community initiatives have also been financed: ADAPT, EMPLOYMENT, INTERREG, KONVER, LEADER, PESCA, REGIS, RECHAR, RESIDER, RETEX, SME and URBAN. For further information, see the homepage of the European Commission's Directorate General for Regional Development.

12   See discussion below.

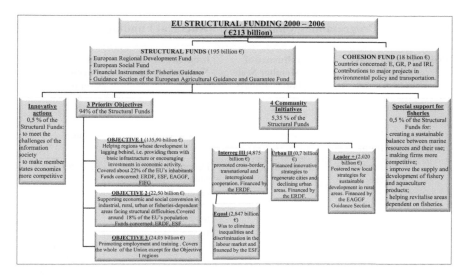

**Figure 3.1    EU Structural Funding 2000–2006**

In her analysis of EC regional policy Tömmel (1992) highlighted that only because of the interaction of three levels – the community level (Commission), the member state (executive) and the sub-national level (regional and local authorities) – can concrete concepts of support and strategies for implementation be developed. This is still valid today. Analysing the political influence the three levels of actors involved in this process can exert on structural policy-making, one can sketch out the three core phases of this policy:

- Negotiation of the financial framework;
- Creation of an institutional context (institutional framework, criteria to provide aid and promotion);
- Creation and implementation of the programmes.

In order to illustrate and simplify the results of his analysis of the different structural funds' programming phases and patterns of influence in this process, Marks created a table,[13] which is slightly modified here in Table 3.1.

According to Marks, the member states are the main actors in the creation of the financial framework. In the case of Germany, for instance, looking at the negotiations over the budget for 2007–2013, the political composition of the government has been one important factor in determining the bargaining strategy. However, the governments of the poorer East German *Länder* took a different stance to that of the federal government even if they were from the same political party.

---

13    The article and table are in German and published in Marks (1996).

**Table 3.1      Programming Phases in EU Structural Funding**

| Programming Phase | | Influence of Member State Governments | Influence of Sub-National Levels | Influence of European Commission |
|---|---|---|---|---|
| *Negotiation of Financial Framework* | | Strong | Insignificant | Weak |
| *Creation of Institutional Contexts* | Institutional frame | Strong | Insignificant | Strong |
| | Promotion criteria | Weak | Depending on Member State, ranging from insignificant to medium | Medium |
| *Programme Planning* | Cohesion Fund | Strong | Insignificant | Depending on Member State, ranging from weak to medium |
| | Community Support Frameworks | Depending on Member State, ranging from weak to strong | Depending on Member State, ranging from weak to strong | Depending on Member State, ranging from weak to medium |
| | Community Initiatives | Weak | Weak | Strong |

The core of the first phase of the process of working out structural funding consists of negotiations between the member states' governments regarding the overall budget, then the distribution of the funds. According to Marks, the influence of the Commission is rather weak while that of the sub-national level is unimportant. One might disagree with this conclusion. This issue is very case-specific and needs to be more accurately elaborated.[14] Ultimately, however, Marks is probably right in that the position of the governments prevails over that of their regions.

The second phase is interesting in so far as the Commission is and was able to push for new and efficient strategies although the member states persevere with their positions and sometimes act in a very reserved way (e.g. Tömmel 1992: 198). Looking at the historical development of structural funding, one can see that the Commission often had problems in convincing the Council to accept its new concepts. Negotiation and bargaining often turned out to be a long process. This is because, as Marks demonstrated, both levels involved in this phase – member states and their executives in addition to the Commission – are strong players.

---

14    Marks (1996: 329) provided another table in which he looked at the member states in particular.

During the phase of programme planning, the member states are, according to Marks, strong players, and the influence of the sub-national levels is insignificant. The issue of power in the programming phase of the CSFs very much depends on the member states in question. Marks emphasised that all the actors become equal players during this phase. The influence of member states will be weak, medium or strong depending on the member state's structure, i.e. whether it is a federal or unitary state. The influence of the sub-national level ranges from weak to strong and that of the Commission from weak to medium. Tömmel (1992) made similar observations. According to her, in processes of administrative interaction between the EC and institutions of the member states, new modes of operational procedures emerge, which replace formalised allocation of competence and top-down steering.

Tömmel and Marks analysed situations in which the member states are forced to realise incisive reforms which have the capacity to transform and modernise policy fields and profiles of performance. They locate those reforms in the context of the community initiatives. Marks perceived the role of the Commission as strong while those of sub-national and member state levels are seen as weak. Mainstreaming the public-private-partnership approach implemented by LAGs as well as the principle of tri-partition – a determining factor of the LAGs' composition – was one such development in transforming rural-development policy in Finland. Another Finnish example is the creation of new tiers of governance, namely the Regional Councils, for implementing EU Regional Policy.[15] Without the will to transform the state structure to accommodate this new level of governance that some key civil servants in Finland had, this would not have been possible, at least not with the same qualitative and quantitative range. How powerful those new tiers of governance are, is another question, which is answered in the empirical study below.

The EU functions as a system of multi-level governance with supranational, national, regional and local actors, at least on paper, jointly responsible for the organisation and shape of structural policy. Actors from different levels of the EU can influence the process of structural funding with varying success in different areas and depending on the programme phase. Baldersheim (2002: 209) argues that 'more, not fewer levels of government are being established to cope with the exigencies of modern societies; more complex social and economic patterns require more complex modes of governance'. One example from Finland is the Regional Management Committees where central state actors participate. These committees are responsible for coordinating the implementation of structural fund programmes and the financing of regional strategic programmes. Although appointed by the

---

15 At the Finnish regional level, the Regional Councils (*Maakunnan liitto*) and the Centres for Economic Development, Transport and the Environment (*Ely-keskus*) are links between the local and the national levels. The Regional Management Committees *MYR – Maakunnan yhteistyöryhmä*) as well as their rural subunits are important in this context, too. There are, however, differences between areas in the country.

Board of the Regional Council the participation of the central state is secured.[16] According to Ståhlberg (1999: 203–204), the planning and implementation of regional development programmes 'are only loosely coupled and coordination of the programmes seems, in the final analysis, to be a state matter'.

In that sense, it is important to realise that member states still influence this policy field. They act as 'gatekeepers', as Bache (1998, 1999) has demonstrated in several studies on England. As far as Germany is concerned, *Länder*-level authorities, as Benz and Eberlein (1999: 337) argue, 'quasi-monopolize arena linkages between domestic and European funding'. Furthermore, central ministries in Finland and *Länder* ministries in Germany have important functions in coordinating and managing rural policies and structural funding. According to Benz and Eberlein (1999: 344), the national coordination of the structural funds does not take place outside the 'shadow of hierarchy'.

Furthermore, even though, as in the case of Germany, the Federal level not necessarily involved in managing or implementing Regional Policy and structural funding, central states remain in a central position because they are engaged in negotiating the overall financial framework. Yet, the member states rank not 'above' the Commission but are very strong actors in negotiating the financial framework. The Commission has the most weight in initiating policy or setting the agenda. As far as Community initiatives such as LEADER+ are concerned, it had an almost exclusive right to initiate policy and worked together with public and private experts. Allen (2000) argues that the Commission had considerable autonomy here since the initiatives were drawn up by the Commission alone. However, he also stresses that the member states' governments had set up a Council Committee on Community Initiatives 'to tighten member governments' control'. The Commission has strong influence but no authority over implementing the structural funds. The sub-national levels have responsibilities in implementing programmes, and, in several member states, act as managing authorities of the funds. Decentralisation to sub-national and local actors in implementing the structural funds – often in connection with subsequent monitoring by higher-level administrative units – has the advantage that local-level actors, such as the LAGs in LEADER, know the local needs much better. For local residents this means that decisions are made by institutions that are close to them. Regional, national and supranational authorities profit from the fact that local peculiarities might be taken into consideration more effectively and they can rely on endogenous knowledge.

All levels are highly interwoven and form a very complex system of governance. This is also the case in terms of the distribution of power. Tömmel (1992) saw this as a process of decentralisation in which the interests of local and regional actors are increasingly involved. Pitschas (1994) raised a fundamental point in arguing that the inclusion of social elements in policy-making has to be fostered to a greater extent. Structural policy is not only meant to distribute funds

---

16   See §17 of the Act on the National Management of Structural Fund Programmes (1353/1999).

but support structural cohesion. The partnership principle, especially the Finnish variant being based on the principle of tri-partition, is a step in the right direction.

In sum, there is an increasing number of actors with different backgrounds – such as public administration, local residents, private companies etc. – involved in the process of implementing structural funds and in rural policy. They are organised at or try to exert influence on three levels of administration – supranational, national and sub-national. The status and inclusion of these different actors depends on the development of the process and the programming phase. While Scharpf (1995) in analysing the process of European integration observed similarities to developments in decision-making in the Federal Republic leading to obstacles and possibly into the joint-decision trap, other studies (e.g. Schmid 1987) tried to demonstrate that the European multi-level system of governance and policy-making within networks of public and private partnerships does not necessarily lead into the joint-decision trap. As Marks and Tömmel pointed out, actors become equal players with no single player able to dictate the outcomes. That coincides with what Benz (1998) observed in his analysis of 'negotiation systems', but Benz was much more cautious in arguing that there still is the shadow of hierarchy. Those 'negotiation systems' tend to favour some actors over others and even exclude actors. That is not only the case with the German *Länder* in LEADER+ but also the case, for instance, with the Greek sub-national level and the administration of structural funds.[17] In addition, multi-level governance scholars risk overseeing the 'reassertion of member states' government control' by only highlighting the positive aspects of the implementation of the funds with regional and local levels and especially non-public actors being increasingly included in different stages of the policy process (Bache 2001: 380). Furthermore, the system of multi-level governance often tends to become so complex that it is hard to locate responsibilities, accountability and power structures, at least with conventional approaches, such as multi-level governance.

## LEADER

> Projects must be elaborated locally and not anywhere else ... The principle of partnership must not only be maintained but also reinforced.[18]

The basic rationales of the LEADER approach can be traced back to 1988, when the European Commission published 'The future of rural society' (*COM (88) 501 final*). This was at a time when the limits of top-down steering and the predominant community method – the Common Agricultural Policy following the logic of

---

17   According to Heinelt (1998) and during the 1990s, only 20% of the structural funds were transferred to the regions while the central state kept the rest.

18   Former EU-Commissioner Franz Fischler in 'Special LEADER Symposium Towards a new Initiative for rural development: 800 leaders give their views'.

this policy mode – became visible. Highlighting the need for a *European* rural-development policy, the European Commission saw the participation of different actors from the rural communities as a basic principle for the period 1991–1994, a first test and experimentation phase. For the period 1991–1994, 10% of the structural funds were used to experiment with new approaches to fostering cohesion throughout the EC. The implementation of these new approaches was through the four community initiatives. As far as rural governance is concerned, the most important leitmotif is the area-based approach, that is, the involvement of local communities (public, private and economic players/local enterprises) through local networks and partnerships.

During the LEADER II phase (1995–1999), the areas covered were increased to approximately 50% of rural Europe. Furthermore, a more intense cooperation was one of the key foci. That meant the inclusion of local-level public administration and transnational cooperation. In his study of endogenous development, social capital and social inclusion in LEADER in England, Shucksmith (2000: 213) refers to an earlier study by Asby who argued that 'LEADER I was more innovative, until it became regarded as important, which led to efforts to control LEADER II more closely'. Shucksmith observed that the '"capturing" of LEADER by other agencies and authorities has been a feature of LEADER II in many parts of the UK, exacerbated by the rules requiring matching national funding and the difficulties of attracting this at a time of public expenditure restraint'.

LEADER+ followed LEADER II and was implemented in 2000–2006. LEADER+ was part of the Commission's strategy and goal to foster a more coherent EU and improve living conditions in the peripheries of the EU for marginalised groups. It was one of four community initiatives and financed by the Guidance Section of the EAGGF.[19] Of the Structural Funds, 5.35% (€10,44 billion),[20] were concentrated on these community initiatives. Within LEADER+ and during the period 2000–2006, the EU contributed €2,020 billion[21] to foster new local strategies for sustainable development. If one adds co-funding from public and private sources, a total sum of €5,0465 billion was available under LEADER+. While during the first round of the Community Initiative LEADER (1991–1994) €417 million was available for co-financing rural-development measures, LEADER II (1994–1999) had a budget of €1,755 billion. Also the number of sponsored LAGs rose from 217 in 1991–1994 to more than 1000 in 1994–1999 before slightly falling back to 843 in 2000–2006.

LEADER+ was structured around three 'Actions' in addition to technical assistance. The lion's share of the LEADER+ budget, that is 86.75% or €4,377.6 million[22] was spent on Action 1. Action 1 provided support for integrated

---

19   See Figure 3.1.

20   Seehttp://europa.eu/legislation_summaries/regional_policy/provisions_and_instruments/160014_en.htm.

21   See http://ec.europa.eu/regional_policy/archive/atlas/factsheets/pdf/fact_eu25_en.pdf.

22   See http://ec.europa.eu/agriculture/rur/leaderplus/intro_en.htm.

territorial development strategies of a pilot nature based on a bottom-up approach and implemented by LAGs. LAGs were also responsible for implementing action 2, i.e. they received support for cooperation between rural territories. The overall budget for action 2 was €504.8 million[23] or 10% of the overall budget for LEADER+. The amount spent on action 3, that is networking, was €68.7 million.[24] Networking was implemented by National Network Units. Action 3 was an OMC-type soft form of policy-making that aimed at collecting and analysing data on LEADER+ implementation in order to exchange knowhow, make out best or good practice and learn from each other's experiences.

There were three categories of criteria that were applied to the selection of LAGs. Criteria related to the partnerships, that is, qualitative criteria on the assessment of the partnerships and their organisation, criteria related to the territory concerned and socio-economic criteria, such as unemployment. Furthermore, the Commission laid down four community themes:

- Making the best use of natural and cultural resources, including enhancing the value of sites;
- Improving the quality of life in rural areas;
- Adding value to local products, in particular by facilitating access to markets for small production units via collective actions;
- The use of new know-how and new technologies to make products and services in rural areas more competitive.

## LEADER+ in the Member States

The member states only added a few national themes to these community themes. According to an interviewee from the Commission (Interview 16), some states were much attached to this thematic approach of the strategy, whilst others were more attached to the innovation of the method, to governance. A good example of the latter is the mainstreaming of the LEADER+ approach, i.e. covering the whole countryside with LAGs financed by national sources, and the principle of tri-partition in Finland.

The main reason for the application of different approaches was the budget made available for LAGs that were to implement LEADER+. Sweden, for instance, had given on average about €10 million per LAG. This meant that LAGs were in a position to cover almost all the issues of rural development. A stark contrast is France. French LAGs had a very small budget, only about €1.5 million per LAG. This meant that LAGs in France had to limit their actions to specific themes.

Throughout the EU there were 882 LEADER+ LAGs. There were no LAGs in the new member states. However, funding was available for LEADER+ type measures, such as the acquisition of skills by training and building local development partnerships (so-called 'Scheme 1') or projects under local development strategies

---

23    See http://ec.europa.eu/agriculture/rur/leaderplus/intro_en.htm.
24    See http://ec.europa.eu/agriculture/rur/leaderplus/intro_en.htm.

(so-called 'Scheme 2'). Six of the ten new member states chose to implement these measures sponsored by Objective-1 money.[25]

As indicated in Table 3.2 (below), the member states differed in the number of LAGs per country, which reflected variations in population and territory. Variations in the programming level are remarkable. There were 9 member states that had a national programming level and only 7 member states with a regional programming level. From a multi-level governance perspective it is interesting to note that the 'regionalisation' of EU-sponsored rural-development policy also meant the creation of several regional programmes within some of the member states. In the UK for instance, there were four regional LEADER+ programmes. Regional authorities in England, Northern Ireland, Scotland and Wales were responsible for implementing the regional programmes. There were two LEADER+ programmes in Belgium; one in Wallonia and one in Flanders. Interestingly, also in the Netherlands, a unitary state, there were 4 regional programmes. In the quasi-federal structures of Spain and Italy the autonomous regions and provinces implemented regional LEADER+ programmes. There were 17 programmes in Spain (plus one national programme) and 21 programmes in Italy.

The programming level in Germany was at the regional level, resulting in 13 regional LEADER+ programmes implemented by the *Länder* executive, in addition to one national programme. Although regional authorities were responsible for implementing LEADER+ in some countries, the empirical analysis and comparison of Germany, a federal state with a regional programming level and Finland, a central state with a national programming level shows, that decentralisation and the influence of local-level actors was much greater in Finland than it was in Germany (Chapters 5 to 11).

LEADER+ covered between 7% (Belgium and UK) and 37% of the national populations in various EU countries. The figure for Germany is 13% and for Finland 31%. One has to note two important things. First, there were regional differences within the countries. Second, it was possible that national or regional programmes complemented LEADER+, as was the case in Finland, where the whole countryside was covered by LAGs to implement projects of rural development.

The ratio of the sources of funding depended on the one hand, as far as the EU share is concerned, on the categorisation of the area in terms of EU Regional Policy Objective regions. On the other hand, national co-funding and the use of private funds was decided by the managing authorities. If the LAG was situated in an Objective-2 area, the EU provided up to 50% of the funds. For LAGs in Objective-1 zones, the EU provided 75% of the funds. The figures provided in the table above are thus the average for the countries in question. With 61%, the highest average EU share was in Spain and Portugal. The lowest average EU share was in Luxembourg with 23%. On average, in Finland, the EU share was 34%, other public funds 34% and private funds were 33%. German interviewees from decision-making authorities that took part in the empirical analysis criticised the

---

25  Czech Republic, Estonia, Lithuania, Latvia, Hungary, and Poland.

reluctant use of private sources. On average, only 17% of LAG budgets came from private sources, while the EU share was 51% and other public funds 32%.

Above all, the ratio of different sources for funding LEADER+ projects depended on the different national and regional programmes. In some countries they focussed more on the private economy, in others more on public infrastructures, on problems the population in dense areas faces or public services. Other countries limited LEADER to the renovation of villages and basic services, that is, on more public-orientated projects with public funding. Others projects with a focus on tourism or on the food sector saw a higher presence of the private sector.

According to a civil servant from the Commission's DG Agriculture, Leader+ did not strengthen the Commission's position. As for the new member states and the programming period 2000–2006, the fact that measures for rural development were not within the framework of the community initiative even weakened the position of the Commission. The Commission had fewer tools to monitor because it did not approve the programmes as such but some of the measures only. Thus, as far as the new member states are concerned, the Commission was, according to a Commission official (Interview 16) 'in a weaker position'. The informant continued by arguing that interaction between the Commission and the LEADER+ managing authorities in the member states was cooperative rather than competitive. This concerns, above all, interaction within the EU LEADER+ Steering Committee. However, the LEADER+ Observatory received complaints from managing authorities because the Commission was very ambitious as regards international cooperation of the LAGs.[26]

Cooperation between the Commission and the decision-making authorities of the member states took place within the EU Leader+ Steering Committee. As decision-making in LEADER followed the principle of subsidiarity, the Commission had no influence on the actual decision-making process. Once the programmes were approved, they were implemented by the managing authority or the public authorities designated in the national or regional LEADER+ programmes. The managing authorities designated the public body to implement the programme. The Commission was not involved in the implementation of the programmes, but received monitoring data. LEADER+ was a pilot programme for the use of monitoring data, i.e. the LEADER+ Observatory received very detailed monitoring data compared to other EU programmes.

The rural development approach of all three LEADER rounds (LEADER, LEADER II and LEADER+) and the current LEADER axis was and is based on a number of principles. The area-based approach with the broad inclusion of local actors with different backgrounds stands at the core. LEADER has been and continues to be implemented by locally-based public-private partnerships, the LAGs. The LAGs exist to develop and implement the 'local action plan'. In this local action plan, the group agrees upon several priorities. In a multi-sectoral

---

26  Within the context of international cooperation there was a joint action which was more demanding than under LEADER II.

**Table 3.2    The Community Initiative Leader+ in the EU Member States**

| Country | Number of LAGs | National population covered by LAGs (%) | Programming level | Sources of funding (%) | Managing authority | Paying authority |
|---|---|---|---|---|---|---|
| AUSTRIA | 56 | 26.8 | National | EU = 47 Other Public Funds = 17 Private = 36 | Federal Min. of Agricult., Forestry, Environment & Water Management[a] | Federal Min. of Agricult., Forestry, Environment & Water Management |
| BELGIUM | | | | | | |
| *Flanders* | 5 | 7[b] | Regional | EU = 46 Other Public Funds = 46 Private = 8 | Min. of Flanders region | Min. of the Flanders region |
| *Wallonia* | 15 | 7[b] | Regional | EU = 46 Other Public Funds = 46 Private = 8 | Min. of Walloon region, Directorate General of Agricult. | *Ministère du Budget de la Région Wallonne* |
| DENMARK | 12 | 11 | National | EU = 28 Other Public Funds = 28 Private = 45 | Directorate for Food, Fisheries & Agri Business/Ministry of Food, Agricult. & Fisheries | |
| FINLAND | 25 | 31 | National | EU = 34 Other Public Funds = 34 Private = 33 | Min. of Agricult. & Forestry | Min. of Agricult. & Forestry |
| FRANCE | 140[c] | 12.7 | National | EU = 50 Other Public Funds = 44 Private = 6 | National centre for the development of the structures of agricultural holdings (CNASEA)[d] | |

| | | | | | |
|---|---|---|---|---|---|
| GERMANY | 148 | 13[e] | Regional | EU = 51<br>Other Public Funds = 32<br>Private = 17 | *Länder* administrations, in most of the cases ministries responsible for agricult. & forestry | *Länder* Administrations of the, in most of the cases ministries responsible for agricult. & forestry |
| GREECE | 40 | 20 | National | EU = 50<br>Other Public Funds = 19<br>Private = 31 | Min. of Rural Development & Food | Min. of Rural Development & Food |
| IRELAND | 22 | 37 | National | EU = 44<br>Other Public Funds = 23<br>Private = 33 | Department of Community, Rural & Gaeltacht Affairs | Department of Community, Rural & Gaeltacht Affairs |
| ITALY | 132 | 18 | Regional | EU = 59<br>Other Public Funds = 41<br>Private= 0 | Regional Administrations and Autonomous Provinces for the 21 regional LEADER+ programmes, Min. of Agricult. & Forestry for the network programme | Regional Administrations and Autonomous Provinces for the 21 regional LEADER+ programmes, Min. of Agricult. & Forestry for the network programme |
| LUXEMBURG | 4 | 22 | National | EU= 23<br>Other Public Funds = 68<br>Private = 9 | Min. of Agricult., Viticulture & Rural development | Min. of Agricult. Viticulture & Rural development |
| NETHERLANDS | 28 | 11.6 | Regional | EU = 41<br>Other Public Funds = 32<br>Private = 27 | Four regional administrations (Randstad, Oost, Noord and Zuid)<br>Min. of Agricult., Nature & Food quality to coordinate the programmes | Four regional administrations (Randstad, Oost, Noord and Zuid) |
| PORTUGAL | 52 | 32.5 | National | EU = 61<br>Other Public Funds = 23<br>Private = 16 | Institute of Rural Development & Hydraulics[f] | Institute of Rural Development & Hydraulics |

| Country | Number of LAGs | National population covered by LAGs (%) | Programming level | Sources of funding (%) | Managing authority | Paying authority |
|---|---|---|---|---|---|---|
| SPAIN | 145 | 14 | Regional | EU = 61 Other Public Funds = 38 Private = 0 | Min. of Agricult., Fisheries & Food had overall responsibility for managing EAGGF-Guidance in Spain. In addition to 1 national programme, there were 17 regional programmes. Autonomous regions had managing authorities for the regional programmes. | Ministry of Agricult., Fisheries & Food |
| SWEDEN | 12 | 8 | National | EU Share = 28 Other Public Funds = 40 Private = 32 | Swedish National Rural Development Agency (*Glesbygdsverket*) | Swedish Board of Agriculture (*Jordbruksverket*) |
| UK | | | | | | |
| *England* | 26 | 7[g] | Regional | EU = 43 Other Public Funds = 45 Private = 12 | Department for Environment, Food & Rural Affairs (DEFRA)[h] | Resource management division of DEFRA |
| *Scotland* | 13 | 7[i] | Regional | EU = 43 Other Public Funds = 45 Private = 12 | Scottish Executive | Scottish Executive |
| *Wales* | 7 | 7[i] | Regional | EU = 43 Other Public Funds = 45 Private= 12 | National Assembly for Wales/ Welsh European Funding Office | National Assembly for Wales/Welsh European Funding Office |

| Northern Ireland | 12 | 7[i] | Regional | EU = 43 Other Public Funds = 45 Private = 12 | Rural Development Division/ Department of Agricult. & Rural Development Northern Ireland | Rural Development Division/Department of Agricult. & Rural Development Northern Ireland |
|---|---|---|---|---|---|---|

*Notes*: [a] The Responsible Programme Units within the governing authority of the *Länder* formally approved projects selected by LAGs and were responsible for the implementation of the national programme. [b] The figure is for Belgium as a whole. [c] Including 4 LAGs from the overseas territories of Guadeloupe, Guyane and Martinique. [d] *CNASEA* alongside the Delegation for the regional development and action (*Délégation à l'aménagement du territoire et à l'action régionale – DATAR*) chaired the national Leader+ monitoring committee. The Ministry for Agriculture developed the programme together with *DATAR*. [e] The figure is for Germany as a whole. [f] The institute chaired the managing authority which was composed of representatives of the Institute of Rural Development and Hydraulics, the Planning and Agroalimentary Cabinet, the Regional Agriculture Directorates as well as the Governments of the autonomous regions of Azores and Madeira. [g] The figure is for the UK as a whole. [h] DEFRA had also overall responsibility for managing the UK Leader+ as a whole, including the awarding and monitoring of the UK Leader+ network contract. LAGs were selected initially by regional selection panels, then by national ones with the final selection made by the Minister. [i] The figure is for the UK as a whole.

approach, the LAG seeks to link different projects while implementing them. This linking concern the LAG as such, LAGs from the same region, country-wide or Europe-wide. Especially during the 2000–2006 period (LEADER+), national network units in addition to the Brussels-based 'LEADER European Observatory', which was organisationally part of the DG Agriculture and Rural Development, assisted LAGs to find transnational cooperation partners abroad.

Former Commissioner Franz Fischler sees the strength of the community initiative LEADER+ in the partnership principle and the inclusion of local-level expertise.

One interviewee (Interview 16) contributing to the empirical analysis summarised this core principle of LEADER policy-making as follows:

> Those implementing the projects (funded by LEADER) are highly motivated for their projects, they know the local conditions and also how to best realise them. Only they can render the whole project possible and successful. Organs situated above have to control. But they should not be too far away from the events.

By including local-level actors, the EU Commission can foster the effective implementation of EU policies. With the involvement of non-public actors, according to the partnership principle, even local residents can participate in EU policy-making. Furthermore, the inclusion of individuals at the local level is an opportunity to enhance the visibility and perhaps also the legitimacy of the EU.

LEADER and LEADER+ are important and useful tools for improving Europe's rural areas. For the areas where LAGs were selected to implement projects funded by LEADER, the additional resources made available by the EU were very significant. They helped to create new jobs, restructure the local economy or created new and qualitative space for the local residents, such as houses for youth to meet or community centres.

*LEADER+ Statistics for Finland and Germany*

According to statistics provided by the EU Commission summarised in Table 3.3 (below), 69 out of 148 LAGs in Germany were also beneficiaries under LEADER II. In terms of sustainability, Finland's figures are slightly better with 15 out of 25 LAGs having already participated in LEADER II.

The most popular theme in Germany was *Theme 4: Making the best use of natural and cultural resources*. Theme 4 was very popular in Finland, too, but the most popular theme chosen by LAGs was *Theme 2: Improving the quality of life in rural areas*.

While a striking majority of heads of LAGs in both countries were men, the imbalance as regards the management is not that striking in Germany. In Finland, there were more female managers. Looking at the function and professional backgrounds of the heads/chairmen of LAGs' executive committees, the very high number of those working for public administration is striking. In

Germany, 91 out of 148 heads/chairmen of LAGs had a background in public administration. In Finland, although the data was not comprehensive, at least 36% of the heads/chairmen of LAGs' executive committees had a background in public administration.

The interviewee from the LEADER+ Observatory (Interview 16) saw the LAGs as the most important players within LEADER+. He was also of the opinion that the bottom-up principle has been successfully realised throughout the EU. While (German) managing authorities have been criticised in this study (Chapter 5) by decision-making authorities for being too influential and also for misusing their positions (selection of LAGs was politically motivated, 'selective' information policy, setting 'too high' standards for international cooperation, recentralisation of decision-making power etc.), the LEADER+ Observatory did not receive many complaints from LAGs.

*The Administration of LEADER+ in Finland*

The construction of rural-development policies started during the 1980s, but policy makers were faced with a lack of financial means. Also in the early1990s, the contextual environment for fostering rural-development policies was rather ambivalent. While the EU Commission and the Council of Ministers were pressing for this, Finnish conditions hindered more comprehensive approaches. According to Uusitalo (2004: 5) this was because the 'industrial and administrative sectors continued to protect their own territories instead of viewing the rural areas as a whole'. In 1991, when the first Rural Policy Programme was completed, Finland was not a member of the EU.

Ten years later, and after joining the EU in 1995, the indexed budget for LEADER+ in Finland was €167,858,644. The total area covered by LAGs in Finland was 124,238 km². This represented 41% of the whole country. LAGs in Finland covered roughly 1,595,000 persons, which was 31% of the population. The average population density of a LAG's area in Finland was 12.8 inhabitants/km².

As far as the administration of LEADER+ is concerned, the model for administering rural policy under this Community initiative is visualised in Figure 3.2 (below).

The managing and paying authority for the LEADER+ programme in Finland was the Ministry of Agriculture and Forestry. An important early step in LEADER+ policy-making was taken by the ministry when it set up the so-called Working Group for LAGs *(Toimintaryhmätyöryhmä)*. Among the Work Group's most important functions was the preparation of the national 'LEADER+ Programme for Finland' and the national selection criteria for LEADER+ groups. In addition, the Work Group nominated potential LAGs to the Ministry of Agriculture and Forestry. Looking at the composition of the Work Group, the diversity of actors and levels is striking. It consisted of social and economic partners such as the Central Organisation of Agricultural and Forestry Producers, the Federation of

**Table 3.3    LEADER Statistics for Germany and Finland**

| | Germany | Finland |
|---|---|---|
| Beneficiaries under LEADER II | 69 out of 148 | 15 out of 25 |
| Theme: 1. The use of new know-how and new technologies | 12 | 3 out of 25 |
| Theme: 2. Improving the quality of life in rural areas | 53 | 10 |
| Theme: 3. Adding value to local products | 19 | 2 |
| Theme: 4. Making the best use of natural and cultural resources | 76 | 9 |
| Management | Male: 73<br>Female: 72<br>No Information: 3 | Male: 22<br>Female: 23 |
| Head/Chairman by Gender | Male: 101<br>Female: 20<br>No Information: 27 | Male: 17<br>Female: 8 |
| Head/Chairman by Function | Public Admin.: 91; that is 44 County,[a] 40 municipality, 1 District; 6 *Land* Agencies<br>Private: 23<br>No Information: 34 | Public Admin.: 9 (municipality)<br>Private: 3<br>Firm: 3<br>No Information: 10 |
| Form of organisation | Registered Associations: 29<br>Registered Associations (non-commercial, non-profit): 25<br>Limited Liability Company (GmbH): 2<br>Special Purpose Association: 2<br>Without own legal form: 80 | LAGs were registered associations which were open to all local people and organisations |

Budget [b]

Overall indexed budget for Germany (2000–2006):
€ 513 172 391
EU share: € 262 910 244 (51%)
Other public funds: € 162 498 240 (32%)
Private co-funding: € 87 763 907 (17%)

Indexed budget for Finland (2000–2006):
€ 167 858 644
EU share: € 56 378 322 (34%)
National co-funding and other public funding amounted: € 56 378 322 (34%)
Private funding: € 55 102 000 (33%)

*Notes*: [a] In Baden-Württemberg, for instance, all the heads were county counsellors. [b] Source: European Commission/Leader+ Observatory Contact Point, 2005.

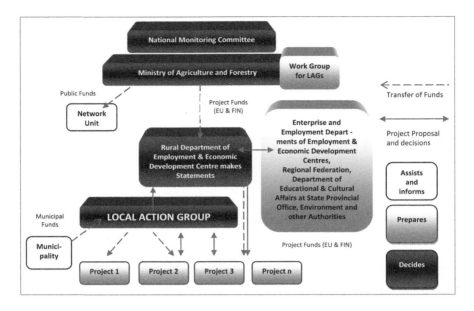

**Figure 3.2    The Administrative Model for Leader+ in Finland**
*Source*: © Finnish Ministry of Agriculture and Forestry.


Finnish Enterprises and the Finnish Village Action Movement. Municipalities were represented by the Association of Finnish Local and Regional Authorities as well as the Regional Councils. In addition to social partners, private actors and local-level public authorities, delegates from several ministries, such as the Ministry of Agriculture and Forestry, the Ministry of the Interior, the Ministry of Labour, the Ministry of Trade and Industry, the Ministry of Education and the Ministry of the Environment, participated in the Work Group and its early tasks in LEADER+ policy-making. As the managing and paying authority, the Ministry of Agriculture and Forestry determined the annual financial framework for each LAG. Importantly, it authorised decision-making authorities to grant payments.

The Rural Departments of the Employment and Economic Development Centres[27] (*TE-Keskus*) were the decision-making authorities in Finland. They decided on granting financial assistance to projects proposed by the LAGs. This

---

27    The Employment and Economic Development Centres were situated in the regions. Set up by and responsible to the Ministry of Trade and Industry, the Ministry of Agriculture and Forestry and the Ministry of Labour, there were 15 such centres countrywide to advise businesses, entrepreneurs, and private individuals in, for instance, promoting and developing farming and rural enterprise activities. For the tasks of the Employment and Economic Development Centres in the LEADER+ Programme, see 'Leader+ Programme for Finland', p. 82.

concerns both the national share and the share from the EAGGF. The most important tasks of Finnish Employment and Economic Development Centres as LEADER+ decision-making authorities were handling project applications, checking that they contain no measures which laws and acts do not allow, preparing their decisions (i.e. approving or changing project proposals) and also participating in meetings of the LAGs.

The answer to the question whether decision-making authorities were supervisors or coordinators was answered slightly differently by various Finnish interviewees. Most interviewees saw their role as 'coordinators and not supervisors' (Interview 11) or 'on some issues a supervisor and on some issues a coordinator' (Interview 8). However, decision-making authorities were very interested in good cooperation with the LAGs and the successful implementation of the funds. As an interviewee from an Employment and Economic Development Centre in Central Finland (Interview 8) nicely summed it up: 'With rural development both the LAG and us, we were aiming at the same target, side by side'.

Within the application process decision-making authorities had a supervisory function since the final decisions were taken by them.[28] However, if problems arose, it has been stressed by many interviewees from decision-making authorities that they were easier to solve collectively, that is, by decision-making authorities and LAG members together and if the decision-making authority acted as a coordinator. An interviewee from Southern Finland (Interview 7) put it like this: 'We from the Employment and Economic Development Centre looked at solving problems. It would have been bad if we had said: "You must not do it like this".'

Decision-making authorities in Finland also supported the LAGs in their activities, for instance, by supporting the exchange of knowledge and of information between different LAGs and by supporting them in international network activities.

Analysing the institutional setting for implementing structural funds in Finland, it is noteworthy that new entities, such as the Regional Councils, have been created. While, for instance, in Objective-1 and Objective-2 programmes, the Regional Councils were, at least on paper, a key institution for the implantation of structural funds, in LEADER+, the Employment and Economic Development Centres were the decision-making authorities. In an interview, an official of the managing authority (Interview 6) was asked why this is different from Regional Policy implementation. His response was the following:

---

28  One interviewee (Interview 11) also reported that 'we only once declined the decision of one LAG's steering committee on funding'. Normally, the interviewee explained, 'we approved, sometimes demanded alterations, but normally approved'. The board for complaints was appealed and also refused to approve the application. As the application was for a lorry for the containment of oil used by the local auxiliary fire brigade, the interviewee added that he told the applicants that 'this belonged to the sphere of responsibility of the municipality and not to fostering rural development'.

the Employment and Economic Development Centres were central government authorities in the Regions, and the Regional Councils were municipal bodies. But I think it is not up-to-date anymore to think of public power (at the regional level) in two forms. Both can be replaced by a third form. We have in Finland very many fights, lobbying and tugs-of-war, especially at the regional level. International comparisons show that our regional administration is tremendously stupid and this is how it is. It is so messy because there are bodies from both (central and municipal) levels. The central state authorities have money. More decision-making power is transferred to the municipal level, which does not have money. One has the power and the other the money. The Regional Councils don't have money so they cannot help the Ministry of Agriculture and Forestry but in the Toimintaryhmätyöryhmä they have a position.

Above all, it is important to note what a civil servant from an Employment and Economic Development Centre in Western Finland (Interview 11) said: 'The independence of the groups was an important feature (as was) the grass-root thinking. Our whole region except Seinäjoki (city) was covered with LAGs'.

In Finland, LEADER is not only perceived as a decentralised grass-root approach. In addition, mainstreaming and covering the whole countryside with LAGs is a central basic rationale of the Finnish translation of LEADER.

For implementing rural-development policy projects within the context of LEADER+, 25 LEADER+ LAGs had been set up in Finland (Table 3.4).

**Table 3.4     LAGs in Finland**

| LAG | Municipalities/Regions Covered |
| --- | --- |
| Peräpohjolan kehitys ry | Keminmaa, Ranua, Simo, Tervola, Kemi rural areas, Rovaniemen mlk (parts) |
| Kainuun naisyrittäjyys LEADER Plus | Hyrynsalmi, Kuhmo, Ristijärvi, Sotkamo, Suomussalmi |
| Oulujärvi LEADER ry | Paltamo, Puolanka, Vaala, Vuolijoki, Kajaani rural areas |
| Nouseva rannikkoseutu ry | Hailuoto, Liminka. Lumijoki, Pattijoki, Pyhäjoki, Rantsila, Ruukki, Siikajoki, Temmes, Tyrnävä, Vihanti, Raahe rural areas |
| Pirityiset ry | Halsua, Kaustinen, Lestijärvi, Perho, Toholampi, Ullava, Veteli |
| NHS – LEADER II ry | Haapajärvi, Haapavesi, Kestilä, Kärsämäki, Nivala, Piippola, Pulkkila, Pyhäjärvi, Pyhäntä, Reisjärvi |
| Rieska-LEADER ry | Alavieska, Himanka, Kalajoki, Kannus, Kälviä, Lohtaja, Merijärvi, Oulainen, Sievi, Ylivieska |

| LAG | Municipalities/Regions Covered |
|---|---|
| Aisapari – Härmänmaan ja Järviseudun Kehittämisyhdistys ry | Alahärmä, Alajärvi, Evijärvi, Kauhava, Kortesjärvi, Lappajärvi, Lapua, Vimpeli, Ylihärmä |
| Suupohjan kehittämisyhdistys ry | Isojoki, Jurva, Karijoki, Kauhajoki, Teuva |
| Kalakukko 2006 ry | Juankoski, Kaavi, Nilsiä, Rautavaara, Tuusniemi, Vehmersalmi, Kuopio and Siilinjärvi rural areas |
| Maaseudun kehittämisyhdistys VIISARI ry | Kannonkoski, Karstula, Kinnula, Kivijärvi, Kyyjärvi, Pihtipudas, Pylkönmäki, Saarijärvi, Viitasaari, Äänekoski rural areas |
| RaJuPuSu LEADER ry | Juva, Joroinen, Puumala, Rantasalmi, Sulkava, Virtasalmi |
| Maaseudun kehittämisyhdistys Keski-Karjalan Jetina ry | Kesälahti, Kitee, Rääkkylä, Tohmajärvi, Värtsilä |
| Joensuun seudun LEADER – yhdistys ry | Eno, Kiihtelysvaara, Kontiolahti, Liperi, Outokumpu, Polvijärvi, Pyhäselkä |
| Vaara-Karjalan LEADER ry | Ilomantsi, Juuka, Lieksa, Nurmes, Tuupovaara, Valtimo |
| Pomoottori ry | Juupajoki, Kuhmalahti, Luopioinen, Längelmäki, Orivesi, Pälkäne, Sahalahti |
| Kantri ry | Kangasala, Lempäälä, Pirkkala, Vesilahti, Ylöjärvi, Nokia and Tampere rural areas |
| Aktiivinen Pohjois-Satakunta ry | Honkajoki, Ikaalinen, Jämijärvi, Kankaanpää, Karvia, Kihniö, Kiikoinen, Lavia, Merikarvia, Parkano, Pomarkku, Siikainen, Suodenniemi |
| Karhuseutu ry | Harjavalta, Kokemäki, Kullaa, Luvia, Nakkila, Noormarkku, Ulvila, Pori rural areas |
| Varsinais-Suomen jokivarsikumppanit ry | Alastaro, Aura, Karinainen, Koski, Kuusjoki, Loimaa, Loimaan kunta, Marttila, Mellilä, Oripää, Pöytyä, Somero, Tarvasjoki |
| I samma båt – Samassa veneessä rf | Dragsfjärd, Särkisalo, Houtskari, Iniö, Kemiö, Korppoo, Kustavi, Merimasku, Nauvo, Parainen, Rymättylä, Taivassalo, Velkua, Västanfjärd, Bromarv village |
| Etelä-Karjalan Kärki-LEADER ry | Parikkala, Rautjärvi, Ruokolahti, Saari, Uukuniemi, Imatra rural areas |
| Kehittämisyhdistys Sepra ry | Anjalankoski, Hamina, Miehikkälä, Pyhtää, Vehkalahti, Virolahti, Kotka rural areas and parts of Ruotsinpyhtää |
| Päijät-Hämeen maaseudun kehittämisyhdistys ry | Asikkala, Hartola, Padasjoki, Pertunmaa, Sysmä, Heinola rural areas |
| Pomoväst rf | Hanko, Inkoo, Karjaa, Pohja, Siuntio, Tammisaari rural areas (without Bromarv), Kirkkonummi rural areas |

The LAGs assisted in drafting applications by 'a single natural person or several natural persons jointly, by associations governed by public or private law, as well as foundations'.[29] They also evaluated project applications and raised awareness about LEADER+ in their regions. The principles of partnership and tri-partition were important as far as the composition of the LAGs' executive committees are concerned. The LEADER+ Programme for Finland defined partnership as 'extensive co-operation on an equal standing in the composition and activity of the LAG'.[30] The LAGs were 'open to all local persons and organisations who are interested in rural development'.

Tri-partition supposed to guarantee 'openness and equitability in the decision-making required in the LEADER+ programme as well as the involvement of new people in the local development work'.[31]

The LAGs' executive committees decided whether a project should be financed and submitted project applications together with a statement of reasons to the relevant Employment and Economic Development Centre. In contrast to Germany, if 'the area where the LAG operates extends to the territory of more than one (decision-making authority), the decision is made by an authority in whose territory most of the municipalities covered by the LAG are located'.[32] An important feature of rural development in Finland is the fact that the LEADER approach was a role-model for national programmes of rural development. During 2000–2006, 419 of all 444 Finnish municipalities were covered by LAGs. In addition to 25 LEADER+ LAGs, 23 other LAGs were sponsored by national funds or from the ERDF. As a result, all the parts of the country eligible for structural funding had been covered by dense networks of LAGs. This is the result of intensive efforts of the Rural Policy Committee[33] (*Maaseutupolitiikan yhteistyöryhmä – YTR*) and its head.

*The Administration of LEADER+ in Germany*

One important difference between Germany and Finland in the administration of LEADER+ is that all 13 *Länder* participating in the community initiative LEADER+ had their own programmes. In addition to those 13 core programmes, there was one national programme which was specific to network activities

---

29   See 'Leader+ Programme for Finland', p.82.

30   See 'Leader+ Programme for Finland', p.72. The other general eligibility criteria for LAGs were as follows: the area must be rural, the area must be the appropriate size, strategic cohesion in the development plan and the development strategy must be consistent with one or two themes. These themes were listed in the LEADER+ Programme.

31   See 'Leader+ Programme for Finland', p.72.

32   See 'Leader+ Programme for Finland', p. 83.

33   This committee aims to promote rural areas in various ways. Appointed by the Finnish Government, more than 500 persons from several ministries and other organisations participate in its work.

in Germany. As can be seen from Table 3.5 below, each *Land* had its own managing authority, which was not necessarily situated within the Ministry of Agriculture.

**Table 3.5    Leader+ Managing and Decision-making Authorities in Germany**

| Land | Managing authority | Decision-making authority |
|---|---|---|
| Baden-Württemberg | Ministry of Food and Rural Development | District Level: *Regierungspräsidium/Landesamt für Flurneuordnung und Landentwicklung* |
| Bayern | Ministry of Agriculture and Forestry | 7 District Governments |
| Brandenburg | Ministry of Rural Development, Environment and Consumer Protection | **Land agency:** *Amt für Flurneuordnung und ländliche Entwicklung* (6) |
| Hessen | Ministry of Economics, Transport and State Development | Investmentbank Hessen AG 16 Rural District Offices oversaw the LAGs |
| Mecklenburg-Vorpommern | Ministry of Food, Agriculture, Forestry and Fisheries | Same as managing authority |
| Niedersachsen | Ministry of Rural Areas, Food, Agriculture and Consumer Protection | First municipal level administration (13 counties, 2 *Samtgemeinde* and one city). One Land agency did conformity checks afterwards |
| Nordrhein-Westfalen | Ministry for the Environment, Agriculture and Consumer Protection | District Government (*Bezirksregierung*) |
| Rheinland-Pfalz | Ministry of Economics, Transport, Agriculture and Viniculture | **Land agency:** *Aufsichts- und Dienstleistungsdirektion (ADD)* |
| Saarland | Ministry for the Environment | Same as managing authority |
| Sachsen | Ministry for the Environment and Agriculture | **Land agency:** *Amt für Ländliche Entwicklung* |
| Sachsen-Anhalt | Ministry of Agriculture and the Environment | District Level: *Landesverwaltungsamt* Counties make predecisions |
| Schleswig-Holstein | Ministry of Interior | Municipalities (4 counties one *Amt*) |
| Thüringen | Ministry of Agriculture and the Environment | District Level: *Landesverwaltungsamt* |

The managing authorities were responsible for the effective and orderly administration and implementation of the LEADER+ programme in their region. They interacted with the European Commission, Federation, other *Länder* and other departments of administrations of the *Land* level. Among their most important tasks were the following:

• Adjustment and amendment of programme planning,
• Determination of processing and monitoring standards (including the monitoring of the EU guidelines),
• Surveying of financial and statistical data and indicators for monitoring,
• Evaluation, preparation and presentation of annual reports,
• Organisation and management of the monitoring committees.

Decision-making authorities were situated at different levels. While in most *Länder*, district governments were responsible for deciding on the applications forwarded by LAGs, in some *Länder*, municipal-level administrations (county, *Samtgemeinde*, city etc.) made initial decisions. The rationale was that those authorities that made initial decisions were to co-finance approved projects. As outlined above, in Finland, these decisions were made by a single authority.

Decision-making authorities interviewed in Germany thought that advising LAGs on funding and coordinating between different actors were their most important functions. An interviewee from a decision-making authority in Sachsen (Interview 13) described her function as follows:

> I was responsible for coordination between the management of the LAG and the administrative unit, the ALE[34] ... We verified conformity with the LEADER concept, as well as what the management did before, in doing a kind of revision. We also checked conformity of the application with different directives and laws, such as budget or EU law.

Before the administrative machineries were set into motion and the project proposals made their way through the official channels, informal steps to coordinate potential future applications were taken by all the decision-making authorities interviewed (Interview 13):

> The LAG management gave us the project proposals, and we did a kind of pre-evaluation and gave recommendations so that the projects would be eligible for funding. If the coordination committee (Koordinierungskreis) made a positive decision that the project was worth being funded, the applicant prepared the papers and submitted the application with all the necessary attachments.

---

34  ALE stands for *Amt für ländliche Entwicklung*. This was one of the decision-making authorities in Sachsen and the authority the interviewee worked for.

An interviewee from Niedersachsen stressed that it was important to work quickly and in an unbureaucratic manner in coordinating between the project-executing group,[35] the administration and the LAG since the project executors had to provide funding for their projects themselves in advance to be reimbursed later on.

Mediation between the applicant, the regional management and the standards written down in the rules was also an important function in decentralised LEADER+ structures such as Schleswig-Holstein. This helped ordinary people file applications and showed them various options and alternatives. For instance, if project executors were in fact not permitted to be applicants, as some interviewees reported was the case, for example with the church or a club, the decision-making authority[36] looked for a municipality to be the project's backer.

Finally, decision-making authorities supported LAGs and project executors in handling projects and coordinating their implementation.

As was observed in the Finnish case, as well, the number of staff employed dealing with LEADER+ varied. The amount of LAGs each member of staff employed in a decision-making authority was responsible for was also diverse. In the German case, some of the staff responsible for LEADER+ were also engaged in the implementation of other programmes such as those launched by the *Land* or those receiving EU Regional Policy Objective-2 funding. One interviewee from Niedersachsen (Interview 15) reported: '25% of my position was dedicated to LEADER+ and for instance 20% to Objective 2-funding'.

A colleague from Sachsen (Interview 13) had a slightly different portfolio: 'I myself was only responsible for LEADER+, but I had 5 other colleagues who were responsible for other programmes, too. In our area there were 4 LAGs but this number differed from Amt to Amt, one had 2, one had 3 and we had 4'.

The interviewee from Schleswig-Holstein perceived the role of decision-making authorities as supervisory. But as the regional management and the decision-making authority were both situated at the county administration, cooperation was very informal. This also applied to the common search for guidelines and their definitions. Questions such as 'what is your opinion on this or that?', 'if we do it this way, does it work out or not, or are there better alternatives?' were characteristic of their daily interaction. One civil servant (Interview 17) described the administration of LEADER+ in his region as

> ideal since we threw the ball to each other. We had outstanding cooperation between the regional management, the head of the LAG, the executive committee and the decision-making authority. This was an interlocking system with a very smooth flow of information although the system was of course de jure separated.

Similar to the Finnish case, the self-perception of German decision-making authorities was that of a kind of soft-supervisor, with slightly more emphasis on the

---

35   Projects were not executed by the whole LAG but by project groups.
36   In a concrete case from Schleswig-Holstein.

supervising function. However, unofficial interactions between decision-making authorities and LAGs and a good working climate were often characteristics of the day-to-day working relations between decision-making authorities and LAGs. The coordination of functions was a core responsibility but decision-making authorities saw themselves, above all, as a public authority approving and, in a few cases, dismissing applications or asking the applicants to amend the applications. An interviewee from Baden-Württemberg (Interview 12) made this point quite clear:

> I would have preferred to see myself as coordinator but in point of fact we were more like supervisors. This was because we had to check the applications and say this doesn't work, the application has to be amended to make it eligible for funding. So we were more a supervising authority.

The inclusion of authorities to make initial decisions in addition to the decision-making authorities in some *Länder* resulted in much more complex decision-making structures compared to those in Finland. The fact that two authorities were involved in making initial decisions if the geographical area of the LAG included more than one co-financing authority added to this complexity and the duration of the decision-making process was much longer.

In some of the *Länder*, the managing and decision-making authorities were one and the same organisation. There was also one case where the decision-making authority was an investment bank. The LAGs in the *Land* of Hessen might have profited in this administrative model in terms of efficiency (e.g. the expertise of the bank's staff) and financially since a connection with loans was possible.[37]

The total number of LAGs in Germany was 148 and varied regionally between 1 (Saarland) and 45 (Bayern).[38] LAG membership was generally smaller than in Finland. One LAG from East Germany, the LAG '*Mittlere Altmark*', for instance, had 26 members, while the average membership of the executive committees of Finnish LAGs was 15–20. In Finland, there were groups with well over 200 members. Thirty-six per cent of Germany was covered by LAGs (129,629 km²). The population of the area covered by LAGs was 10,483,350, which represents 13% of the whole population. The average population density of a LAG's area was 80.9 inhabitants/km².

It is important to underline what an informant from the managing authority in Niedersachsen stressed; namely that it was possible that the internal structures of individual LAG's and their legal form were different, as were the tasks of the head of the LAG and the executive committees.

---

37  Decision-making is realised jointly with 16 rural district officers. The *Investitionsbank Hessen AG* is not a private bank.

38  A table indicating the number of LAGs per Land is in the appendix.

Another important characteristic of rural-development policies in Germany is a trend to professionalisation.[39] An increasing need for specialised regional managers fostered the development of special postgraduate degrees.[40] Thus, the construction and maintenance of policy-community-type networks were advanced through institutionalised vocational training or regional manager networks.

As far as the scope of duties and the status of regional managers in German LEADER+ programmes are concerned, there were substantial national and regional differences. Some regional managers only advised and provided information for the actors in the LAGs, others took a more active part in the application procedures.

According to the partnership principle, economic and social partners as well as associations should have made up at least 50% of the members of the executive committees of the LAGs. This means that half of the members should have been from local public authorities, which would have been a higher proportion than in Finland. In contrast to Finland there was also no principle of tri-partition defining the composition of the executive committees. This means that the participation of local residents was not assured.

As the following empirical chapters of this book show, the success stories of LEADER are success stories of all the people in rural Europe who have dedicated themselves to make life in their home regions pleasant and nice. This applies to LAG members, LAG managers, the staff in decision-making authorities and the open-minded actors working in managing authorities, who regard the countryside and its people as more important than paragraphs and prestige and have a clear understanding of local needs in a holistic perspective. Solutions that are imposed from above in a top-down manner are ill-suited. In order to achieve a more inclusive and sustainable development of rural areas, national and EU-level policy-makers need to rely on endogenous knowledge which is based on the specificities on the ground and the experience of all those active people in the countryside. On the following pages, they share these experiences with us.

---

39   For more on the professionalisation of rural-development policies in Germany, see *Leader Forum* (2005: 32).

40   While in 1993 there was only one option for obtaining a degree in *Regionalmanagement/Regionalberater* (*Akademie der Katholischen Landjugend in Bad Honnef-Rhöndorf*), during 2000–2006 future regional managers had at least half a dozen options. While some institutions provide a certificate, it is also possible to receive an MA from polytechnics and universities.

# Chapter 4

# Studying the Status of Local Actors in the Community Initiative LEADER+ – A Methodology for an Empirical Analysis of Germany and Finland

The empirical study of LEADER+ in Finland and Germany (Chapters 5 to 11) is informed by multi-level governance and structural constructivist approaches to European integration and policy making. The findings contribute to a more nuanced picture of how the local level of governance (public and private sector and civil society) in Europe's remote areas is integrated in the EU and how it is part of one of its public policies. The study shows how local actors are organised in multi-level decision-making and how one particular form of organised local actors, the LEADER+ local action group, is integrated in the multi-level structure of LEADER+ decision-making and implementation. Issues relating to intra-institutional relations, such as which group of actors is the most influential within the LAG are covered. In addition, it will be seen how those groups cooperated with other administrative units within the LEADER+ administrative chain and how their scope of influence was restricted, not only by predefined operational procedures but by the day-to-day implementation of the programmes. Another crucial point of investigation was the interaction of the LAG with public and private actors outside the LAG, especially local residents. The study wanted to discover if these new governance-type forms of interaction and cooperation attracted the attention of a wider local audience and if local residents participated in the work of the LAG. A related question is whether this LAG approach succeeded in bringing the EU closer to local residents in rural Germany and Finland.

The study began with exploratory interviews with the head of the executive committee and the LEADER+ manager of the LAG *'Mittlere Altmark'* from Sachsen-Anhalt, situated in the author's home region. In order to receive a more in-depth picture of the position of LAGs in the LEADER+ administrative chain, a questionnaire – also informed by the exploratory interviews – was designed and distributed to all the members of this LAG for pilot testing it.

This questionnaire contained five chapters on:

1. Personal Data,
2. The LAG's Creation,

3. Cooperation with other Administrative Units within the LEADER+ Administrative Structure, and Networking,
4. Functionality/Operational Procedure and
5. The LAG and the Public.

After the pilot testing a final questionnaire was constructed and was sent to LAGs from all over Germany to participate in a survey based on this questionnaire.[1] The respondents were in most cases members of the executive committee. The data on German LAGs used in the following analysis comes from 53 questionnaires.

For Finland, the questionnaire was only slightly modified in order to reflect the different structures of the state or educational system.[2] The questionnaire was sent to all members of the executive committees of all 25 Finnish LEADER+ LAGs. Only the executive committees were covered because of the large number of members – in some LAGs more than 200 – which would have made handling all the data too complex.[3] All in all, 59 responses were received from Finland.

The survey was supplemented and completed by interviews based on an evaluation of the results of the questionnaires. LAG members, LAG managers, several civil servants from Finnish and German decision-making and managing authorities and from the EU Commission were interviewed.[4] Interviewees received the questions before the interviews were conducted and were also informed about the survey results and invited to comment them.

Annual reports and position papers published by LAGs in addition to local newspapers, press reports and mid-term evaluations of the LEADER+ programme in Finland have been included in the analysis as well. An interesting detail regarding the collection of the data was that the Finnish mid-term reports were easily accessible and available on the Internet, while in some *Länder* in Germany

---

1    The focus was on the 13 *Länder* that implement a LEADER+ programme via LAGs. Sixteen LAGs from all over Germany took part: Altenburger Land (Thüringen), Burgwald/ Entwicklungsgruppe Region Burgwald e.V. (Hessen), Hildburghausen-Sonneberg (Thüringen), Hohenlohe-Tauber (Baden-Württemberg), Holsteins Herz (Schleswig-Holstein), Isenhagener Land (Niedersachsen), Mittlere Altmark (Sachsen-Anhalt), Naturpark Frankenwald e.V. (Bayern), Naturparkregion Uckermärkische Seen (Brandenburg), Nordseemarschen (Niedersachsen), Rügen (Mecklenburg-Vorpommern), Schlei-Region (Schleswig-Holstein), Sächsische Schweiz (Sachsen), Vogtland (Sachsen), Impuls Westallgäu 10+ e.V. (Bayern), Nordschwarzwald (Baden-Württemberg). Some LAGs that were contacted did not want to participate. Local actors from 16 German LAGs participated in this survey and filled in the questionnaire.

2    Regarding the state structure, the unitary Finnish state does not have counties or different forms of municipal organisations, as Germany has. The politico-administrative system (federal state, central/unitary state) and the degree of local and regional self-government are important background conditions when considering the implementation of rural policy.

3    Five LAGs did not want to participate or did not respond to several invitations.

4    The appendix contains a list of interviews.

those reports were classified as confidential. Thus, in the process of 'public' policy-making, the 'public' was more involved in Finland than in Germany. Furthermore, this also shows that German managing authorities were much more eager to maintain a government-dependent policy-style, while in Finland ideas on 'new' governance (e.g. partnership) seem to fall on much more fertile ground. The elaboration on different national contexts – for instance, different cultures, such as administrative culture, or practices of cooperation (i.e. competitive, goal-oriented, existence of hierarchical thinking etc.) paved the way for such a finding.

The focus on individuals was very important for conducting this empirical study. In Rhodes's (2000: 86) succinct phrasing, individuals as 'bearers of traditions enact and remake structures in their everyday lives. So, governing structures can only be understood through the beliefs and actions of individuals.' Bevir made another powerful argument that underlines the importance of focussing on the actors' positions and beliefs and how they interpret their role in a given situation. According to Bevir (2010: 261) 'reasoning is always local in that it occurs in the context of agents' existing web of beliefs. While the content of the relevant web of beliefs varies from case to case, there is no possibility of reasoning outside of any such backgrounds'.

If we believe Rhodes and Bevir, for understanding the functioning of a particular policy, in the current case LEADER+, we need not only to map the structures but we have to focus on how individuals engaged in policy-making interpret those structures and their own position in these settings. What is more, individuals in key positions as well as those that implement policy in their day-to-day action do not necessarily follow a well-designed path towards a clearly defined goal (Mérand 2011: 183).

In that sense, studies of multi-level governance could benefit from the application of structural constructivist methodology that is an additional and careful focus on individuals, on their feel for the game, their networks and strategies to utilise opportunities and their perception of their place in the institutional (multi-levelled) structures of governance – all of which are key elements in the shaping of policy (see also Bourdieu in Mérand 2011: 183). In approaches dealing with 'Governance and Political Struggle', the role and impact of ideas is of particular importance, too. This approach, as Wæver (2009: 169) put it, 'has grown around the concept of (multilevel) governance' and 'deals with political choices in different political settings'. Importantly, these choices are subject to political struggles for legitimacy and are not necessarily open and visible (Wæver 2009: 170). Highlighting the ideas that form the discourse on rural-development policy outlined below helps to make those struggles visible. The 'Governance and Political Struggle' view is useful in this context since it analyses 'national debates, and is interested in explaining, understanding or problematizing national policies on Europe' (Wæver 2009: 177). Actors from different territories form a national discursive community. The two national discourses analysed in this book are close to what Schmidt (2008) has defined as a coordinative discourse and encompass actors who deal with rural development in various different capacities, for instance, as policy makers or as practitioners. Schmidt (2008: 313) argued that in the EU, coordinative discourses among political and administrative elites are more common than communicative discourses involving the public. As far as the latter is concerned, elites or in-groups communicate their ideas to the public. However, it is precisely this lack of communication that is causing problems regarding legitimacy. Debates on policy reforms, often highly technical in nature, take place behind closed doors and escape the public view. Furthermore, there are several disconnected spheres in discourses (Schmidt 2008: 311). By focussing on national discourses in Finland and Germany some light is shed on how and where ideas that emerge in different national discourses on the state and the future of rural-development policy differ, but also on the issues they share. Yet, as Schmidt (2008: 307) and Kull (2009: 30–31) have argued, it is not necessarily the case that ideas or good practices that are seemingly more appropriate to the needs of society will prevail and finally be implemented. One problem in policy analyses feeding into policy making is the move away from a Lasswellian approach of deliberation and mediation between academics, decision-makers and citizens towards what Fischer describes as a growing emphasis on 'rigorous quantitative analyses' and the search for 'generalizable findings whose validity would be independent of the particular social context from which they were drawn' (Fischer 2007: 98). A structural constructivist reading of the current situation of multi-levelled rural governance serves to avoid such mistakes and helps to better understand the power structures as key features of the field of rural policy. Through the application of qualitative techniques such as group discussion and interviews or observations as applied in this study it is possible to see which groups possess more power as they can 'rely on a variety of social resources and institutionalized processes to protect their status and increase their power' (Kauppi 2011: 152). This means that the (reform) path chosen in a distinctive environment very much depends on the individuals occupying key positions in responsible institutions (see especially Chapters 5 and 6). Individuals responsible for institutional reform can and do select strategies from culturally specific repertoires. Being aware that culture-specific norms and ideas have an impact on actors and drive their action is important in order to understand why different approaches to policy reform occur in different member states, even in policy fields that are seemingly quite coherent in nature and categorised under the label of a 'Community Method' (Wallace et al. 2005: 49–92). Norms, ideas and symbols matter but it is important to keep in mind that norms, ideas and symbols are not free floating and only make sense in specific contexts (Mérand 2011: 180). To highlight and analyse these 'specific contexts' is what structural constructivists and this book are interested in. By studying political institutions and unmasking (hidden) mechanisms that determine the distribution of political power the empirical chapters are meant to fill a gap left by some multi-level governance scholars, social constructivists and other approaches interested in the study of the process of European integration and polity-building. The results of the empirical study are presented in Chapters 5 to 11.

Chapter 5 deals with actors and power relations in LEADER+ local action groups. In this chapter different issues concerning the internal structures of Finnish and German LAGs are examined, such as gender distribution, the interaction of actors within executive committees or between members and management. The influence of different actors within the LAGs is analysed, too. Members that had particular social or functional backgrounds were able to dominate administrative processes, or were at least perceived as being in more influential positions than other members.

In Chapter 5, 'LEADER+ – Actors, Local Action Groups and Power Relations', Finnish and German LAGs are positioned in the overall administrative structures of the Community Initiative LEADER+. This enables an analysis of how independent LAGs acted and reveals whether (actors from) other levels were able to restrict the power of LAGs. To that end, the LAGs' cooperation with other administrative units is discussed, such as with decision-making and managing authorities. In order to further illustrate the rather abstract and general act of cooperation, the questionnaire sent to the LAGs contained a number of concrete dimensions to shed more light on different aspects of cooperation. Respondents were asked to evaluate the formation of the LAG and the different authorities' information policies during this phase. In addition, they were asked to outline how they perceived the support of their LAG at the time the development plan was drafted. Furthermore, the questionnaire invited respondents to characterise the information policies of institutions from different levels. Last but not least, LAG members were invited to assess the impact of decision-making and managing-authorities on the time it took to process applications. Information policies of those latter authorities and the LAGs' networking strategies and experiences in international cooperation are discussed as well. In addition to the presentation of the results of this survey, this chapter also presents the comments of staffs from decision-making and managing authorities on this survey.

Chapter 7, 'Local Action Groups and the Public', positions LAGs in the broader local context beyond the institutionalised LEADER+ context. The LAGs' information policies and its relations to local residents are discussed. In addition, this chapter elaborates on whether or not local residents were interested in the work of the LEADER+ LAGs or in becoming members of such LAGs. One topic of discussion is whether or not the LEADER approach in EU-sponsored rural-development policies succeeded in bringing the EU closer to local residents living in Europe's countryside. In addition to local residents, this chapter is targeted at other regional actors that were not part of LEADER+ projects, for instance social institutions or trade associations.

Chapter 8, 'Cooperation beyond Local Action Groups – Decision-Making and Managing Authorities', stems from the need to assess the cooperation between decision-making and managing authorities. This is in addition to the positioning of the LAGs in the overall administrative structures in the previous chapter. In Chapter 8, the differences between Germany and Finland in terms of the independence of decision-making authorities from managing authorities at the top-end of the LEADER+ administrative structure are revealed. One conclusion is that the will to empower lower units and refrain from unnecessary and time-intensive control mechanisms was much more distinct in Finland than in Germany.

Chapter 9, 'Efficiency and Decentralisation', is meant to shed some light on the efficiency of the decision-making and implementation structures of LEADER+. In this context, taking a closer look at decentralisation makes sense, too. In Germany, the complexity of decision-making with several levels involved and the partial duplication of functions lead to situations with many actors being responsible without anyone really feeling so. Thus, decentralisation needs to be discussed by looking at examples from some German *Länder*, Finland or Ireland. This discussion also focuses on some of the negative aspects of decentralisation, such as the accumulation of power in the hands of local political elites and the danger that the LAG approach will be dismantled with the LAGs turning into governmental institutions.

Chapter 10, 'LEADER+ LAGs on the Move to the Next Programmatic Period – Hopes and Expectations for 2007–2013', looks into the expectations LAGs had for the future of EU-sponsored rural development in the funding period 2007–2013.

Chapter 11 summarises the main findings discussed in all sections. The results discussed in Chapters 5 to 11 are the ideas, hopes and critical views that were part of the various discourses around LEADER+, discourses between different actors engaged in rural development. In addition to representatives from the grassroots level civil servants ranging from the municipal level to officials from the European Commission, politicians and practitioners with various functional backgrounds were involved in elaborating their ideas on the future of rural-development policy.

# Chapter 5

# LEADER+ – Actors, Local Action Groups and Power Relations

This chapter starts at the bottom of the LEADER+ decision-making and implementation structure and analyses different issues regarding the internal structures of Finnish and German LAGs, the different forms of social and cultural capital possessed by the members of LAGs and their power relations within the LAGs. Of the questions asked in this context, the members' motivation to engage in the LAG, gender, age distribution and education are highlighted. Looking at these characteristics helps to unmask the 'inequalities and power relations between social actors within a "community" the territorial approach tends to mask by employing a consensus perspective' (Shucksmith 2000: 209).[1] Shucksmith (2000: 209) has argued that 'differences according to class, ethnicity and gender' can be 'obscured' in such communities.

To reveal the differences and power relations, this chapter looks first into gender, age and motivation of LAG members. The second section discusses the institutional backgrounds of LAG members and how this determines their weight in these institutions. After that, patterns of intra-institutional collaboration are highlighted.

## Gender, Age and Motivation

Analysing the composition of executive committees, there was a clear male dominance in Germany and Finland as far as the number of heads of LAGs is concerned. Seventeen out of 25 Finnish LEADER+ LAGs were headed by men and only 8 were headed by women. In Germany, 101 heads of executive committees were men and only 20 were women (Figure 5.1 below).

In her study of the composition of the LAG boards in the 2007–2013 Danish Rural Development and Fisheries Programmes, Thuesen (2010: 31) found a similar pattern for Denmark, where 'most of the board members are extremely well-educated older men who hold many other posts in society'.

Looking at the function and professional backgrounds of the heads/chairmen of LAGs' executive committees, the very high number of those working in public administration is striking. In Germany, 91 out of 148 heads/chairmen of LAGs, which is more than 61%, had this background. The Finnish case is an interesting

---

1   See also Curtin, Haase and Tovey (1997).

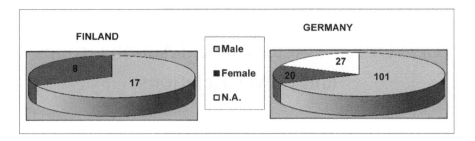

**Figure 5.1     Gender Distribution of Heads/Chairmen of LAGs' Executive Committees**

contrast to Germany. Whilst the data received was not as comprehensive as in the German case, at least 36% of the heads/chairmen of LAGs' executive committees had a background in public administration.

The majority of LAG members that answered the questionnaire were between 50 and 59 years old. This was the case both in Finland and Germany. The assumption is that these figures are very similar to the general situation in most German and Finnish LAGs.

LAG members were highly educated. Fifty-one per cent of the German LAG members that participated in the survey had a university degree. An additional 24% of all members had *Abitur*.[2] In Finland, 47% held a university degree and an additional 15% of the members held the *ylioppilastutkinto*.[3]

The majority of the members of Finnish LAGs said that the main reason for their joining the LAG was to be part of the development of the rural area (30%) or to play an active part in decision-making regarding rural development (19%). For 10% of the respondents, rural development was part of their profession (Figure 5.2 below).

The figures for Germany presented in Figure 5.3 (below) are very similar to those in Finland. Thirty-eight per cent of the respondents mentioned the development of the rural area as the number-one priority for their joining the LAG. An additional 7% wanted to foster sustainable development in their home region. For 11%, rural development was part of their work.

Many actors that were organised in LAGs were also engaged in the public life of their community and occupied important positions in their community. In his study on LEADER in England, Shucksmith made a similar observation. He also found that it was rather difficult to get everybody in the local community to participate in the development process. Instead, local elites, or local notables, were usually the most active figures in LEADER as well. According to Shucksmith (2000: 209) their accumulation of symbolic capital in the hands of a few people can lead to the 'exclusion of marginalized individuals and groups', and this is

---

2   Put simply, the final secondary school examinations that qualify the student to study at university.

3   See previous footnote.

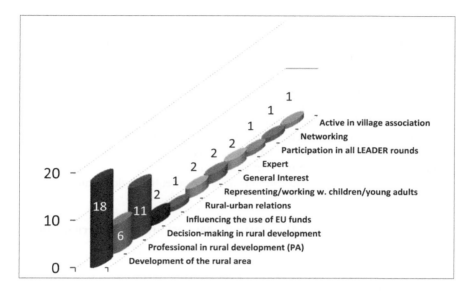

**Figure 5.2    Main Motivation for Joining The LAG (Fin)**

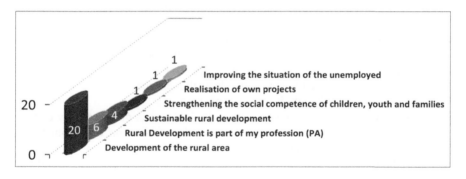

**Figure 5.3    Main Motivation for Joining the LAG (D)**

shown more explicitly below. The authors of the mid-term evaluation of the Finnish LEADER+ Programme came to a somewhat different conclusion. In their view, LAG activities have strengthened civil society. Especially in LEADER+, if compared to the other structural-funds implementation, the bottom-up approach and local orientation are more advanced. However, they also observed regional differences in that 'participation does not always expand dynamically: it seems that, in some areas, the same actors are always involved in development projects'.[4]

4   See 'Suomen LEADER+ Ohjelman Väliarviointoraportti 2003', p. 10.

These observations lead to one of the most interesting questions in terms of interaction within systems of governance and the cooperation of actors with different social backgrounds. What is the status and influence of those actors and are there any hierarchies both in terms of intra- and inter-institutional relations? Are those relations dominated by a group of people or even a single person or does cooperation function without domination, outside the 'shadow of hierarchy'? While some scholars perceive public-private partnerships as typical examples of governance institutions that are based on non-hierarchical coordination (see Rosenau and Schäferhoff in Börzel and Risse 2010: 115) access to knowledge and information as well as the professional background of members in LAGs does create situations in which certain groups have the potential to dominate others.

## Patterns of Collaboration – How Institutional Backgrounds Determine the Weight of Actors

To receive an impression about how Finnish and German members of LEADER+ LAGs perceive intra-institutional relations, questions were posed about the general working atmosphere within their LAG and the cooperation between the executive committee and other members. In addition, there is an interest in finding out whether there were certain groups that dominated decision-making processes within LAGs. Finally, there was a particular interested in the interaction and cooperation between LAG members and their management.

Most respondents from German LAGs took the position that the working atmosphere within their LAG was positive (positive 52%, very positive 38%). Forty-seven per cent of the Finnish respondents thought their working atmosphere was positive, and 37% thought it was very positive.

To discover whether interaction within the LAGs was dominated by certain groups, several questions were asked concerning the cooperation, on the one hand, between members of the executive committees and other members of the LAGs – and how the executive committee considers other members' concerns – and, on the other hand, between heads of the executive committee and other members of the executive committee. In addition there was an interest in which group of actors had the most weight and which group should be further empowered.

As an example of decision-making in a LAG, one LAG manager from Eastern Germany was asked to outline the decision-making procedure in his LAG. In this particular case the executive committee had three members (one head and two deputies). In cooperation with the LAG management the executive committee prepared LAG meetings and discussed applications to be forwarded to the decision-making authority. Specific work groups were created if needed, for instance on 'Culture and Education' or 'Tourism'. Decisions on forwarding the applications were made by all 28 LAG members during the LAG meetings. All the members had one vote. At the time the interview was conducted, 60% of all the members of this LAG were economic and social partners, and 40% were from the public sector.

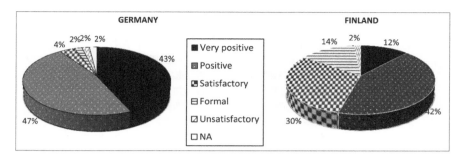

**Figure 5.4    Cooperation between Executive Committees and other LAG Members**

Overall, most members of the German LAGs characterised cooperation between the executive committees and other members of the LAG as either very positive (43%) or positive (47%) (Figure 5.4 above). A dominance of one group over another was not perceived. Finnish respondents painted a slightly more negative picture than their German counterparts. While the majority of them described cooperation between the executive committee and other members as good (41%) or very good (12%), 31% characterised it as satisfactory.

One reason for the difference between Finland and Germany is the larger number of members in Finnish LAGs, which made coordination more complex.

The majority of respondents from both countries were of the opinion that the executive committees considered the other members' concerns always or with only a few exceptions (Figure 5.5 below). Almost half of the German respondents said that the executive committee always considered other members' concerns (Finland 24%), and 45% said that this is always so, with only a few exceptions (Finland 58%). Six per cent of the German and 15% of the Finnish respondents said that the executive committees do not always consider the other members' concerns. The differences between Germany and Finland reflect the larger number of members in Finnish LAGs.

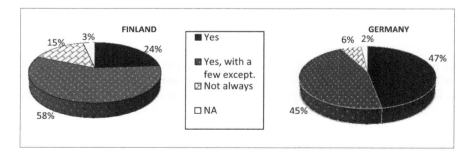

**Figure 5.5    Does the Executive Committee Consider other Members' Concerns?**

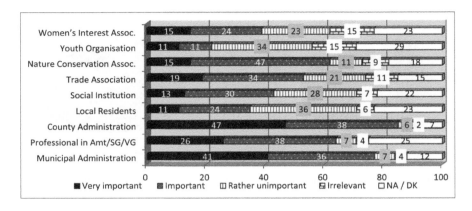

**Figure 5.6    Importance of Different Actors within German LAGs in Relation to their Affiliation/Functional Background**

The majority of the respondents from both countries gave a positive or very positive assessment of the cooperation between the heads of the executive committee and other members of the executive committee. Forty-three per cent of the Finnish respondents said that cooperation was very positive (Germany 35%), and 39% said it was positive (Germany 49%).

The empirical analysis of intra-institutional relations, such as working atmosphere within LAGs or the cooperation between executive committees and other members shows that interaction and persuasion is a social process of interaction 'where one agent convinces the other through principled debate'[5] rather than through manipulation or the use or misuse of a powerful position. However, as demonstrated above, there was a differentiated distribution of social capital such as gender and education and more studies of those characteristics are needed. Furthermore, in the context of hierarchical relations within governance units, the question as to how members perceive the influence of actors with different institutional and social backgrounds is also of interest. According to Bell and Newby (1971) and Shucksmith (2000: 208), 'communities of place are far from homogeneous and include many "communities of interest", with highly unequal capacities to act'. The evaluation of the answers received in this study of LEADER+ in Finland and Germany support this observation. Representatives of public administration had the most weight in German LAGs. As indicated in Figure 5.6 (above), a large majority of all respondents said that members employed with a municipality were important or very important. Most German respondents (85%) said that LAG members employed by their counties were even more important.

---

5    On the differences between a rational-choice reading of persuasion as manipulation and the constructivist view of persuasion as principled debate, see Checkel (2001a: 220–223).

When asked to comment on the perceived importance of members from the public sector, one interviewee (Interview 5) stated that members employed in the public administration:

> shape the opinion within the LAG. They know the day-to-day business, for instance the legal dimensions of funding, and those from the non-public sector subscribe to their opinions. There was one civil servant employed by the county who was a leading figure in writing the Regional Development Programme.

Another respondent linked the perceived high influence of members with a professional background in public administration to this group's access to information. The fact that members of those professional groups occupied more than one position, that is they were members of the LAG and worked for public administrations, this 'multipositionality', as Kauppi (2002: 26) has called it, provided them with access to important additional resources, such as information. Information was more accessible for them due to their professional knowledge of the subject and terminology and was ideally forwarded to other members that lacked this sort of professional capital. This means that members working in public administration have more influence in the LAG. In one respondent's view, this situation was: 'absolutely justified since they knew how things work'.[6]

Additionally, some German respondents argued that civil servants mastered the complexity of bureaucracy more easily since 'they' had the necessary routine.

Interestingly, and in stark contrast to Finnish LAGs, local residents were very poorly involved in German LEADER+ LAGs. One interviewee discussed the formation and composition of his LAG and the difficulties in motivating local residents: 'it was not that complicated to recruit members from the public sector, but to involve and motivate private actors was ... There are only a few local residents involved. They [local residents] are mainly stakeholders for different groups'.

These findings are similar to those found in the UK. In his analysis of LEADER in the UK, Shucksmith (2000: 210) found not only that a few groups were the most influential but that 'in many instances existing power-holders became more powerful, partly as a result of the failure to consider systems of governance and the dimension of power (Wight 1990). The more articulate and powerful individuals and groups were better able to engage with programmes and to apply for grants and submit proposals, while others lacking the former's capacity to act were unable to benefit from such capacity-building initiatives'.

Finland is very different from Germany and the UK in this respect. For instance, the answers to the question about the influence of different actors within LAGs were very different in Finland compared to those in Germany. Fifty-eight per cent of the Finnish respondents said that members of municipalities were very important actors within LAGs. The majority of the Finnish respondents (78%) said that local residents were very important. Reflecting on the research conducted by

---

6    The respondent was a member of a LAG from Sachsen-Anhalt.

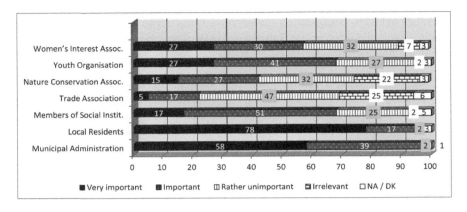

**Figure 5.7    Importance of Different Actors within Finnish LAGs in Relation to their Affiliation/Functional Background**

Shucksmith, the analysis of the Finnish case leads to the view that the capacity building of individuals (local residents) was much more advanced in Finland than in Germany. In Finland the 'capacity of "communities" (of place or of interest)' (Shucksmith 2000: 208) had been strengthened, while in Germany, quite often, actors from public administrations were in key positions. As Figure 5.7 (above) indicates, members of social institutions, youth organisations and women's interest organisations were perceived as important, too. This reflects the diversified communities in Finnish rural areas as opposed to the powerful position local notables occupy in German LAGs.

The differences between Finnish and German LAGs, especially as far as the much higher number of local residents in Finnish executive committees is concerned, can be explained by the principle of tri-partition, laid down in the Finnish LEADER+ programme, on the one hand and by the size of the LAGs on the other hand. While the findings do not necessarily show that any one group dominates intra-institutional interaction, they do reveal that certain groups were potentially more powerful. In addition to members with a background in public administration, nature-preservation associations played a major role in LEADER+ financed rural development in Germany. Sixty-two per cent of respondents said that members who were engaged in nature-preservation associations were important or very important. More than half of the German respondents expressed the opinion that members of trade associations were important, too.

In addition to the *perceived influence* of different actors, this study is interested in the members' views on which groups *should have more influence* in the LAGs.

Almost 40% of the Finnish respondents said that local residents should be more influential, and 20% said that members who worked for municipalities should be. The German answers were very different in that the members supported the status quo. Only 14% of the German respondents said that local residents should be more important, while 36% thought that members employed by local public administrations should be more important within the LAGs. Some German respondents thought that the existing situation was satisfactory, such as this respondent, who said: 'I think that all the members are equally influential. Cooperation is very constructive'.[7]

*The LAG Management*

An important institutional factor within LAGs was the LEADER+ management. It fulfilled a number of crucial tasks, such as advising the LAG, assisting in drafting and forwarding applications and acting as a mediator between the LAG and public-administration institutions. As an interface between the LAG and the authorities above, the management was in a key position. It often is 'the central operational unit' and functions as 'the motor of regional development'.[8] The managers were responsible for important administrative functions and were often key communicators with the decision-making authorities. An interviewee from an Employment and Economic Development Centre in Southern Finland (Interview 7) estimated that more than 95% of the interaction between the Employment and Economic Development Centre and LAGs in their region is with the manager, who is, according to the interviewee, 'in general the workhorse' of the LAG.

Almost all LAG members participating in this study said that their management was doing a good or very good job. In addition, respondents from both countries perceived cooperation with the management as good or very good. The majority of respondents from Finland and Germany stated that the management had contributed a great deal to the success of project applications and mediated well between the LAG and other actors. A member of one German LAG summed it up by saying: 'We always have the full support on the spot and within a very short time. My conclusion: The management is very positive for our project'.[9]

The figures below show that a large majority of Finnish and German LAG members was convinced of the work performance and necessity of the LAG management. Sixty per cent of all German respondents characterised both their management and cooperation with their management as very positive. The figures from Finland are very positive as well. Fifty-four per cent of all respondents said that their management and cooperation with their management was very positive, and 30% said that cooperation with the management was positive.

Regional management and the creation of regional-management networks as forums for exchanging ideas and experiences or for extending education are important organisational details in rural development in Germany, and not just for LEADER+.

---

7  The respondent was a member of a LAG from Sachsen-Anhalt

8  Jahresbericht (annual report) 2004 der LAG Entwicklungsgruppe Burgwald, p. 2.

9  The quote comes from a questionnaire filled in by one member of the LAG 'Mittlere Altmark' from Sachsen-Anhalt.

As to the conceptualisation of MLG and the establishment of networks as a feature of governance, one respondent's answer (Interview 1) is of interest:

> (Public authorities) have a great deal of experience with different regional management networks, for instance with Städtenetz (Cities Network), Regional Management Altmark, Regionen Aktiv, and tourist management. Due to this experience they know what they want, and above all what they want when selecting applicants. Since early 1994, structures have been further developed and working relations are tightly knit.

*Partnerships and Power Structures*

The statement above is a good example of the ambivalence of EU-funded rural-development policies in Germany. On the one hand, these policies are clearly for the good of selected LAGs. On the other hand, there is a sour note of densely knit structures leaving little room for others to enter. Considering the work of Giddens, his analysis of institutions is a very suitable explanation for the ambivalence of networks of modern governance. Giddens (1991: 6) argued that 'modernity produces difference, exclusion and marginalization. Holding out the possibility of emancipation, modern institutions at the same time create mechanisms of suppression, rather than actualisation, of self'. One of the interviewees contributing to the study of LEADER+ in Finland and Germany would not go this far but critically reminds us that old-boy networks (*alte Seilschaften*) exist not only as far as LEADER+ is concerned. According to him (Interview 3), those 'are a feature found at every level of decision-making in the Federal Republic of Germany. It is obvious that some actors are more equal than others. To assume something else is foolish'.

One important characteristic of governance in the multi-levelled EU is the inclusion of different actors in policy-making and especially in implementation. In Finland, the composition of the LEADER+ LAGs' executive committees and the principle of tri-partition reflect this characteristic. In Germany, the participation of public administration as well as economic and social partners followed different rules. For instance, the LEADER+ programme of the *Land* Sachsen-Anhalt laid down that at the decision-making level of the LAG at least 50% of the members in the executive committees had to be economic and social partners. Furthermore the programme demanded a fair balance of gender.[10]

Former Commissioner Franz Fischler once said that

> The partnership is in my view a fundamental part of LEADER and the future Community Initiative for rural development. The projects must be elaborated

---

10    See *Programm zur Gemeinschaftsinitiative LEADER+*, p. 56.

locally and not anywhere else. The principle of partnership must not only be maintained but also reinforced.[11]

According to an interviewee from the EU Commission's LEADER+ Observatory (Interview 16), partnership had been reinforced over the years. The main reason for and most obvious example of this is the 50% rule, whereby no more than 50% of LAG members can be from public administration. This 'golden rule and one of the core elements of the LEADER method' is, according to the interviewee, accepted throughout the EU. In addition, there is a tendency in an increasing number of countries to cover the whole country with LEADER groups. In some countries, there is a tendency to mainstream the partnership principle as regards other policies as well. However, while groups engaged in rural development can actively 'build on people's wish to believe in their "community",' by 'encouraging and developing its symbolic construction', there is the danger that other groups, such as local residents, who do not take part in this process, are disempowered and excluded 'if they do not feel affinity with the constructed cultural identity' (Shucksmith 2000: 210).

Overall, looking at the Finnish LEADER+ programme, the composition of the executive committees of the LAGs and the daily interaction of actors that participated in the empirical analysis, the conclusion is that in Finland the government component was not central and that the inclusion of local residents was much more advanced than in Germany. The principle of tri-partition and the LEADER method as practised in Finland was perceived to be built according to the needs of both practitioners at the grassroots level and policy makers in the decision-making and managing authorities. However, vertical networks, for instance, were mentioned for not working well enough at times. This is subject of the analysis carried out in the next chapter dealing with the interaction between LAGs and actors from different administrative levels that are part of the decision-making and implementation structures of LEADER+.

---

11   See 'Special LEADER Symposium Towards a new Initiative for rural development: 800 leaders give their views'.

# Chapter 6

# LAGs in the Administrative Structures of LEADER+ – Vertical Power Relations

This chapter contains three sections and begins with LAG members' perception of their cooperation with different actors within the LEADER+ structure. The perceptions expressed in the survey are analysed in the section 'Cooperation with Other Administrative Units'. Actors from different decision-making and managing authorities will have the space to comment on these assessments. The section is structured in such a way that after presenting the empirical results of the survey, the focus shifts to the comments of civil servants from decision-making authorities followed by the comments of staff from managing authorities. As information and the control of information are a very important aspect of the distribution and manipulation of power, especially in the conception of structural constructivism, one section is dedicated to information policy.

Networking and the construction of networks is an important feature of multi-level governance. The section on networking is a critical analysis of the realisation of national and international networks in LEADER+ and a discussion of the control mechanisms that had been imposed in some of the German *Länder*.

## Cooperation with other Administrative Units

Due to its proximity to the LAG, survey respondents judged the local level of public administration to be better than the regional or *Land* level in Germany and the central state level in Finland. Respondents viewed relations with managing authorities more critically than relations with other units in the LEADER+ structures. In Finland, the managing authority was situated at the central state level, and the programming level was national, while the German programming level was regional, and the managing authorities were situated at the *Länder* level (see Chapter 3). However, while the administrative structure was at first sight more decentralised in Germany without the federal level being involved, German respondents were much more critical in their assessment of cooperation with managing authorities than the Finnish respondents. Thirty-two per cent of the German respondents described cooperation with these authorities as good, 2% as very good. Thirty-eight per cent in total thought that cooperation needed to be improved; requires improvement (30%), was bad (2%) or very bad (6%) (Figure 6.1 below). As documented in Figure 6.2 (below), the majority of the Finnish respondents said that cooperation with the managing authority was very

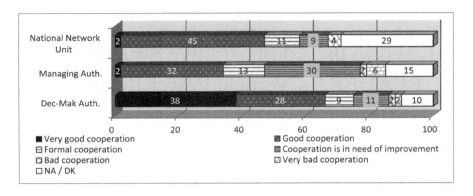

**Figure 6.1    Cooperation with other Administrative Units (D)**

good (39% very good and 7% good), while 7% of those respondents would like to improve cooperation with the managing authority. In contrast to Germany, nobody was of the opinion that cooperation was bad or very bad.

Overall, members of both Finnish and German LAGs painted a rather positive picture in terms of their cooperation with decision-making authorities. The majority of the German respondents perceived cooperation with decision-making authorities as good or very good. Fifteen per cent of those respondents were critical saying that cooperation has to be improved (11%) or that it was bad or very bad (4%) (Figure 6.1). Critical positions towards decision-making authorities mainly came from *Länder* where the decision-making authority was situated at the ministry level, such as in Mecklenburg-Vorpommern. The duration of processing applications was given as one reason for critical assessments.

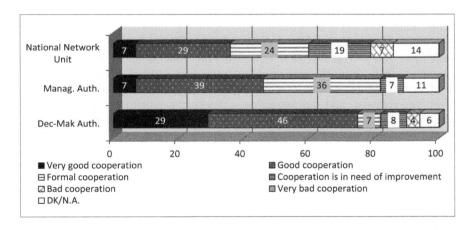

**Figure 6.2    Cooperation with other Administrative Units (Fin)**

The majority of Finnish respondents described cooperation with the decision-making authorities as good, too. Twenty per cent of the Finnish respondents said that cooperation with the decision-making authorities was very good (44% good), while only 8% took a critical view (bad) (Figure 6.2).

*Decision-Making Authorities and the LAGs*

Before discussing the results on the cooperation between LAGs and managing authorities, more light will be shed on the interaction of LAGs with decision-making authorities as this is, in terms of implementation, a more direct form of cooperation within LEADER+.

An important pre-condition for positive assessments of cooperation with staff from decision-making (and managing authorities) was the establishment of 'good relations' between actors from the LAG and individuals in key positions in those authorities. One German respondent explained that it was important to have good contacts with: 'the administrative personnel employed there and to interact well with them'.[1]

In addition to the perception of LAG actors, interviews were intended to shed light on how staff employed in decision-making authorities evaluated their cooperation with LAGs. This would provide a more balanced picture of the interaction of LAGs and decision-making authorities. Consequently, several decision-makers in Finnish and German decision-making authorities were invited for an interview.[2] All the interviewees were provided with information on how LAG members perceived their position *vis-à-vis* other actors. Interviewees were then asked to comment on these perceptions of cooperation between LAGs and other administrative units in general and decision-making authorities in particular.

The results of the LAG survey corresponded, according to the interviewees from both Finland and Germany, with their own experience. According to the interviewees from Finnish decision-making authorities, cooperation between the Employment and Economic Development Centres and LAGs with the administrative procedures was good. An interviewee from an Employment and Economic Development Centre in Central Finland (Interview 8) claimed that good cooperation was 'necessary and wise (and) people usually realise that good relationships make the work easier'.

A colleague of his from Southern Finland added that good cooperation was fundamental since the amount of bureaucracy is huge and both the Employment and Economic Development Centre and the LAGs have few administrative resources. According to him, if there was a delay in processing applications, the effects for the LAGs were substantial.

The quality and quantity of cooperation depends a lot on the personal chemistry between individuals in important positions or even the nature of certain groups of people. As an interviewee from Eastern Finland (Interview 10) argued: 'There

---

1　The respondent is engaged in a LAG in Eastern Germany.
2　A complete list of all interviews is in the appendix.

was very good cooperation because people here in Southern Karelia are not very formal. There was very warm cooperation'.

However, cooperation must function in two or more directions. This concerned the rural sub-committee (*maaseutujaosto*[3]) and its function as an advisory committee in the execution of the programme. Rural sub-committees were composed of representatives from public authorities, municipalities and various social partners and representatives from LAGs. A civil servant from an Employment and Economic Development Centre in Western Finland noted that the size of the rural sub-committees should not be any bigger than they were. In his view (Interview 11), larger rural sub-committees might cause problems in terms of coordination and bargaining, since:

> the rural sub-committee was probably a bit too big. While there were all kinds of political streams who wanted to stick their noses into everything ... luckily the political level did not participate. All expert organisations were involved, and local educational institutions were involved and so forth. So in practice the right people were selected.

One important reason for the positive evaluation of relations between LAGs and decision-making authorities was the professional support provided by decision-making authorities as public authorities, who were in most cases very valuable complements to the LAGs as public-private partnerships with the voluntary engagement of actors with different backgrounds.

Looking at the situation in Germany, one interviewee from Baden-Württemberg described the decision-making authority as a supportive coordinator:

> The people in the LAGs were often in charge of something entirely new for them. They didn't know what was written down in the budget regulation of the Land or what had to be taken into account when filing the application. So they had a totally different approach to LEADER than we had. And I think they were thankful that we took over this rather unpleasant job for them.

The personnel in decision-making authorities had specialist knowledge as regards the modalities of funding and the legal foundations. They 'succeed with things that

---

3   The rural sub-committee was established in connection with the Regional Management Committee (MYR). It was set up at the suggestion of the rural department of the Employment and Economic Development Centre (*TE-Keskus*). The Rural Development Plan for Finland defined the composition and functions of the rural sub-committee as follows. The rural sub-committee 'will be chaired by the head of the rural department. The task of the division is to monitor the progress of programme implementation, to handle programme amendments, and to coordinate the views, operations and funding of different financiers and players to create an appropriate unity in order to develop the rural areas of the region according to the regional development strategy'. See Ministry of Agriculture and Forestry Finland (2002: 84).

are in fact impossible', said one interviewee from Northern Germany. Furthermore, decision-making authorities also acted as the interface between the ministry (as the managing authority) and the LAGs.

Reportedly, in Sachsen, apart from a seminar, which was organised once a year and where the ministry also participated, 'there were no contacts between the LAG and the ministry'. Thus the decision-making authority filled an important gap. A similar problem concerning the cooperation between LAGs and the managing authority, the Ministry of Agriculture, was perceived by an interviewee from Niedersachsen. According to this interviewee, relations between actors from both levels were slightly reserved. This was a structural problem, as there were two administrative levels between the LAG and the ministry. Some members of the LAG, so the interviewee claimed, did not comprehend this constellation, and the decision-making authorities had to function as mediators between the LAGs and the public authorities and utilised their contacts to the *Land* parliaments and the *Land* government. An interviewee from a decision-making authority (Interview 15) reported:

> We did not have any fear of interaction with Land institutions; for instance, we visited the Land parliament or talked to the Minister. After that, the near impossible was suddenly possible. We had good relations, and we were in the fortunate position that four members of parliament were from our region, and we had to utilise those contacts simply to get the best we can for our region.

The cooperation between decision-makers and the heads of the LAGs, in addition to the managers and the project executors, was another important aspect of the relations between LAGs and decision-making authorities the interviews addressed. Decision-making authorities had close contacts with the heads of the LAGs, the managers and the project executors. The closest working relationship, as far as the processing of applications is concerned, was, according to most interviewees, with the LAG managers. As far as the implementation of projects is concerned, there was close cooperation with project executors. Informal meetings prior to the submission of the actual project application were of fundamental importance. An interviewee from a decision-making authority in Baden-Württemberg (Interview 12) elaborated:

> We exchanged information very often and outside the official channels. For instance, they asked in advance whether we could check if a project had a chance, or if it was eligible for funding if they launched it. And we said yes or no. So there was very close and good cooperation, also with the heads of the LAGs. Unofficial cooperation was very important. This concerns not only the LAGs but also, for instance, the mayors. There have been cases where mayors were pressed into choosing a project that they couldn't in fact support due to a lack of resources. As we know the mayors very well we gave them a quick call and asked 'are you serious about your application?'

Decision-making authorities and project-executors interacted directly with each other, not only during the implementation of the project but also as far as modifications and adjustments of the applications are concerned. An interviewee from a decision-making authority in Sachsen preferred direct interaction with project executors since, in her view, the inclusion of the management would be too time-intensive.

Another form of unofficial cooperation had been established between staff from decision-making authorities and their colleagues from other public authorities. They conducted *ex-ante* verifications whereby before the actual application was filed officially, the decision-making authority tried to find out whether or not the other authority was willing to approve the potential project. For instance, if a project was targeted at young people, the youth welfare office was consulted by the decision-making authorities. Whilst this mode of administration enhanced efficiency, it required a very good working relationship between individuals from different institutions. Otherwise, pragmatic actions outside the official channels such as a quick phone call to ask 'I have an application on my desk. I will send it to you. Could you have a look?' would not have worked. In addition, and usually as a first step, the management ensured that applications were complete and in such a form that they were eligible for funding. If some documents were missing, there was also interaction between the decision-making authority and the project executing group. This means that the management was not necessarily too involved. According to the interviewee from Sachsen (Interview 13), the managing authority would have liked to see this changed, but based on her practical experiences she argued that this would have been too time-intensive. While some interviewees thought that acting through unofficial channels was more efficient than following the official paths, others regretted that there was not more time to provide LAGs with additional information in advance. Both Finnish and German interviewees complained that there was a lack of resources, such as staff and time, which prevented them from fully supporting LAGs with official administrative processes.

In sum, decentralised decision-making authorities (in Germany, the counties) received the best evaluation by the respondents taking part in this survey. One of the reasons for this was that they were much closer to the LAGs, and the intensive cooperation often went beyond interaction within the LEADER+ context. Everyday contacts in routine working relationships were of great importance. Members with a professional background in public administration were able to profit from work-related contacts with their counterparts from higher levels. This shows that the construction of rural-development policies does not just depend on the LEADER structures. Routine interaction between actors with different backgrounds and positions outside the LEADER context was and is of paramount importance too.

*Managing and Paying Authorities and the LAGs*

Managing and paying authorities in Germany were different ministries at the *Land* level. Respondents from those *Länder* which had a more simplistic and decentralised administrative structure to implement LEADER+, such as Sachsen and Schleswig-Holstein, were less critical in their evaluation than those respondents faced with a high number of additional administrative levels. An informant from the managing authority in Niedersachsen argued that due to differences in the internal structures of individual LAGs and their legal form it was not possible to make universally valid statements regarding cooperation with the key actors of the LAGs such as the manager or the head of the executive committee. However, as a whole, the informant from the Ministry (Interview 14) explained that 'one can say that cooperation was businesslike and goal-oriented'.

The Finnish respondents painted a more positive picture when it came to evaluating cooperation with the managing and paying authority (Ministry of Agriculture and Forestry) than the German respondents. Confronted with the positive results, an official of the Ministry (Interview 6) argued that 'the situation was good'. However, he also outlined some of the problems that occurred in the first years of Finland's EU-membership. According to him, there were disagreements between the municipalities and the central government over the distribution of decision-making power.

> during 1996, 1997 and also during 1998 there were a number of municipalities where the municipal government said, 'yes we will participate in the LAG but we will decide on the projects'. I told them 'you can do so but then you can operate with 1 Finnish Markka only. Then you will not receive the additional 4 Finnish Markka of EU co-funding. Your intention is not according to the LEADER principle'. And then everybody agreed. Occasionally, there were civil servants from municipalities who opposed the fact that the municipality could not fully decide. There have been some minor problems but in general it worked well.

According to the interviewee, the situation has improved over the years:

> After some years many of those civil servants who had disagreed came to me and said: 'you were right'. They realised how much power there was in fact for the LAGs to decide themselves. In general in Finland, the municipalities have a problem, in that they have wide-ranging competence but no doers. Municipalities are sponsors, experts. One third of the executive committee (in the LAG) were municipal functionaries. Should there have been even more?

*Alternative Structures?*

Taking up the previous argument and looking at the institutionalisation of the implementation of EU structural funds in Finland, it is notable that new entities, such as the Regional Councils (*Maakunnan liitto*),[4] have been

---

4  For some scholars such as Ryynänen (2003: 167), the Regional Councils are the 'real regions' in Finland. They are 'joint municipal boards of which the *municipalities* in

created. However, as far as the administration of LEADER+ is concerned, the Regional Councils were rather unimportant players on paper. In spite of this, they participated in the rural sub-committees of the Regional Management Committee (MYR) and were composed of municipal deputies. Municipalities were included in the LAGs' steering committees. Despite the fact that Regional Councils were not part of the decision-making and implementation structure, staffs from the decision-making authorities, which were also situated 'in the regions', were asked how they see an empowered Regional Council taking over more tasks in LEADER+.

An interviewee from a Southern Finnish decision-making authority (Interview 7) argued that municipalities were included in the LAGs' steering committees and, according to him, 'this worked fine and was local. The Regional Councils are not that local'.

Due to the composition of the Regional Councils, he and others did not see them as appropriate actors in LEADER+, potentially replacing the Employment and Economic Development Centres. One argument was that the Employment and Economic Development Centres – acting as a public authority – were more neutral if compared to the Regional Councils. Some interviewees also argued that in addition to their representation via municipalities in the LAGs' steering committees, actors from Regional Councils also took part in the rural sub-committees of the Regional Management Committee (MYR). Although the interviewee from the Southern Finnish decision-making authority could have imagined including the Regional Councils instead of the Employment and Economic Development Centres, he explained that 'we were the public authority. In our rural committees representatives of the Regional Councils were always present. In these committees they had the possibility to influence and they were the experts of their own area and they were important there'.

Another critical aspect was raised by an interviewee from Western Finland (Interview 11). Due to their poor financial resources and lack of human resources, Regional Councils were, according to him, ill-suited to act as decision-making authorities. The development work within Regional Councils was rather modest with few staff and fewer resources: 'There was no staff, and there were no experts to handle this work. If their role was to be made stronger, then the Regional Councils would need much more resources'.

---

the region *must be members*' (Finnish Regional Development Act 602/2002). Its highest decision-making body, the Assembly, is indirectly legitimised in that it consists of delegates being members of the municipal assemblies. They are delegated to the Regional Council Assemblies. Among the main tasks Regional Councils are responsible for and involved in are the development of regional development plans, the co-ordination of EU regional development programmes and planning of the regional infrastructure (see also OECD 2010).

**Information Policy**

For the majority of German respondents (59%), the decision-making authorities were the key institutions to satisfy the need for information (Figure 6.3). The second most important source of information in Germany was the municipalities. The majority of the Finnish respondents (53%) said that the Employment and Economic Development Centres were the most important source of information, at least as far as questions on funding were concerned (Figure 6.3). In addition to the more or less intense information policy provided by decision-making authorities, the ministry and the national network unit provided LAGs with information, too. In comparison to Germany, the managing authority played a more important role in providing information.

According to the survey, 20% of respondents from Finnish LAGs said that the information policies of the decision-making authorities were very positive, and 44% said that they were positive, while 7% of them thought they were bad and 2% very bad. The managing authority received a fairly good evaluation, too. Forty-one per cent of the Finnish respondents were of the opinion that the managing authority's information policy was good (13% very good).

Decision-making authorities in Germany received a positive response, as well. Eleven per cent of all German respondents said that their decision-making authority conducted a very positive information policy, and 41% were of the opinion that it was positive. German respondents were much more critical than Finnish LAG members towards managing authorities. While 23% were of the opinion that managing authorities' information policies were positive, 28% of the German respondents had a critical standpoint saying that the information policy of their managing authority was either negative (21%) or very negative (7%). For some German respondents, there was a critical structural issue regarding the large number of levels and actors of decision-making involved. Complex structures led to a slow flow of information. An annual report summarised these shortcomings: 'there is a stronger need for information in the *Land* Hessen as concerns current

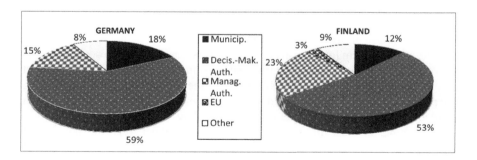

**Figure 6.3     Searching for Information on Funding, Which Level is Most Important?**

funding possibilities within regional development policies'.[5] Many respondents and interviewees argued that the situation had improved by the end of the funding period.

According to respondents and interviewees, information policy in Finland had improved, too. This is the position taken by many interviewees from decision-making authorities and the staff of the Ministry of Agriculture and Forestry as the managing and paying authority. For example, interviewees mentioned the improved quality of applications.

Despite a trend towards better performance, the lack of resources resulting in understaffed decision-making authorities was seen as a major problem and future challenge in Finland and Germany. As an interviewee from a Southern Finnish Employment and Economic Development Centre (Interview 7) reminds us:

> At the beginning there was a lack of resources, and providing information was kind of an extra job. Processing applications was our principal duty. If there was not enough time to handle information policy, this was a bad thing. Information policy needed to be improved.

The shortage of personnel was another problem, according to this civil servant. He was responsible for five LAGs, and his main function was to evaluate and approve applications. The high number of LAGs did not leave much time for information policy. However, in order to inform the broader public on LEADER+ in their region, the Employment and Economic Development Centre sponsored a bulletin for all LAGs out of its own development funds. LAGs from the whole region cooperated in publishing this bulletin.

It was difficult to find out how much time civil servants in Employment and Economic Development Centres invested in providing information. The general picture received from the interviews was that Finnish decision-makers thought there was not enough time for information purposes and would have liked to spend much more time on information policy. A lack of staff and their daily workload prevented them from doing more to provide information. A civil servant from South-East Finland (Interview 10) complained: 'I didn't have enough time. I had more than 10cm of post that came in every day. I think the provision of information was less than 5% of my work'.

The main problem for Finnish decision-makers was the lack of resources. While processing applications was their principal duty, information policy was regarded as something extra, an additional job. Some of the problems that occurred during the processing of applications could have been avoided if more resources had been available for conducting a proper information policy.

Reflecting on their information policy *vis-à-vis* the LAGs, the position of interviewees from German decision-making authorities was similar to that of their Finnish colleagues. Above all, they regretted the lack of time available. This

---

5   Jahresbericht 2004 der LAG Entwicklungsgruppe Burgwald, p. 10.

was propelled by a lack of staff in addition to ever higher standards in public administration, such as the necessity to document more than before every little step in detail. The answers to the question how much time decision-making authorities invested in providing information on funding varied. While some interviewees saw the provision of good information as their principal task and thought that it accounted for more than 50% of their work, others estimated that it represented no more than 15–20% of their work.

According to most of the German interviewees, the LAG management is an important mediator of information between the LAG and the decision-making authority. One interviewee (Interview 17) explained that:

> The manager and I, we met one whole day per week and exchanged our ideas. This was the minimum. In addition there were LAG meetings. In the meeting of the steering committee we discussed relevant issues in advance. We jointly sought out information on funding. We also went, together with the potential project executors, to the respective authorities to receive the green light that the project was eligible for funding.

In Niedersachsen, an important institution for exchanging ideas and information was the LEADER+ steering committee (*Lenkungsausschuss*). Representatives from all the LAGs in addition to all the *Land* agencies that took part in LEADER+ as well as the decision-making authorities participated in the meetings of this body. Meetings were organised several times a year. According to one informant from the managing authority, the steering committee was a platform for coordinating the actions of the LEADER+ regions in Niedersachsen. In addition, it served as a forum to exchange experiences and information amongst all the actors involved and between the LAGs. As a result, the informant (Interview 14) saw a 'steady flow of information between the different levels involved in the administrative procedures'. An interviewee from Schleswig-Holstein reported that the exchange of information between local actors and institutions and the decision-making authority functioned very well.

*Information Policy during the LAGs Constitutional Phase[6]*

To reflect in more depth the area of information policy, this study was interested in the respondents' perceptions of managing and decision-making authorities' activities during the constitutional phase of LEADER+ LAGs. There is an imbalance in the answers provided in terms of information provided by decision-making and managing authorities during the constitutional phase of LAGs. While 26% of German respondents said that the information provided by decision-making authorities was useful or very useful, the same number of respondents said the

---

6   Constitutional phase means here the time the LAGs started their preparations to apply to become a LEADER+ LAG.

information was not very useful or insignificant. A slightly more negative picture was painted as regards the managing authorities. While only 15% of all German respondents assessed the information provided by managing authorities as useful or very useful, 36% said the information was not very useful or insignificant.

Fourteen per cent of Finnish respondents said that the information provided by Employment and Economic Development Centres during their constitutional phase was very useful, 24% said that it was useful and 20% that information was neither useful nor useless. Only 12% of the respondents were more critical saying that information provided during the constitutional phase was not very useful or insignificant (3%). As far as the managing authority is concerned, 29% of Finnish respondents said the managing authority's information was useful or very useful.

Almost the same number of Finnish respondents assessed the information provided by the managing authority as not very useful or insignificant (25%).

The figures show that in both countries at the beginning of the LEADER+ programming period (2000–2006) decision-making authorities were much more important partners for the LAGs than the managing authorities. In addition, survey and interview data shows that managing authorities in Finland had much closer contacts to the LAGs than was the case in Germany.

Interviews with staffs from different decision-making authorities revealed that there were some regional differences in the amount of information provided in Finland. These variations were due to differences in the financial resources available to the individual Employment and Economic Development Centres and the amount of staff dealing with LEADER+. For instance, in the area where one of the interviewees from Southern Finland worked, at the beginning of the programming period 2000–2006, there were a number of new LAGs that did not participate in LEADERII. Due to the lack of resources, the interviewee (Interview 7) describes a rather limited interaction with them in terms of personal exchange. However, as she also outlined, they

> were with them (LAGs) in spirit and also answered questions if asked, but we did not manage to do more. We from the administration did not go there to tell them what to do. And there were not enough resources to go even though they had invited us.

In contrast to the situation in Southern Finland, a civil servant from an Employment and Economic Development Centre in Western Finland (Interview 11) said that they provided a moderate amount of support to LAGs during the constitutional phase. He said that the two LAGs that had already taken part in the previous funding period (LEADERII) were supported as far as the Employment and Economic Development Centre's abilities allowed. In his view, the new LAGs 'didn't face any problems, they received all the support they needed'.

While most interviewees from German decision-making authorities saw their information policy during the constitutional phase as relatively good, they pointed out shortcomings as regards the managing authorities' information policies. Harsh criticism that supports the thesis that the *Land* level was the dominant actor in LEADER+ came from Baden-Württemberg, Sachsen-Anhalt and Niedersachsen. According to an interviewee from Baden-Württemberg (Interview 12), the selection of LAGs was highly politically motivated. One interviewee said that

> we have the impression that the constitutions of the LAGs are political tales. That means that the ministry has cooperated directly with the District Administrators and decided it will set up a LAG in this district. We were only informed later on the selected areas. Seeing this is sometimes hair-raising because we know the areas and their peculiarities and cannot understand why, for instance, this municipality has been included and the other not, or why the LAG border divides a municipality. I would have liked us to have been included more extensively but we have the impression that the decisions were politically motivated.

Critical issues were also reported from Northern Germany. According to an interviewee from Niedersachsen (Interview 15), the responsible managing authority was too optimistic, almost naive as to the scope and coverage of the programme, and gave a misleading message to potential LAGs:

> In June 2002 when the managing authority initiated the programme it said that you can do anything you can imagine. As a result, many groups started. Later they faced a big problem. The minister said you can do whatever you want in the beginning! And then, little by little the ministry (managing authority) said, this doesn't work.

According to this interviewee, a misleading information policy in the early days of LEADER+ led to LAG applications that were not in accordance with funding rules. The interviewee explained and stressed that it would have been better if, having realised some of the problems during the first review of the applications, the ministry would have suggested some minor amendments. He explained that

> The region had been selected but 50% of the projects in their application were not eligible for funding. That is impossible! They (the ministry as the responsible managing authority) should have said, 'this one yes, this one no'. 'The heck with it!' In my view, during the first review they should have said, 'you need to rework this a bit, since at least 50% of the projects suggested according to the implementation rule are not eligible for funding'.

The managing authority (Interview 14) being criticised here painted a different picture arguing that during the constitutional phase, 'the work in the LAGs and in the decision-making authorities had been supported in numerous meetings, and we arranged further education'.

The heads of municipal administrations that did not participate in LEADER+ criticised the fact that information policy during the constitutional phase of the

LAGs was, contrary to what was announced in LEADER+ programmes, selective rather than comprehensive. Confronted with such statements, an informant from the managing authority in Niedersachsen (Interview 14) responded very evasively arguing that 'the area of additional information was fairly wide, and the thematic fields were very ample'.

Switching to Sachsen, some minor problems experienced in the early phase reportedly reflected a lack of experience with the programme. The officials in the managing authority wanted to get acquainted with what lay ahead. As regards the upcoming programming period 2007–2013, many issues, most importantly the budget, were, similar to the LEADER+ round, rather ambiguous half a year before the start of the new period. However, an interviewee from a decision-making authority in Sachsen (Interview 13) supported the managing authority's position and behaviour:

> They knew that there is a programme being launched, but they did not exactly know the details. They were in the starting blocks and would have liked to start but could not because not all the preliminary work had been finished. They probably would have liked to run a more intense information policy but were not sure whether the programme would live up to its promise to satisfy people's expectations.

Schleswig-Holstein is an interesting case since no decision-making authorities had been set up during the start-up phase of LEADER+. LEADER and LEADER II were conducted by the managing authority without an additional decision-making authority. Decision-making authorities were set up during the LEADER+ programme. Insiders reported that this led to a situation where individuals' activity and their access to the 'right people' were important pre-conditions for successful selection and participation in LEADER+. As one interviewee from Schleswig-Holstein (Interview 17) reports: 'As I was personally involved in setting up a LAG, I can say we have done all this alone, without a decision-making authority. We had some contacts with the Ministry but did most of the work on our own'.

In analysing the function of governmental institutions and the transformation of LAGs after the construction of the LEADER programmes in Germany, Bruckmeier (2000: 221) argued that

> rural development projects became more politically controlled, standardized and administered; the independent actors and action groups have, in effect, become 'Quangos' (quasi-non-governmental organizations). The influence of governmental institutions has thus been strengthened and the financial basis enlarged; the programme has 'golden chains'.

The impression received from interviewees and questionnaire respondents regarding the 2000–2006 programmatic period comes closer to this observation than to hypotheses claiming that the EU polity is non-hierarchical and post-political. German managing authorities were very important actors that controlled processes and monopolised power (see also Böcher 2008). The Finnish case looks slightly different despite the fact that some issues, such as the time available for providing information or the allocation of resources has been criticised, too.

### Networking

An important trend in European rural development is that LAGs increasingly combine their efforts and create synergies. Networks are organised nationally and internationally. Respondents from Finland and Germany stressed the importance and value of networking, a position shared by the Commission. Forty-four per cent of the German and 52% of the Finnish respondents said that networking was very important, and an additional 28% of the Finnish and 23% of the German respondents argued that networking was important (Figure 6.4). For 8% of the German respondents networking was unimportant. For 13% of the Finnish respondents networking was unimportant or totally unimportant.

German LAG members were more satisfied with their LAG's networking strategy than their Finnish counterparts were with theirs. The majority of the German respondents said that their LAG's networking strategy was good (41%) or very good (19%). Looking at Finland, 43% of all respondents appreciated their networking strategy, stating that it was good (36%) or very good (7%). Nineteen per cent of the Finnish respondents would have liked to see more efforts in terms of networking, and 12% of them were not aware of any networking strategy.

At the national level, institutions – national network units – had been set up to assist LAGs in finding partners for cooperation. At the EU level, LAGs were able to use the European Database for Cooperation to find LAGs with similar interests willing to cooperate Europe-wide. Interesting differences became visible in terms of the LAGs' usage of the national network unit and the European database for cooperation to help find partners. While about half of all Finnish respondents regarded the national network units as being a more important player, 42% of them

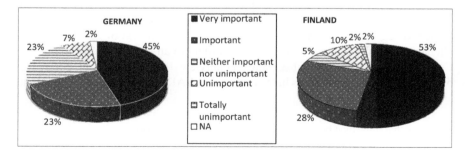

**Figure 6.4     How Important is Networking?**

expressed the opinion that both national and community-level institutions were relevant. Only 11% of the German respondents shared this view. For 21% of the German respondents, both the national network unit and the European Database for Cooperation were irrelevant in helping to find partners.

German LAGs from Niedersachsen criticised restrictions imposed by the managing authority that resulted in serious problems as regards international networking. An interviewee from an LAG in Niedersachsen critically stressed that the managing authority had imposed regulations for financial support of networking there were so strict that they made cooperation almost impossible (Interview 5). There had to be a clear added value from cooperation. Meetings aimed at finding common interests and mapping possible areas of cooperation were apparently not possible.

As far as international cooperation is concerned, the behaviour of the managing authority in Niedersachsen was also perceived as problematic by an interviewee from a decision-making authority from another region in Niedersachsen. According to his information, which was confirmed by other decision-makers, LAGs in Niedersachsen did not conduct much international cooperation during the 2000–2006 programmatic period. The interviewee observed that towards the end of the LEADER+ programming period, the managing authority became more active. One reason, according to this interviewee, was that the budget of the LEADER+ programme contained a sum for supporting international cooperation, which had not been fully used by the managing authority. As the Commission wanted some explanations for that in its evaluation of the programme's implementation, the managing authority showed more activity at the very end of the funding period.

This demonstrates how influential and powerful the *Länder* level was and how much it was able to restrict the core actors in LEADER+, namely the LAGs. While networking and transnational cooperation were important features of LEADER+ and favoured by the EU Commission, the national and in this particular case the *Länder* level had the option of formulating strict rules and preventing the full and unrestricted implementation of policies. They did not renounce their influence and gate-kept EU law.

Other problems that became visible in the construction of networks related to the budget for LEADER+. Countries which had a very small overall budget tended to neglect the importance of networking in the context of LEADER+ and allocated (too) few funds to this issue. According to an interviewee from the EU Commission's LEADER+ Observatory (Interview 16), an important difference between the EU member states in the context of LEADER+ concerned cooperation and networking[7]:

> I see that some member states clearly did not attach much priority to international cooperation. Although we have said clearly that for the Commission it was a

---

7   On the different LEADER+ actions, see Chapter 3.

priority. It was the European dimension. It was clear that it was a European initiative and maybe they (the national authorities, esp. the managing authorities) stressed more the method, the tool as such but not so much the cooperation element.

The interviewee added that based on his experience with other community initiatives, some areas in Europe are more cooperative than others. Cross-border cooperation between neighbouring regions has a certain tradition in the Baltic area, Scandinavia and the Mediterranean. There is a long tradition of cooperation between neighbouring countries. According to the interviewee from the LEADER+ Observatory, cross-border cooperation was the European dimension of the LEADER+ programme, and the authorities should have encouraged rather than obstruct, as observed in the Niedersachsen case, cooperation. The neglect of cooperation, a key dimension of LEADER+, was problematic since in structural funded rural development, INTERREG and LEADER only were the available tools to fund cross-border cooperation between local actors.[8] However, convinced of the benefits from cooperating with international partners, LAGs pragmatically approached restrictions in cross-border cooperation by using their own resources for networking.

Overall, looking at the vertical power relations in LEADER+, the member states remain in core positions, be it, as is the case in Finland, in trying to construct a broad involvement of different groups and to mainstream the programme, or, as is the case in some German *Länder*, in supervising, steering and controlling, and in constructing and maintaining a government-dependent policy instead of encouraging autonomous regional and local development.

---

8   While LEADER could have been used as a complementary tool to INTERRREG under some conditions, in INTERREG only a few activities were eligible for funding in the context of rural development.

# Chapter 7
# Local Action Groups and the Public

In this chapter, the local and regional contexts of the LAGs are analysed, by shedding some light on the relations between LAGs and other individuals and groups. First, the LAGs' openness in terms of their readiness to accept new members is looked at. Second, the information policies and strategies LAGs used to inform the public about their work is discussed. Third, the mobilisation of local residents to become members is analysed, including the extent local residents have been interested in the work of the LAG. Finally, differences between Germany and Finland in terms of the LAGs' success in bringing the EU closer to local residents are shown.

## LAGs and Local Residents

For local residents access to a LEADER+ LAG was different in Finland and Germany. In Finland, LAGs were generally open to new members, and local residents were able to join relatively easily, for instance, via the Internet. In Germany, at least in some cases, membership was restricted. In one LAG from Sachsen-Anhalt, for example, all members decided whether or not to accept new members by simple majority after the managing and decision-making authorities had approved enlargement. To the question whether it was difficult to attract new members, one respondent from the same LAG (Interview 4) answered that obstacles to potential members joining were often economic in nature. She explained that 'Financial contributions to be paid when joining the LAG, for instance, to finance the LAG management discouraged potential members'.

Looking at Germany as a whole, 74% of the German respondents said that their LAG was open to new members, while 17% said it was not. Reflecting on the differences mentioned above, it does not come as a surprise that the figures for Finland reflect more openness. Eighty-eight per cent of the Finnish respondents said that their LAG welcomed new members. Openness, in this context concerning membership, is a general problem facing systems of governance. As this example shows, network-type units for solving functional problems are not open to new members to the same degree.

The European Commission has discussed the problem of openness in European governance in the White Paper on European Governance, in the Report from the Commission on European Governance and in the White Paper on Multilevel

Governance.[1] The former two documents failed to fully address some of the core aspects of the problem of openness in systems of governance, as many observers and practitioners have criticised.[2]

Once the problem of efficiency is tackled and solved by involving experts from the locality, openness and accountability may suffer, as the German example demonstrates.

In addition to membership, another important issue in terms of the linkage between an LAG and its local and regional environment is the LAG's information policy targeted at local residents. A large majority of Finnish and German respondents – 87% of the members of German LAGs and 88% of the members of Finnish LAGs – stated that their LAG organised information events to inform the public about its activities and projects. LAGs used various tools, such as Internet platforms, to inform people about their work. In Finland, all but one LAG had a homepage. LAGs also used newsletters and the local press to communicate with local residents about their work. They also participated in or organised local or regional events such as exhibitions. While most LAGs actively informed the public about their work and activities, the survey contained a question concerning the interest of local residents in the work of the LAGs and in becoming members. The majority of Finnish and German respondents painted a rather negative picture when asked whether there was any interest in the work of the LAG or in joining the LAG. Forty-three per cent of the German respondents said that local residents were not very interested or not interested at all in the work of the LAG (21% said they were interested). More than 60% of those respondents said that local residents were not much interested or not interested at all in membership.

According to the survey data, most Finnish LAGs conducted an intense information policy, too. However, as Figure 7.1 indicates, most of the members of Finnish LAGs were of the opinion that local residents were only slightly interested in membership and only moderately interested in the work of the LAG. Twenty-one per cent of the Finnish respondents said that local residents were not interested or not interested at all in the work of their LAG. Twenty-seven per cent of the Finnish respondents had a positive image of local residents and their interest in the work of the LAG. The majority of the Finnish respondents (53%) were of the

---

1    See European Commission (2001). For a summary of the reactions to the White Paper see European Commission (2003). Information about the White Paper on Multilevel Governance is available at http://cor.europa.eu/en/activities/governance/Pages/white-pape-on-multilevel-governance.aspx. For a discussion of rural implications see Chapter 2.

2    See, for instance the following documents: Association of Finnish Local and Regional Authorities: 'The Position of the Association of Finnish Local and Regional Authorities on the Reform of European Governance'; Eurocities: 'Eurocities Response to the Commission's White Paper on European Governance'; German Association of Cities and Towns: 'Statement on the White Paper on *"European Governance"*'; German Association of Towns and Municipalities: 'Position paper of the German Association of Towns and Municipalities (DStGB) on the European Commission's White Paper on European Governance'.

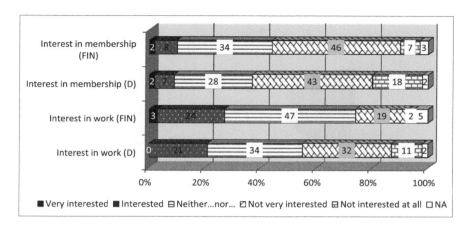

**Figure 7.1    Public Interest in the Work of the LAGs and Membership**

opinion that local residents had no interest or no interest at all in membership. One respondent to the questionnaire summed this up: 'Honestly, there was no real interest'.

Many actors in Finnish and German LAGs sought to improve this situation. To achieve this, LAGs in both countries developed numerous strategies to improve public interest and attract new members. They organised open days or were represented at regional events. One LAG invited local residents and rural actors to take part in a 'Future-Conference' and invited participants to express their views on how to develop the region.[3] Another example was a youth exchange programme between German and French pupils fostered by the same LAG.[4]

An interviewee from a decision-making authority in Schleswig-Holstein was also convinced that local residents had become more interested in the work of the LAG over time. He observed that sometimes there were more people at LAG meetings than at normal county council meetings. The local and regional press were very interested in and reported on LAG meetings. The interviewee (Interview 17) described the LAG meetings thus:

> Local newspapers reported on the meetings. The meetings were open to the public and people came because they knew that something was going to happen. Sometimes there were up to 40 non-members, and this was very positive because it showed us that our work went down well with the public. In comparison, sometimes there were only 1–2 people at meetings of some committees of the county council. This is nice, but of course public relations can always be improved.

3    See 'Jahresbericht 2004 der LAG Entwicklungsgruppe Burgwald', p. 4.
4    See 'Jahresbericht 2004 der LAG Entwicklungsgruppe Burgwald', p. 6.

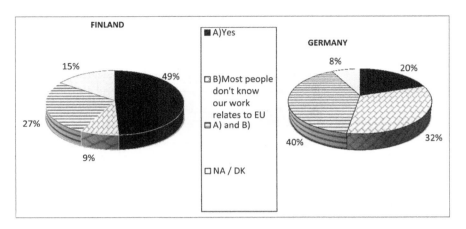

**Figure 7.2     Success in Bringing the EU Closer to Local Residents**

As far as information policy and the interest of local residents in the work of LAGs are concerned, an interviewee from a LAG in Sachsen-Anhalt (Interview 4) was positive and optimistic about the future: 'Well, local residents were interested in receiving information. We regularly communicated via the press or our "Newsletter". There was increasing interest in our work'.

She added that in addition to the measures mentioned above, it was important to indicate when projects are financed by LEADER+ money, for instance by adding labels to LEADER+ sponsored projects. She concluded that the LAG had 'succeeded in bringing the EU closer to the local residents'.

This position was not shared by all respondents, especially not by those from Germany. While half of Finnish LAG members thought that their work had brought the EU closer to local residents, 27% were of the opinion that most local residents were not able to relate the work of the LAG to the EU. German LAG members were much more pessimistic. Only 20% thought that they had succeeded in bringing the EU closer to local residents. Thirty-three per cent were convinced that most people in rural Germany did not know that the LAGs' work related to the EU.

**Cooperation with other Regional Actors**

In addition to questions about the LAG members' perception of their interaction with local residents, the questionnaire contained questions about how the LAG members assessed their cooperation with other actors from their region. A list of social groups and institutions was provided to the respondents and they were asked whether cooperation with the various groups was very good, good, formal, sufficient, in need of improvement, bad or very bad.

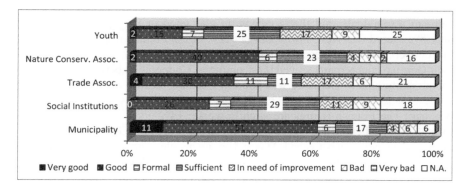

**Figure 7.3    Cooperation with other Regional Actors (D)**

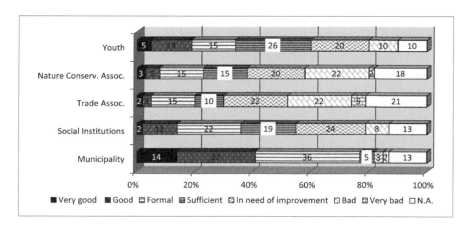

**Figure 7.4    Cooperation with other Regional Actors (Fin)**

Due to the principle of tri-partition and the mainstreaming of the LEADER approach in Finland, the inclusion of different groups in the LAGs was much more developed in Finland than was the case in Germany. The evaluation of the interviews supports this argument as well. As is documented in Figures 7.3 and 7.4 below, LAGs from both countries cooperate fairly well with municipalities. Sixty-two per cent of German respondents said that cooperation with municipalities, which were not part of the LEADER+ administration, was good or very good. Forty per cent of the Finnish respondents shared this position. Thus, in Germany, cooperation was slightly better. One explanation is the higher number of civil servants from municipalities involved in LAGs and their work-related contacts to other municipalities.

There is a stark contrast between Germany and Finland in the perception of the LAGs' cooperation with nature-preservation associations. While 42% of

German respondents said that cooperation was good or very good, in Finland only 8% shared this view. Forty-four per cent of the Finnish respondents argued that cooperation was in need of improvement, bad or very bad, while only 13% of their German counterparts voiced these opinions. Cooperation between LAGs and social institutions in Germany was good in the view of 26% of the respondents, while 29% saw it as sufficient, 11% thought it needed improving and 9% said it was bad. The Finnish figures are slightly worse: 14% good or very good, 22% formal, 19% sufficient, and 8% bad. Seventeen per cent of the German respondents evaluated cooperation between LAGs and young people as good or very good, 25% as sufficient, 17% wanted to improve it and 9% said such cooperation was bad. The Finnish figures are quite similar. Nineteen per cent of the respondents saw cooperation between their LAG and young people as good or very good, 26% sufficient, 20% in need of improvement and 10% were critical, saying cooperation was bad.

Chapter 8

# Cooperation beyond Local Action Groups – Decision-Making and Managing Authorities

This chapter sheds some light on the interaction and cooperation between decision-making and managing authorities. It discusses whether the managing authorities were in a dominant position or whether the relations were, as some multi-level governance scholars perceive the EU's multi-level system of governance, structured without hierarchies or an accumulation of power at the top-end in the national LEADER+ setting. To that end, interviewees from several Employment and Economic Development Centres and German decision-making authorities were asked to characterise their cooperation with the managing authority. Did the managing authority act as a superior or a colleague? Were there any serious problems in these relationships? If so, what were the reasons for those?

The relations between Employment and Economic Development Centres as decision-making authorities and the Ministry of Agriculture and Forestry as the managing authority was that the Ministry was a 'soft supervising' managing authority, or as an interviewee from Central Finland (Interview 8) put it: 'The Ministry of Agriculture and Forestry acted like a superior, but like one that listens'.

The overall impression is that the Ministry of Agriculture and Forestry – as managing and paying authority – was accountable for the programme and that it needed to ensure that the LEADER+ programme was properly implemented. This was accepted by the decision-making authorities who adopted the attitude that this put the managing authority in a superior position. While most interviewees argued that relations were cooperative in nature and that there was room for discussion, some critical issues were also pointed out. One problem related to the workload in both authorities caused some delays. A civil servant from an Employment and Economic Development Centre in South-Eastern Finland (Interview 10) reported:

> Civil servants in the managing authority were quite busy people, and when you asked some questions they always gave different answers. Of course, they were trying to do things the same way but I have heard many times that when you asked person A or person B they always gave different answers. In general they were excellent but sometimes we had to wait quite a long time for advising letters.

Her colleague from Southern Finland (Interview 7) was critical of the administrative practices of the staff of the managing authority. He was not satisfied with the administrative culture and practice of the Ministry and reported that he was about to stop asking for advice because he did not receive answers in the past.

He added that sometimes the Ministry did not want to answer him. In his view, the reason for the shortcomings was that the managing authority lacked time since it prioritised relations with the EU. He observed that only after they have dealt with the EU's experts and 'if there was some time left did they then deal with the Employment and Economic Development Centre. That is how the ranking has been'. In his view, an institution that coordinates between the managing authority and the decision-making authorities and fosters understanding between the Ministry and the Employment and Economic Development Centres would have solved this problem. According to him, this could have been either one Employment and Economic Development Centre or the national network unit. One colleague of his was more satisfied with the work of the managing authority. 'Except for the inspectors (of the managing authority)', the interviewee from Western Finland (Interview 11) argued, 'there was cooperation and there was an openness to discussion'. The interviewee was positive arguing that

> the auditing activities also didn't cause any major problems although they meant additional bureaucracy, since inspectors from the Ministry were not experts in this field but they raised questions and wrote them into their reports, and we had to answer those, however stupid they were. But besides this, the cooperation functioned very well.

The impression received from Germany after a number of interviews with decision-makers, LAG members and Commission officials was very different and much further from the ideal of a non-hierarchical, functional type of cooperation than was the case in Finland. Some interviewees perceived mistrust by the managing authority towards the decision-making authorities and lack of understanding. Critical interviewees and respondents criticised the waste of resources and the partial selection of LAGs to become part of LEADER+. As interviewees from German decision-making authorities criticised the administrative practices of managing authorities, they were asked to provide a more detailed evaluation of their daily cooperation with them. If there are any problems, what triggered them?

According to an interviewee from Baden-Württemberg (Interview 12), a serious problem was that the bottom-up approach, a basic principle of the LEADER-approach, was not realised since some decisions were monopolised and depended on one individual person from the managing authority. She also mentioned other problems such as mistrust by the managing authority or 'a lack of assigning personal responsibility to subordinates, in short, the opposite of bottom-up. This was top-down'.

The interviewee painted the picture that the ministry and the individuals employed at the ministry stood at the top of the LEADER+ administrative chain. They were often unwilling and mentally unable to 'level down'[1] influence

---

1    On struggles for prestige and symbolic capital within social spaces, see Bourdieu (2006: 135–141).

to decision-making authorities or LAGs for fear of losing their (symbolic) superior position.

An interviewee from Niedersachsen (Interview 15) reported that at the beginning of the programming period 2000–2006, the managing authority was 'clearly superior, probably even a dictator'. In his view, the situation improved over the years. One major problem, in addition to the *Land's* reluctance to supporting international cooperation, was that within the context of the 2005 administrative reform, institutional structures were changed, as were the responsibilities for LEADER+. The institutional structures were reconfigured with employees able to retire at the age of 50 years and 4 months. As a result, almost at the end of the programming period, new staff had to be hired. These new civil servants lacked the know-how of their predecessors. An informant from the managing authority in Niedersachsen (Interview 14) was not aware of such problems or at least did not comment on them: 'Cooperation between different authorities', he said 'was always dependent on the people working there. Therefore, the quality of cooperation cannot be classified across-the-board. ... We do not recognise system-related problems'.

According to an interviewee from a decision-making authority in Schleswig-Holstein, in addition to the change of staff during the programming period, there were major problems regarding the interpretation of the regulations and how they should be executed (Interview 17). Another problem was what he called over-cautious 'security-thinking', i.e. avoiding pragmatic action and solving major problems due to fear of making tiny mistakes. He provided a detailed description of this problem and how it occurred in the daily interaction between the decision-making and the managing authority:

> As a civil servant I can partly understand that ['security-thinking'] but challenging each and every thing 3–4 times (meaning our suggestions and details of project proposals)? Sometimes it would have been better if we had not asked any questions. But from there [the managing authority] every question was posed. So sometimes we just avoided mentioning some points because we knew that they'd question it and it would take half a year to solve the problem. So we just acted and if a monitoring commission criticised this we said that we'd do it differently next time. Of course they had the responsibility but this envisaged 'total security' was the main obstacle.

Another point of criticism concerned responsibility and its displacement, brought forward by a civil servant from a decision-making authority in Baden-Württemberg (Interview 12):

> The Land officials knew that they had the responsibility but they would have liked to pass it down to others. If the Land said this issue was eligible for funding and later the EU revision proved that it was not eligible for funding, the Land said 'no we never [approved this]'. But if the Land said, this was eligible for

funding, then this was a statement and the Land was liable, no ifs no buts. In this context the Land had massive problems with internal revision. We know that but they had to live with that.

The harshest criticism was reserved for favouritism, both as concerns certain geographical areas and companies that are engaged in the evaluation of the LEADER+ programme and the preparation of the next programme. An interviewee from a decision-making authority in Niedersachsen (Interview 15) reported:

> In the Land, one also liked to remove money to area X [interviewee said where]. You only have to look where all the LAGs were and how much money had been transferred to this area. Look also at which consultancy worked in this area [mentions the name]. Company x had a direct link to the ministry and they also did the evaluation and were engaged in working on the new programme.

Asked whether all this happened on the quiet, the interviewee responded: 'Yes, of course'. An interviewee from Sachsen was less critical of the relations between the decision-making and the managing authorities. According to her, while the flow of information was sometimes slow, the managing authority had a supervisory function and acted in a cooperative manner.

A good forum for exchanging information between all the German decision-making authorities on administrative practice and malpractice in other *Länder* was the German national-network unit, the *Deutsche Vernetzungsstelle (DVNS)*. The interviewee from Niedersachsen (Interview 15) explains the importance of this institution:

> Without the DVNS we wouldn't have received so much information on administrative practice in LEADER+. The Land didn't always like this exchange of information. Many problems and malpractices have been revealed at those meetings. So many things went wrong! But as we are a big family in LEADER, we know the problems.

# Chapter 9
# Efficiency and Decentralisation

This chapter assesses the efficiency of the administrative structures of LEADER+ and the LAG actors' satisfaction with the duration of application procedures. Furthermore, pros and cons of further decentralisation are discussed.

## Efficiency

First, Finnish and German LAG members were asked to share their opinion on the efficiency of the decision-making and implementation structures of LEADER+. If the respondents were not convinced that the structures were efficient, there were invited to elaborate on mechanisms or reforms they wished to see adopted.

Only 20% of the German respondents were convinced that the decision-making structures were efficient. Most respondents suggested empowering the LAG (39% of all answers).[1]

Twenty-six per cent thought that empowering the decision-making authority would be one way to increase efficiency.

Only 8% of the answers of Finnish respondents indicated that the structures for administering LEADER+ funds in Finland were efficient. Sixty per cent of all answers favoured strengthening the LAGs. According to 12% of the answers, the best way to increase efficiency would be to empower the decision-making authority. Four per cent of the given answers preferred a stronger managing authority. According to 4% of all Finnish answers the Regional Councils should be involved in LEADER, too, for instance, as a decision-making authority.

Civil servants from German and Finnish decision-making and managing authorities were asked whether or not the implementation structures were efficient. If this was not the case, the interviewees were invited to outline their preferred reform scenarios for enhancing efficiency.

Similarly to their German counterparts, Finnish decision-makers complained about too much bureaucracy. Better and more easily understandable instructions, better application papers and more resources were among the demands of these decision-makers for future funding periods. Interviewees from some Finnish decision-making authorities argued that they had a better comprehension of the region as a whole compared to both the managing authority and the LAGs and demanded more influence for Employment and Economic Development Centres. An interviewee from South-Eastern Finland explained why she thought the

---

1    It was possible to give more than one answer. Seventy answers were received in all.

Employment and Economic Development Centres were better suited for handling tasks of a decision-making authority than empowered LAG or Regional Councils to replace them would be. Every project application was to be carefully examined by the Employment and Economic Development Centres before decisions on funding were made. This was to ensure that bigger problems would not arise. There had not been any major or scandalous misuses of funds in Finland. According to one interviewee (Interview 10) the tasks of a decision-making authority were broader than that of the LAGs; they were not only multi-level but also multi-sectoral and often tended to stretch beyond simply developing rural areas: 'We looked more at the whole region, while the people from LAG A or B in this region dealt with their local area. I think we should have more information and influence here and discuss our empowerment with the Ministry'.

An alternative option discussed was to follow the Irish procedure and transfer the money directly to the LAGs' bank accounts. They would decide themselves how to use the funds. Spot tests could have been conducted occasionally to ensure that the funds were put to good use and in conformity with the EU's regulations. While there are advantages to this approach, for the managing and paying authority, which has to make sure that the use of funds is moderately controlled, the present approach involving a decision-making authority and not delegating its functions to the LAGs was perceived as the safer approach. According to a civil servant from an Employment and Economic Development Centre in Western Finland, an administrative culture has already been established with positive implications for the collaboration of LAGs and public authority. According to him, the LAGs know all procedural practices and they work well. He added an important pre-condition. In his view (Interview 11) the decision-making authorities should not complicate the lives of LAGs but support them in speeding up the administrative process. He reported that over the course of two programming periods, only one decision that declined an application has been made by his authority. Furthermore, there was one incidence where one LAG's steering committee sacked its manager for his reckless use of municipal money.[2]

An interviewee from a Southern Finnish Employment and Economic Development Centre raised several critical issues, some regarding the actual application process, others concerned with monitoring and yet others concerning the lack of cooperation between Employment and Economic Development Centres on certain issues, such as international cooperation. The interviewee criticised the standard of applications, which was sometimes rather poor. According to him, this was partly because there was a little bit too much money available. The

---

2 The interviewee explained the incident thus: 'In all the projects more municipal money was used than has been budgeted for. This can happen. The apportionment of national and EU funding is very much controlled, and there was no irresponsibility. We do not look at the municipal contributions. This is what the steering committee is responsible for. This is what they did and although there was no fraud and nobody put money in their own pockets, there was a slightly reckless use of money.'

decision-making authority was not forced to select just the best. According to the interviewee (Interview 7), there was no need to prioritise. If the Employment and Economic Development Centre had to compare and choose between larger numbers of applications, this would have improved the quality of applications and would have brought effectiveness. According to the interviewee this will not happen

> if we have to take the view of 'here comes an application, let's approve it', since there are no applications to compare. There are bad applications one should not provide funding for. The problem is that there will be no additional applications and the money should be used so that there will be funds available next year also.

The interviewee concluded that it would not necessarily be a bad thing if there was a little less money available in the future. Both the LAGs and the Employment and Economic Development Centres would learn to deal with the new situation.

Another issue concerns mistakes and problems and the need to be open about them in order to learn from those mistakes. For instance, monitoring reports were only made available to Employment and Economic Development Centres. According to one interviewee, the language used in the reports was hardly comprehensible to anyone else, and nobody except the staff from the Employment and Economic Development Centres was able to read them. Furthermore, reports from the board of complaints were only sent to the Employment and Economic Development Centres. This information should have been available to all the actors concerned. Another problem concerns international projects and the training required for dealing with cross-border projects. 'In six years', an interviewee from Southern Finland (Interview 7) reported,

> I have dealt with one cross-border project. And for this I had to learn completely new tools. This could have been handled by one Employment and Economic Development Centre instead of all Finnish Employment and Economic Development Centres individually.

Thus, certain administrative practices were criticised by interviewees from Finnish decision-making authorities for being very inefficient when everybody accumulates detailed and specific knowledge through training and further education when there is little chance to apply it and without some communication and exchange of experience between staffs.

As far as Germany was concerned, an informant from the managing authority in Niedersachsen (Interview 14) argued that it was not possible to make general assessments on the efficiency of individual operational procedures or how they were to be improved since the realisation of operational procedures very much depended on the individuals in particular stages of those procedures. 'On the whole', the informant argued, in the depiction of the administrative procedures within the 'LEADER+ Programme Niedersachsen', importance was attached to avoiding unnecessary procedures and verifications and that the only activities undertaken are those required to conform with EU rules governing implementation.

However, interviewees from decision-making authorities painted a contrasting picture on what is necessary and what could and must be avoided. In an article published in *Ostsee-Zeitung*,[3] a LEADER manager from Mecklenburg-Vorpommern complained that the decision-making procedures were so complex and the application forms so detailed that many applicants had to fill in and submit the 'gigantic application' four or five times. Some applicants gave up and did not apply. The manager also complained that too many people from a variety of bodies had to give an opinion on the applications. As a result the applications had to be rewritten and amended several times.

Interviewees from *Länder* with lean administrative structures raised a number of critical issues, too. For instance, a civil servant from a decision-making authority in Schleswig-Holstein (Interview 17) criticised the 'flood of regulations', which, compared to other programmes, were unnecessarily complicated. One example is that private capital was not to be used as a source of co-funding in LEADER+ in Schleswig-Holstein.

The neighbouring *Land* Mecklenburg-Vorpommern provided a different and more efficient example. Twenty-five per cent of the project's money was automatically co-financed by the county or municipality in Mecklenburg-Vorpommern. Decision-making authorities in Schleswig-Holstein had to organise project-specific co-funding, be it from municipalities or project-executing groups. There was no national co-funding from the *Land*.[4]

Some German interviewees complained about inefficiency related to territoriality and the function of authorities to make initial decisions that were to be approved by higher levels. For instance, in Sachsen-Anhalt, if a LAG covered more than one county, all the counties in which the LAG was operating were involved in taking initial decisions on funding.

By contrast, a more pragmatic approach was implemented throughout Finland. If the area where the LAG operated extended to the territory of more than one decision-making authority, the decision was made by an authority in whose territory most of the municipalities covered by the LAG were located.[5] In general, there were no problems, or at least no significant ones, in implementing this approach and according to the interviewees. As a civil servant from an Employment and Economic Development Centre in Western Finland reported,

---

3　See 'LEADER-Macher suchen neuen Schwung'.

4　While there was no explicit co-funding for LEADER+, funding for projects was to be combined. For instance, in funding projects for a nature preservation park, funds from both the *Land* and LEADER+ were available.

5　See LEADER+ programme for Finland, p. 83.

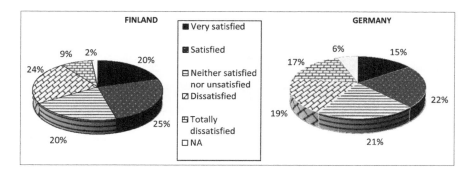

**Figure 9.1    Satisfaction with the Duration of the Application Process**

even in joint projects that included two LAGs and several municipalities – in the sphere of responsibility of two decision-making authorities – co-sponsoring projects collectively, no problems occurred. The interviewee thought that this form of cooperation was transparent. This functioned if cooperation between the Employment and Economic Development Centres was open and goal-oriented, and if a negotiation culture and history had been established. Once this was assured:

> the administration was very easy. Employment and Economic Development Centre X handled one municipality of ours, we handled three of theirs. We trusted them. We also asked the Ministry to transfer parts of our budget to Employment and Economic Development Centre X to finance this kind of projects. It worked well. No problem.[6]

Overall, this position is well in line with the public governance review of Finland carried out by the OECD. One of the main assets of the Finnish governance structures and precondition for the functioning of public administration is trust. According to the OECD (2010: 11) 'the Finnish citizenry today trusts the public administration as a key partner for economic development and service delivery, as well as the mechanisms to realise many Finnish values of social solidarity and equality'. This is also reflected in the LAG members' satisfaction with the duration of the application process. Finnish respondents were more satisfied with the duration of the application process than the German respondents. Forty-six per cent of the Finnish respondents said that they were either very satisfied or satisfied. Only 38% of German LAG members said the same, while 36% of them were dissatisfied or totally dissatisfied. Thirty per cent of all Finnish respondents were dissatisfied to some degree (Figure 9.1 above).

---

6    This statement was made by a civil servant from a Southern Finnish Employment and Economic Development Centre.

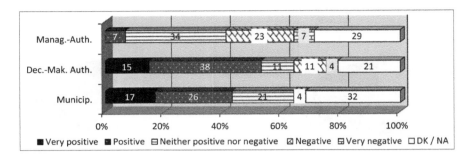

**Figure 9.2    Impact of Different Levels on the Time Taken to Process Applications (D)**

Decision-making authorities in Germany received an overall positive evaluation by the respondents to the questionnaire as to their impact on the time it took to process applications (Figure 9.2 above). Thirty-eight per cent of the respondents were of the opinion that the impact was positive, and 15% said the impact was very positive. Fifteen per cent of the German respondents were critical stating that the impact of decision-making authorities on the time it took to process applications was negative or very negative. This evaluation of decision-making authorities was better than that the Finnish respondents provided. Municipalities have, according to the German respondents a positive impact, as well, despite the fact that they are not necessarily directly and officially involved in approving the applications.

The large number of indifferent answers as far as the managing authorities were concerned was striking. Almost the same number of respondents had a critical image of managing authorities and their impact on the time it took to process applications.

A large number of Finnish respondents had a positive perception of the impact of their decision-making authorities on the time it takes to process applications (Figure 9.3). Twenty-two per cent of them said that Employment and Economic Development Centres had a very positive impact on the time needed to process applications, 20% said that the impact was positive. A substantial share of respondents' answers was negative. Almost one fourth of Finnish participants in the survey said that the impact of Employment and Economic Development Centres on the time it took to process applications was negative and 7% of them perceived it as very negative. The majority of all Finnish respondents were of the opinion that municipalities had neither a positive nor a negative impact on the time needed to process applications.

In Finland, the time that decision-making authorities needed for processing applications was, at times, very short. While according to several sources, the average time was 2–3 months, the approval of project applications was also handled within one hour. Much depended on the project in question, that is, the amount of money applied for, the size of the project and the quality of the application. As decisions by decision-making authorities in some German *Länder* were forwarded for a conformity check to various organs, the application process was considerably longer than in

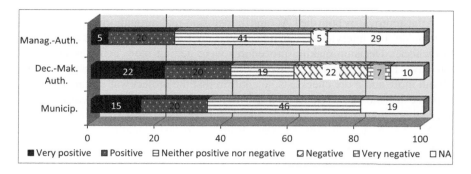

**Figure 9.3    Impact of Different Levels on the Time Taken to Process
Applications (Fin)**

Finland. In Baden-Württemberg, for instance, after the decision-making authorities
had processed the project applications, they had to forward them to a *Land* agency,
namely the LEL, the State Institution for the Development of Agriculture and the
Rural Area (*Landesanstalt für Entwicklung der Landwirtschaft und der ländlichen
Räume – LEL*).[7] Decision-making authorities had to fill out a form stating that they
would approve the application, that the project was eligible for funding and stating the
sum applied for. The LEL scrutinised whether the application complied with the basic
principles of LEADER+. After that, in some cases, the ministry also had to approve the
application. This sometimes required half a year or even longer. In addition to the time
taken by public authorities to handle the applications, the first step in the application
process was a meeting of the LAG which decided whether an application would be
approved as an official LAG project. According to an official of one decision-making
authority (Interview 12), three months was the minimum for the whole application
process in Baden-Württemberg 'but sometimes much longer, too'.

Even though the decision-making structures for examining and approving applications
were very lean in some German *Länder*, such as Schleswig-Holstein and Sachsen, the
process prior to the actual filing of applications, was, at times, highly complex involving
a number of powerful local actors. In Sachsen, for instance, the project applicants first
had to present their projects to the regional coordination committee, an institution
under the District Administrator and, if two counties were involved, with two District
Administrators participating. Additionally, a variety of authorities, associations and
clubs were also represented on this committee. After the committee had decided that the
project was worth funding, the actual project application had to be generated and filed.
According to the interviewee (Interview 12), the problem with these lengthy procedures
was that 'people did not always realise that only after the committee had made its
decision did the actual process start. They also underestimated the work that followed'.

---

7    LEL was responsible for the development of the rural areas and the farming sector
in the *Land* Baden-Württemberg.

After approval by both the LAG and the decision-making authority, amendments were made. The interviewee stated that 'we were surprised how much we still had to recheck'. Decision-making procedures were getting more complex and time intensive. The interviewee criticised these procedures: 'Our Ministry ordered us to fill out more and more checklists, to confirm that the project was sustainable, and to prove this and that. That meant much more work. LAG members were surprised to see this complexity'.

According to an interviewee from a decision-making authority in Niedersachsen, processing the applications in his area was not a problem. Asked how long the average time for approving applications in Niedersachsen was, an informant from the managing authority (Interview 14) was unable to provide a precise answer because

> LAGs and the decision-making authorities were responsible for decision-making procedures and the approval of applications. Statements on the average processing time of applications can only be made on that level, not on the level of managing authorities.

According to an interviewee from a decision-making authority (Interview 15), decision-making authorities in Niedersachsen examined potential projects, and only projects that had been agreed upon in advance with several *Land* authorities, such as ministries, were officially handed in as a project application. To save time, decision-making authorities requested statements from different ministries concerned in advance. According to the interviewee, another important aspect is how well the LAG manager handled the preliminary work prior to filing the application. In this context, the LAG manager and the decision-making authorities regularly cooperated before the application was filed. The interviewee summarised the application process as follows:

> Once the application was with us, I would say we dealt with it for less than a week. Then it went to the Land, and once it returned, the notification of approval was posted in less than a day. Everybody here was very eager for it to be processed immediately. This had priority over other things.

This example shows that a lot of preparatory, unofficial work had a positive impact on the subsequent application procedure. The personal chemistry between actors in key positions was decisive, too. Looking only at institutions as such and the time taken up by official administrative procedures give but a limited picture of the whole process.

Asked about problems and shortcomings in the application process, most German decision-makers complained about the lack of staff, as did their Finnish colleagues. More resources would have helped to speed up decision-making procedures. An interviewee from Schleswig-Holstein (Interview 17) summarised this point:

> I am sure they (interviewees from LAGs) were not satisfied since we, as the decision-making authority, only had one 50% position for administering LEADER+. We needed more staff. We were always at the limit of our capacities, but the county did not approve more hours.

A LAG manager from Niedersachsen (Interview 5) added that due to an administrative reform[8] there were even longer delays. Prior to the reform the county's inspection to see if the application conformed with funding guidelines took approximately 10 days, with an additional eight weeks for various departments within the *Bezirksregierung* to come to a final decision. The administrative reform had changed all that. The decision-making authority, according to the interviewee, was no longer capable of carrying out its main task, namely, making decisions. After the creation of a new *Land* agency, it took 3–4 months to arrive at a decision. The problem was that applications now had to be forwarded by the new agency to *Land* ministries to check that the application conformed to the guidelines. The LAG-manager (Interview 5) criticised the latest institutional reforms. According to him 'conditions and requirements changed. Instead of incremental adaptation, it would have been much better for us if the rules to be applied were clearly defined in advance'.

Another explanation for the longer delays in processing applications was the educational and professional background of the staff at the *Bezirksregierung*, who were specially trained in the legal aspects of funding. They were, according to some interviewees, much more suitable for the job than staff of the new authorities. Another problem, according to some interviewees, was legal in nature. Due to the lack of a clear legal relationship between the LAGs and the managing authority, the managing authority had the power to shape and reshape its positions by issuing new regulations. An informant from the managing authority responsible (Interview 14) had a different standpoint, arguing that

> it is not true that the decision-making authority had been shifted to the ministry. Within the context of an administrative reform the Bezirksregierungen were dissolved as of 31 December 2004. LEADER+ related tasks had been left unaltered and, partly even including the same personnel, assigned to Land agencies. The levels of decision-making and approval remained unaffected. The Bezirksregierungen solely did conformity-checks for submitted projects. Since 2005, these tasks were executed by the corresponding Land agencies.

This is a multi-level governance problem, which concerns what Marks and Hooghe (2003) defined as type-I units and their connectedness and embedding into type-II MLG. Decision-making authorities and LAG managers from different regions of the same *Land* made the same critical observations, which

---

8 On 1 January 2005 the *Bezirksregierungen* were abolished and a new *Land* agency (*Behörde für Geoinformation, Liegenschaften und Landentwicklung*) was created.

were then refuted by the managing authority. However, the informant from the managing authority (Interview 14) admitted that there were 'occasionally some complaints at local levels' that the administrative process was complicated. These complexities were, according to the informant, due to the fact that 'the administration and monitoring system in the EU was comprehensive' and not because of the managerial and administrative structures of LEADER+ in the *Land*. The managing authority in Niedersachsen was not able to provide a clear explanation for the long delays in processing applications that were causing so much dissatisfaction. The informant argued that 'due to the complexity of the administrative procedures predetermined by the EU and based on different *Länder* programmes with sometimes very divergent requirements for their implementation, a general assessment cannot be made'.

As for what the managing authorities could have done to improve the situation, his answer was fairly evasive: 'In general, counties had been designated as decision-making authorities in the LEADER+ programme in Niedersachsen. The Land had very limited influence on the actual decision-making process of individual projects'.

However, as the analysis of the Finnish case or the Irish example shows, the administration can be structured in other ways. This was clearly not a failure of the EU but relates to how the national managing authorities chose to organise the implementation structures.

The interviewee from the Finnish managing authority had a better understanding of the situation and the problems in his sphere of responsibility and was much more open to discussing the kind of problems that can cause delays in the application process. Confronted with the results of the LAG survey's question on the duration of the application process, he spoke fairly openly about what was causing problems and how to avoid them in the future. The main problem in his view was that there was not enough staff at the Employment and Economic Development Centres. This was causing delays. Another problem was that the dialogues between the LAGs and the Employment and Economic Development Centres did not work properly sometimes. These were two obvious problems that had to be improved. A third problem was that the Employment and Economic Development Centres were able to easily say that they could not approve an application because it had not been presented properly. While according to one interviewee (Interview 6): 'there were Employment and Economic Development Centres and LAGs where the interaction and cooperation functioned well, there were still too many (cases) where the application procedure took many, many months'.

Being aware that it sometimes took too long to process applications, Finnish decision-makers identified a number of core problems that, in their view, might explain the dissatisfaction of LAG respondents with the length of the application processes. One problem was the lack of financial resources and related lack of personnel employed in decision-making authorities. The second shortcoming was the quality of applications as, for instance, information was often missing. A third problem was the excessive amount of bureaucracy. Most of the interviewees from

Employment and Economic Development Centres complained about the lack of staff. An interviewee from Central Finland (Interview 8) suggested: 'The best way to improve the situation is to have more personnel in the Employment and Economic Development Centre'.

The situation was most problematic in those institutions where there was only one person responsible for LEADER. An interviewee from South-Eastern Finland (Interview 10) explained: 'When I was not here, nobody else did my job. It was always difficult because everybody had quite a lot of work'.

As far as lack of resources is concerned, in addition to what was mentioned above in terms of provision of information and participation in LAG meetings, the lack of personnel becomes quite evident in the actual process of handling the application. The experiences of two interviewees nicely illustrate this. The first example comes from an interviewee from Southern Finland (Interview 7):

> In the beginning of the 2000–2006 funding period we had a lot of things piling up on the table. For instance, in 2000 we did not manage to approve the applications at all. The whole working time went to finalising the projects of the previous period. We received more applications over all of 2000 so that we could finally handle a portion of them in 2001. The first year was the worst. Later we needed 1 to 2 months to handle the applications. I think this is reasonable, and handling the applications should be not much longer. The people would not be patient much longer. The LAGs, too, would have needed more resources in order to better support the applicants. One person per LAG was not enough. However, financially speaking, 2 or more was unrealistic.

Another problem that was encountered by all the decision-makers interviewed was poor applications. For instance, they might have lacked certain papers or additional information that should have been attached to the applications. While a senior civil servant from a Western Finnish Employment and Economic Development Centre considered incomplete applications as a general problem that led to lengthy application times, he saw a connection between incomplete applications and unnecessary bureaucracy. This concerned, above all, smaller projects. At times, a one-million-Euro project demanded the same amount of paperwork as a ten-thousand-Euro project. Furthermore, the application forms were difficult for ordinary people to deal with. The language, concepts and indicators used were difficult to understand. The head of department of a Western Finnish Employment and Economic Development thought that the application forms were a compromise between vernacular and bureaucratic language with the balance clearly tending towards the bureaucratic. In his view (Interview 11) it would have been better if the managing authority had taken a holistic approach to mistakes in the application: 'All the controllers and examiners of the Ministry were adept at splitting hairs when it came to bureaucracy in that it was always easier to point at a missing form than admit that there were problems with the process itself'.

**Decentralisation**

Based on the interviews with decision-making authorities, a number of core problems that led to LAGs' dissatisfaction with the duration of application processes were identified. Many LAG respondents and decision-makers complained about the complexity of decision-making with several levels being involved. Some German interviewees criticised the duplication of functions that led to situations where people had many responsibilities but nobody really felt responsible. This resulted in a lack of institutional responsibility and accountability. A civil servant from a decision-making authority in Baden-Württemberg (Interview 12), for instance, explained her impression of multi-level interaction, which she saw as devastating for the operation of LEADER+ in her *Land*:

> There was no real responsibility and accountability. In the other programme (a Land-sponsored one) I was the last instance to decide and I had a personal interest that this went off without a hitch. As far as LEADER+ is concerned, the application was forwarded to two additional instances. It eventually came back here and nobody had a clue, who was in charge of the proceedings until the LAG called and asked how things were proceeding and we said 'oh my god, there is still no decision'.

Interviewees from decision-making authorities in Germany criticised on the one hand the complexity of how LEADER+ administration was organised and in particular the duplication of functions on the other hand. In Baden-Württemberg, the responsibility for LEADER+ coordination had been assigned to the *LEL*, the State Institution for the Development of Agriculture and the Rural Area. The *Ministerium für Ernährung und Ländlichen Raum*, which was the managing authority in Baden-Württemberg, had been responsible for coordination. The LEL wrote the rural-development programme, bargained with Brussels, coordinated and monitored. The LEL also supported the LAGs during their constitutional phase. A civil servant from a decision-making authority criticised the creation of an additional administrative unit and the lack of clarity as far as the demarcation of responsibilities was concerned:

> Our experiences with the LEL were not good. It was a third administrative level in addition to the administrative district (Regierungspräsidium) and the ministry. We had different functions but the assignment of our tasks was not clear enough. This resulted in a duplication or triplication of work.

The duplication of functions has been criticised as being inefficient but also because it created situations of unclear responsibility. The interviewee continued:

> We [the Regierungspräsidium as the decision-making authority] and the LEL stood in each other's way because we both did the preliminary work for the

LAGs, and this was inefficient. This was volitional but not anticipated (by the ministry). This was a specialty in our Land. This was a rather bad experience in LEADER+. The problem was that although the LEADER+ related tasks would have been suitable for us we did not have enough staff to deal with them, so we shouldn't be too critical. This doesn't mean we should have swept it under the carpet. I am very convinced that if you asked the LAGs, they would draw a similar conclusion.

According to interviewees from Niedersachsen, the core problems relate to the status of the managing authority in a highly interwoven and complex system of decision-making. Their position is based on a variety of observations. One example is the amount of levels involved in decision-making. They criticised the fact that in 2005, within the context of an overall administrative reform, the *Bezirksregierungen* were abolished and with them the departments responsible for LEADER+. Some staff moved to the new authority, the *Behörde für Geoinformation, Landentwicklung und Liegenschaften (GLL)*. An interviewee from a decision-making authority (Interview 15) thought the new situation was somewhat

catastrophic. But the reason was that person X (interviewee mentioned a name) propagated an administrative reform, but one was not consistent enough in fully implementing it. (Instead of) retiring the people who had the necessary know-how and knew the region, it would have been better if they (e.g. the 50-year-old retirees) had introduced their successors to the job. This would have been good for the Land and the region.

The interviewee argued that the situation deteriorated after the *Bezirksregierung* as the LEADER+ decision-making authority was abolished and replaced with this new *Land* agency. The agency had no decision-making power. Decisions were prepared and had to be forwarded to the ministries for approval. While on paper, the agency was the decision-making authority, in reality the managing authority empowered itself and introduced structural changes. The new agency was apparently restricted in competence and dependent on higher levels. For example, if projects' budgets exceeded €300,000,[9] a *Land* ministry was to issue a certificate that allowed the decision-making authority to approve the project. All this meant a third administrative level was involved.

Mistrust towards those in charge of decision-making and the self-empowerment are examples that demonstrate how the *Länder* level remained in a powerful position and in control. By reforming the overall, type-I MLG administrative structure, it had empowered itself within type-II MLG structures. Such complexities, especially when compared to Finland and some of the German *Länder,* almost

---

9   This concerns the whole budget, not only the funding provided by the public sector, i.e. also private co-funding.

compel one to ask whether leaner structures might improve efficiency. While in the evaluation of Community Initiative LEADER II, the EU Commission had already provided a description of different decentralised models of implementing LEADER, an interviewee from the EU Commission's LEADER+ Observatory (Interview 16) argued that a single authority responsible for the use of EU money and the approval of all public funds 'was the best model for approving both the EU funds and national funds'.

He added that in addition to simplifying structures there should also be more coordination between the authorities that carry out the eligibility checks. This could be institutionalised in a joint inter-ministerial committee but as this is seemingly very bureaucratic, decentralisation would be another alternative. The Irish model is a very interesting example of decentralised eligibility checks but remains an exception and is probably not applicable everywhere. In Ireland the eligibility check was done by the LAGs themselves. This meant in practice that Irish LAGs not only decided on potential projects. Instead of forwarding those proposals to a decision-making authority, they were empowered to do the eligibility checks themselves. There was also an inspection to check if the EU procedures had been implemented properly. But this was an *a posteriori* control, which is done after the projects have received funding. According to a civil servant from the Commission: 'in theory, this would be the best model because the advantage of LEADER is that it is close to the citizen, to local actors and can adapt to different realities and have a process that is quicker than the normal way of implementing programmes'.

Whilst the Irish experience offers an alternative model, there are several important prerequisites if decentralisation is to work. A clearly formulated and comprehensive document with a list of criteria could be developed, which could be imposed as a kind of check-list to be followed by the LAG. Investing more trust in decision-making authorities so that they can make decisions independently is an important pre-condition for the creation of leaner structures. Without conformity tests or verifications by other authorities, such as those some German managing authorities performed in addition to the checks by the decision-making authorities, the administration of LEADER would be more efficient. Double and triple verifications are not only very time consuming, they turn managing authorities into de-facto decision-making authorities and lead to a further empowerment of the managing authorities and thus endanger the bottom-up approach.

When discussing the situation in Germany with a Commission official the fact that some German interviewees complained about the lack of trust on the part of managing authorities as regards the work of decision-making authorities was discussed. The Commission official criticised that in the German LEADER+ structure, there were 'overlays and overlays and overlays'.

However, not all of the interviewed staff from decision-making authorities thought that the operational procedures were inefficient. Sachsen, for instance, had very lean decision-making structures determined by the LEADER+ programme:

1. Within the LAG the projects were discussed and possibly amended by the responsible project-executing group.
2. The regional coordination-committee was to approve the LAG application.
3. The project application was forwarded to the decision-making authority, which was to finally approve it.

The decision-making structures in Schleswig-Holstein were also highly decentralised. After LAGs had decided on their projects, the applications were forwarded to the decision-making authorities. According to an interviewee from one decision-making authority in Schleswig-Holstein, in principle, the LAG approved the project, and the decision-making authority decided on its eligibility. No other institution was involved. The system was, in comparison to other *Länder* such as Niedersachsen or Baden-Württemberg, very decentralised and comparable to that in Sachsen, although in Sachsen the decision-making authority belonged organisationally to the administrative meso-level (the district administration).

In Schleswig-Holstein, the managing authority made random inspections but only after decision-making authorities had made eligibility tests. In principle, the implementation of LEADER+ took place locally, that is at the LAG and county levels, without unnecessary and time-consuming interference from *Land* institutions. While the interviewee from Sachsen said that the lean structures administering LEADER+ in her *Land* had advantages, she was not sure whether this model would be maintained in the next programming period. She thought that one way to enhance efficiency would be to increase collaboration in the regional coordination committees.[10]

Asked whether leaner structures would help to enhance efficiency in Baden-Württemberg, an interviewee from a decision-making authority (Interview 12) answered:

> As far as our Land is concerned, one has to say explicitly that one administrative level has to be abolished. If it was us, although I very much like to do LEADER and I would regret if we were no longer responsible for LEADER, the structures would have to be changed. To give an example, it cannot be that if an application concerns a sum of €20,000 there are 10 highly endowed people dealing with it and decide on the application. That cannot be happening! This is hair-raising if one also thinks about the tax-payers.

A colleague from Niedersachsen (Interview 15) added that if one applied a cost-performance analysis of the administrative structures in his *Land* 'one would

---

10  This means that the authorities and other actors in the coordination committee, for instance the *Regierungspräsidium* or the public saving banks, which in many cases provided temporary finance or credits, would interact more with project applicants, not only after the project application has been filed but after it has been presented within the coordination committee.

tear one's hair out. It would be nice if things ran differently'. In his opinion, the core problem was that the *Land* intervened too much in decision-making procedures and thought 'that it can dominate'. He also criticised that although the municipalities provided *national* co-funding (the *Land* did not provide any co-funding), municipalities did not have the full decision-making powers. The interviewee specified: 'Take a local politician and tell him, you provide funding for a project but you are not the one who makes the decisions on funding. This is strange in terms of public administration'.

Reflecting on decentralisation in Finland, the 'principle of tri-partition' (*kolmikantaperiaatte*) is very noticeable. As one-third of the members of LAG steering committees were from the public sector (municipalities), it would theoretically be possible for the LAG to decide independently on funding. This would mean that the Employment and Economic Development Centres would be abolished as the decision-making authorities in LEADER and the number of the administrative level involved in the administration of the funds would be reduced to two. This would come quite close to the Irish model. On the one hand, there had also been some support from the decision-making authorities and even suggestions to the Ministry of Agriculture and Forestry to remove the Employment and Economic Development Centres from this system. One Finnish LAG manager criticised the administrative process:

> The LAGs' and Employment and Economic Development Centres' intersecting processing of application and payment was unnecessary. The group should have been more independent, equipped with more decision-making power as concerns the applications.

An interviewee from Central Finland (Interview 8) added: 'Two levels (LAG and Employment and Economic Development Centres) had to check the applications, and that was expensive and inefficient'.

On the other hand, there were a number of reasons for preserving the present structures. Above all, there was not enough personnel in LAGs to handle everything as prescribed in the EU's double-check system. In addition to technical problems, giving full decision-making power to the LAGs would compromise the idea that LAGs are public-private partnerships and not public authorities. In one interview, a senior civil servant from a decision-making authority in Western Finland (Interview 11) argued that he and other decision-makers were convinced of the success of the Finnish approach of tri-partition. According to him, the managing authority also continued to favour the limitation of public administration in the steering committee to one-third of the seats. He argued that

> it is quite good that the number of representatives from municipalities, municipal counsellors, was clearly fixed at below half the total membership and that other actors were in the majority. And I share the position of X (senior official of the managing authority) that if more than 50% of the members were representatives

from municipalities, the steering committee would in effect be a municipal board. This was not our intention. The Finnish model continues to be very good.

Furthermore, sometimes the decision was taken to reject applications. It is perhaps better that a neutral instance that is situated somewhere else 'does this dirty job'[11] instead of a LAG. It is easier for a neutral body to reject applications. Overall, the principle of tri-partition is a success in terms of both decentralising decision-making power and including a broad range of different social groups and institutions. Most interviewees from Finland shared this view.

How did staff from decision-making authorities in Germany perceive the principle of tri-partition and would they see it as a good option for the Federal Republic? The answers to this question reflect that on the one hand, decision-makers saw tri-partition as the proper realisation of the LEADER principle. On the other hand, German decision-makers reported that it proved to be difficult to get local residents and entrepreneurs to participate in the LAGs and fill the minimum 50% of places reserved for private actors. Interviewees complained that in many LAGs there were far too few local residents. In addition, fairly often, the people representing social partners were civil servants, too. Some interviewees thought that there was a risk that they pursued partial and functional interests rather than that of a regional community. According to an interviewee from Baden-Württemberg (Interview 12) the situation was sometimes devastating as:

> there were no adolescents, artists etc. Nobody from the 'normal' population is involved. We had 'di-parity' at best and I would have very much preferred to have more local residents involved. This is the main idea of LEADER. I would have liked very much to see this (tri-partition) here.

Her colleague from Niedersachsen (Interview 15) was in favour of the regulation whereby municipalities do not have a majority of seats in LAGs and thought the principle of tri-partition would suit Niedersachsen as well. His main point was that local residents can see problems from a different perspective than an 'inflexible economic or social partner who has no room for manoeuvre'. He continued criticising the poor integration of local residents and argued that 'if one member represents local tourism and the other the peasantry etc., this is not really representative of public opinion. So, I would prefer tri-partition'.

An interviewee from Sachsen (Interview 13) thought that the composition of the regional coordination committees in her *Land* came quite close to tri-partition. As to participation in the LAGs as such, in her region it was also difficult to find private persons or entrepreneurs. 'One had to almost urge them to participate'. For the interviewee, the 50% rule was quite demanding, for instance if a private person or entrepreneur left the LAG to find a substitute with a similar background.

---

11  The quote is from a civil servant from a decision-making authority in Southern Finland (Interview 7).

All in all, she was convinced that this rule had proved its worth. An interviewee from Schleswig-Holstein (Interview 17) added that 'we had a LAG with 51% of its membership from social and economic partners, or even 60%, and 40% from public administration. We had to do something about that. The form of organisation of the LAG is a very topical issue'.

The position of the informant from the managing authority in Niedersachsen (Interview 14) on whether tri-partition would have been an option for this *Land* was that when the LAGs had been formed for the LEADER+ programme,

> the bottom-up-principle was implemented. That means, that a LAG founded and organised itself independently within the framework of the EU guidelines. The crucial point is that the requirement to have more than 50% of the members in the form of economic and social partners, according to EU regulations and the LEADER guideline, was complied with.

Reflecting on the answers above and the problem of motivating local residents or entrepreneurs to participate and to the imbalances in various groups' representation, this answer gives the impression of a managing authority that is remote from local-level administrative processes in its sphere of responsibility.

The answer from a civil servant from the Finnish managing authority (Interview 6) was much more elaborate. In his view, a full-fledged decentralisation that conferred all decision-making power upon LAGs and decoupled the Employment and Economic Development Centres from the LEADER administration was not an option due to the fact that

> we didn't want to turn (the LAG) into a public authority. If the Employment and Economic Development Centres dropped out – and it is unquestionable that some LAGs knew their business so well it might have worked out (in theory) – in practice the LAG would be a public authority and without doubt would affect the groups' activities and lead to a concentration on a few people. It would not be a LAG anymore but 2–3 civil servants. And we don't want this. The challenge was how to arrange the distribution of work between the LAG and the Employment and Economic Development Centres in such a way that the LAG has sovereignty but does not functions as a public authority. This was a difficult question. And this was solved to certain extent.

Within the context of LEADER+, he did not think that it would have been possible to empower the LAGs any further. They had been developed so far that any further step would transform them from a public-private partnership into a public authority. In addition, the degree of decentralisation in comparison to other programmes that functioned under the aegis of one ministry was quite exceptional.

While all the German interviewees very much welcomed an inclusion of more local residents in LAGs, opinions on further decentralisation in terms of empowering LAGs in such a way that they would take over the function of decision-making authorities differed. Some interviewees pointed to technical problems, whilst others had doubts concerning political accountability. German interviewees also argued that a LAG which also acts as a decision-making authority would turn into a new public authority. This is, so the critique, against the LEADER rationale of citizen involvement and well-functioning public-private partnerships.

Based on her experience, a civil servant from a decision-making authority in Sachsen (Interview 13) added another crucial point arguing that a lack of expert knowledge about, for instance, funding regulations would prevent LAGs from taking over the functions of a decision-making authority. Due to their different qualifications and functions, she saw that the managers on the spot were not the right people to handle this task:

> The managers are on the spot, they mobilise, they are creative but they are not administrators. Managers are capable of handling numbers and invoices. They are more creative as far as project design is concerned but they sometimes have problems filing a prudent project application.

In other words, decision-making authorities acted as the interface, as a kind of neutral mediator between LAGs and the managing authorities, between good ideas and the reality of funding guidelines, a reality that tended to become ever more complex.

While the LAG should play a central role, the administration should be organised more centrally, i.e. at least at the level of counties, according to an interviewee from Niedersachsen. Otherwise, one would create a new administrative unit that may lack expertise in a variety of related fields, lack experience and, above all, lack the neutrality of a civil servant employed at a public authority. An interviewee from Baden-Württemberg (Interview 12) put it like this: 'I am sure that the LAGs wouldn't be so keen on doing all this. All the administration is such an unpleasant accompaniment that they willingly leave it to us'.

Above all, assigning all the tasks of a decision-making authority to the LAG would be questionable in that it would raise the whole issue of political influence. The LAGs might ever more turn into political bodies led by a local political elite that does not necessarily have a holistic view of the problems of the whole region. The interviewee from Baden-Württemberg argued in this context that it is better for the implementation of LEADER-type programmes if relatively neutral bodies are responsible for decisions on projects, such as civil servants who have no personal interests and who can be made accountable, as is the case with the *Regierungspräsidium*.

In terms of decentralisation and partnership, putting the principle of tri-partition into practice was perceived by members of Finnish LAGs, decision-making authorities and the Finnish managing authority as a success. Interviewees from German decision-making authorities would have liked to see this kind of cooperation adopted in Germany. But why has this principle not served as a role model here or for other countries? So far, 'local residents' as 'individuals' and not as representatives of a social or economic partner are only represented in Finnish LAGs. In other countries, in addition to public administration, NGOs with different thematic and functional backgrounds are represented in LAGs.

One explanation for the reluctance to adopt the Finnish model relates to the different traditions of public administration in the member states. While most German interviewees said that the Finnish model is attractive and closer to the LEADER rationale of locally based partnership than any other model applied in the EU, they are also aware that managing authorities are reluctant to impose it. In this context Kauppi (2002: 24) argued that each field, in this case the national political field, has

> its own dominant habitus, a culture or internalized set of actions, preferences and evaluations that regulates resource accumulation ... This specific, internalized culture or set of "internalized" institutions constrains and empowers individuals, assigning them roles and providing them guidelines for legitimate behaviour.

As regards LEADER+, 'realistically speaking', reasoned an interviewee of the LEADER+ Observatory (Interview 16), 'I do not see the Finnish model being applied elsewhere. In Finland they spoke about history. In that country, which was between Sweden and Russia, they have this tradition of collective action with a strong involvement of people. So (this model) is very typical of Finland, quite normal'.

To conclude this chapter it is important to see that it does not matter too much whether decision-making is defined as centralised or decentralised on paper or whether responsible managing authorities think the bottom-up principle has been realised. It is of paramount importance to elaborate how particular programmes such as LEADER+ are implemented in daily practice and whether the local level has a fair chance to act independently and in a spirit of partnership. As far as managing and decision-making authorities are concerned, they have to have a clear picture and understanding of developments and problems at the local level. An interviewee from a decision-making authority in Niedersachsen (Interview 15) shared this view:

> The people in charge have to work fast. They have to go out and visit the regions, they have to meet the locals, and they have to visit the LAGs. Whether it is county or ministry, it is important that they come to see the problems on the spot. They have to pay attention.

Chapter 10

# LEADER+ LAGs on the Move to the Next Programmatic Period – Hopes and Expectations for 2007–2013

After the European Commission published a proposal on the new European Agriculture and Rural Development Fund (EARDF) on 14 July 2004, unanimous political agreement was reached at the 2669th Council meeting (Agriculture and Fisheries) in Luxembourg, on 20 and 21 June 2005, on a new framework regulation for the implementation of EU-sponsored rural-development policy for the programming period 2007–2013.[1] This regulation established the EARDF (*11495/04*). The agreement was based on a compromise (*8481/1/05 Rev1*) supported by the Commission.

There were differences between the member states as far as the launching of the new programming period was concerned. In some countries, such as Sweden, the selection of new LAGs took place very early, and this procedure was completed before many other member states. Some member states also had already spent all the money for LEADER+ by mid-2006. Their concern was to start the next programming period very early in 2007 without delay. In other member states, for instance in Italy or Germany, the maximum time to implement LEADER+ funds was used, that is until the end of 2008. This was possible because of flexibility not only within the programming period but also with the transition to the new period. The Commission's 'golden rule' is that before member states can start to implement a new local strategy, they have to complete the previous one. However, the Commission stressed that managing authorities are to inform in a timely fashion and thoroughly about their new programme. The result was that those countries that had not used all their LEADER+ resources by the end of the previous period were forced to start the next period later. What was the situation in Finland and Germany regarding the move from LEADER+ to the 2007–2013 programming period?

In Germany, several LEADER+ practitioners from North-Western Niedersachsen formulated a draft position paper and demanded a transparent selection of LAGs, a reorientation in co-funding and international cooperation as well as simplified and transparent administrative procedures, including a clear legal relationship between decision-making and managing authorities.[2]

---

1    See Council of the European Union, Press release 9991/05 (Presse 143).

2    These and other points for rethinking rural-development policies were raised in the draft position paper 'Die Gemeinsame Agrarpolitik der europäischen Union 2007–2013'.

As far as the selection of potential LAGs is concerned, for the programmes, the Commission has demanded that a broad inclusion of local and regional levels had to be ensured and that there would be enough time for them to express their positions instead of the managing authorities only offering very few appointments for hearings.[3] This was another important point supported by a working group consisting of actors from several *Landkreise*, *Bezirksregierungen* and regional chambers of agriculture in North-Western Niedersachsen raised in an unpublished draft position paper.

Finnish Employment and Economic Development Centres participated in developing the national development plan, and most LAGs had finalised their own programmes quite early on. According to a civil servant from an Employment and Economic Development Centre in Western Finland (Interview 11): 'this process was very much bottom-up. As I was at a seminar in Germany I can say that, in comparison, we were in a class of our own'.

At the time Finnish actors had finalised their programmes, managing authorities in some of the German *Länder* were still fighting about details in the *Länder* programmes, such as the minimum limit of the number of inhabitants a LAG area may cover.

For the programming period 2007–2013, Finnish and German regions had to face a situation of operating with a reduced budget. Both decision-makers and managing authorities were asked to outline how they would cope with the new situation and, if they could choose, which of the following they would opt for:

• More national co-funding;
• A bigger budget for national programmes;
• Reduction/merger of LAGs;
• Something else.

All the interviewees from Finland clearly preferred more national co-funding to enable them to continue and sustain the present kind of rural development implemented throughout the whole country. An interviewee from Western Finland stressed that one of the key principles in Finland was that the policy should cover all of rural Finland. If the amount of money for each LAG was going to be reduced, more national funding needed to be made available, according to most decision-makers. If resources from the EU were reduced, national resources would have to be increased. An interviewee from Southern Finland (Interview 7), for instance, preferred the idea that national programmes would fill the gap.

Another envisaged, less costly method of coping with reduced EU funding was to introduce a stricter system of priorities when choosing projects. According to an interviewee from Southern Finland, enough money to fund projects was available during the LEADER+ programming period, but administrative implementation, that is the technical part, was not always without mistakes. Decision-making authorities

---

3   See 'Die Gemeinsame Agrarpolitik der europäischen Union 2007–2013'.

could have prevented some of those mistakes, however minor they may have been, if they had been given enough resources to inform and activate the LAGs.

While increased national co-funding or establishing alternative national programmes was the number one priority for a decision-maker in South-Eastern Finland as well, she thought that funding other areas more extensively, for instance local companies or cities that can have a positive impact on the economy of the surrounding rural areas, could help to solve the problem of disinvestment in rural-development policies. In her opinion (Interview 10):

> rural-development policies are very important but if we want to be more competitive in the future, we have to think a little differently. I think that not all the projects that received funding under LEADER+ were very useful and sometimes I think the money would be better placed in some companies doing research.

The LAGs' reactions to the reduced budget were contradictory. Some regions can clearly profit from their geographical situation. For instance, rural areas of *Uusimaa* in Southern Finland are 'a showcase for the people from the capital region, bilingual, a lot of beaches and many international contacts and interactions'.[4] An interviewee from an Employment and Economic Development Centre in South-Eastern Finland (Interview 10) looked optimistically into the future, too:

> I think the situation in our Employment and Economic Development Centre, and the two Regional Councils that it covers, is quite good because Russia is quite near and Helsinki is also quite near. So there are good possibilities for companies and rural people and people working in agriculture to make a better future. I think the new programme is very important because the main idea is developing the economy.

For an interviewee from the Finnish managing authority the division of work between the public and the third sectors should have been revised in 2007–2013. This applies not only to Finland but probably even more so to other EU member states. He criticised a lack of trust by the public authorities in the third sector. According to the interviewee, this relationship was not in good trim, despite every effort to reach a balance that empowers the third sector, for instance by including its representatives in LAGs according to the principle of tri-partition.

Rural regions in Germany had to face a reduced budget, as well. Decision-making authorities from different *Länder* were asked how they thought this situation could best be addressed. Would they favour:

---

4   This citation comes from an interviewee from an Employment and Economic Development Centre in Southern Finland.

- more co-funding from the *Land*;
- increased national support;
- a reduction or merger of LAGs;
- a higher minimum limit as regards inhabitants per LAG; or
- something else?

Being aware of the budgetary constraints some of the *Länder* were facing, interviewees expressed doubts that the *Länder* could provide additional resources. The informant from the managing authority in Niedersachsen, for instance, argued that due to the financial configuration of the *Land* Niedersachsen, assistance via *Land* funds would not be possible and the promotion of LAGs could only be realised via EU programmes. The funds that would be made available in the context of these EU programmes, determined the amount of LAGs. However, with corresponding financial backing, the informant (Interview 14) said, 'an area-wide formation of LAGs is conceivable'.

The positions of interviewees from wealthier *Länder* (Interview 12) were different: 'The Land has to provide more funds. In 2000–2006 the contributions were ridiculous, way too little. I think the Land has to take its responsibility more seriously'.

Some of the funding policies found in some *Länder*, for instance in Bayern where 20% of national co-funding came from private sources, were useful examples for the future period. For an interviewee from Schleswig-Holstein (Interview 17) the best option was to involve more private money and to incorporate funding from enterprises that are willing to co-sponsor certain projects and thereby foster economic development in the region.

A stronger involvement of the private sector and co-sponsoring from private firms are options favoured by the Commission. According to an interviewee from the LEADER+ Observatory (Interview 16), it is an asset for public administration to get used to working with the private sector in the field of rural development. The benefit for the public sector is that there are 'many more ideas, many more initiatives etc. taken by the private sector. It is really an added value for public administration. But they often tend to think in a traditional way'.

An important approach to dealing with reduced budgets, which was discussed in Finland as well, was to prioritise. This meant only selecting LAGs with a clear integrated and holistic development strategy, i.e. groups that had developed programmes aimed at fostering the region as a whole. As far as the selection process of LAGs is concerned, this would include, for instance, an efficient selection procedure such as scrutinising whether the concept is specific to regional demands. It would also include ensuring that decisions are based on administrative necessities rather than on political connections. In favour of such an approach as well, an interviewee from Sachsen (Interview 13) argued this would mean turning down programmes that had been:

developed somewhere by a regional planner with a good lobby and good connections to the public authorities. Since he wrote the concept it will be approved because he has good relations with the District Administrator or some other public authority.

Based on its perception of governance, the Commission would like, as a long-term objective, to have much more of Europe covered with LAGs. The situation in Germany under LEADER+ was very different. Due to the upper limit of 100,000 inhabitants to be covered by LAGs, the situation was problematic. There were some villages of some regions that were covered by LEADER+ funding while others of the same region were not. This demonstrates how European integration can also foster disintegration at the same time. A different approach would be in order, an approach that reflects more explicitly the meaning of a region in its cultural and historical dimension, instead of creating new entities based on numerical considerations. But can it be guaranteed that more coherent LAGs are created in the future and that the dissection of regions – some villages are included in LAGs while their neighbouring villages are not – is avoided? This was one of the questions posed to German interviewees from managing and decision-making authorities. For the informant from the managing authority in Niedersachsen (Interview 14) and as regards 2000–2006, the spatial demarcation of a LAG resulted from the various processes involved in finding partners. 'The main focus here was on spatial and thematic similarities as well as the common interests and goals of LAG members. A limiting external factor was the quota of 100,000 inhabitants, according to EU guidelines'. The informant highlighted positive aspects of LAGs as newly constructed areas arguing that they 'helped dissolving "Kirchturmdenken"[5] and fostered the goal- and future-oriented work'.

Critical of dissecting historically recognised regions, an interviewee from Baden-Württemberg (Interview 12) argued that 'in parts, dissecting them was bosh. I do not like to dissect areas since they have to be homogenous'. She also mentioned that the construction of LAGs had a positive impact in that LAGs included municipalities from different counties into one LAG. The result was that counties did not see themselves as competitors but as partners in cooperation. This had positive impacts on other sectors, as well, such as tourism and health care.

While the interviewee from Schleswig-Holstein (Interview 17) and one LAG he was responsible for and that operated across county borders sometimes faced some problems, he drew a positive conclusion since: 'we were able to solve them and profited from synergy-effects of being situated in two counties'.

Another reason for not including whole municipalities in LAGs, but only parts of them, was provided by an interviewee from Sachsen. This concerns city districts which were situated in rural areas. The rural areas were eligible for funding, while the city as such, categorised as an urban or high-density area, was not.

---

5   This means fostering thinking 'beyond the steeple', i.e. enlarging the horizon.

For the programming period 2007–2013, the Commission, aware of the challenges involved in covering large parts of Europe with LAGs, was hoping that member states would put more effort into targeting support to key priorities. The key priorities in the community strategy guidelines for LEADER are endogenous development and governance. A more medium-term objective is to improve the valorisation of local resources. This is, according to a Commission official (Interview 16), 'because the richness of the European territory is its diversity. Strong rural territories are those which are based on their specificities'.

As a 'European answer to the process of homogenisation in the global economy', LEADER fostered the development of local products, the diversification of local production and the use of cultural heritage, all of which were a value-added of LEADER. As local development under the LEADER approach is, according to an interviewee from the Commission, 'a tool to differentiate production in the global market', this tool should also be applied in the future so as to use more local expertise to involve local people more intensively and to enable them to develop their home region according to the socio-economic needs of that area.

# Chapter 11
# Empirical Findings and Discussion

Chapter 11 is a summary and discussion of the main findings from Chapters 5 to 10. Chapters 5 to 11 offer new and additional empirical knowledge on local dimensions of EU policy-making and give new input to theorizing on European integration. Through the analysis of power structures in rural governance based on a combination of multi-level governance and structural constructivism, these empirical chapters fill an empty gap left by mainstream European integration theories. Rural-development policy is analysed by taking different contexts into consideration. Different rural areas need tailor-made policy tools. Furthermore, the environments in which policies are implemented and institutional reforms are to take place are often subject to power struggles. To better understand these struggles the focus was on individuals who construct and implement rural policy – actors from multiple levels of governance who contribute to the European integration process on the ground.

## Intra-institutional Relations in LEADER+ Local Action Groups

LEADER+ was implemented through LAGs. What were the power relations in these institutions? The proportion of non-governmental actors in German LAGs was slightly higher than that of actors from public administration. In Finland, the LAGs' executive committees were composed according to the principle of tri-partition (one-third local residents, one-third public administration and one-third local businesses). There was a clear male dominance in Germany and Finland as far as the heads of LAGs are concerned.

Most Finnish respondents described the working atmosphere within their LAGs as positive (47%) or very positive (37%). German respondents came to similar conclusions (positive 52%, very positive 38%). Most respondents from both countries provided a positive assessment of cooperation between the executive committee and other members of the LAG. According to the respondents, members working in public administration had the most influence in German LAGs and should have been even more important. Finnish respondents argued that local residents had the most influence within LAGs. The majority of Finnish respondents said that local residents should have been even more influential. Interestingly, the majority of German respondents said that local residents were rather unimportant within their LAGs.

Almost all LAG members participating in this survey stated that the LAG management was an important mediator between the LAG and higher authorities. According to the answers received, the management did a good or very good job, was very cooperative and considered the concerns of LAG members.

## LAGs in the Administrative Structures of LEADER+

Respondents described cooperation with actors from different institutions of public administration as positive. The local level was, due to its proximity to the LAG, better assessed than the regional or *Land* level in Germany and the central state level in Finland. The perception of respondents who participated in the survey was shared by interviewees from Finnish Employment and Economic Development Centres (decision-making authorities) and by German civil servants employed at decision-making authorities. Finnish respondents had a positive perception of cooperation with the managing and paying authority (Ministry of Agriculture and Forestry), while German respondents were more critical. German respondents from *Länder* which had a more decentralised administrative structure to implement LEADER+, such as Sachsen and Schleswig-Holstein, provided a more positive evaluation of relations between their LAG and managing authority than respondents faced with a large number of (additional) administrative levels. Decision-making authorities in both countries often act as the interface and mediator between LAGs and managing authorities. The closest working relationship as far as the processing of the applications is concerned was, according to most interviewees, between decision-making authorities and LAG managements.

## Information Policy

Decision-making authorities received positive criticism from German and Finnish respondents as far as their information policies are concerned. German respondents were much more critical towards managing authorities' information policies than Finnish respondents. A critical issue raised by some German respondents was the slow flow of information and the provision of information. A major problem in Finland and Germany in terms of the provision of information was a lack of resources resulting in decision-making authorities being understaffed.

German interviewees from decision-making authorities reported shortcomings and major problems in the managing authorities' information policies. Harsh criticism was levelled at the selective nature of information policy and even the lack of information. On a related issue, the selection of LAGs at the beginning of the programming period was said to be highly politically motivated at least in one *Land* (Niedersachsen), where information was provided to actors with the 'right' party affiliation. In addition, misleading information policies in the early days of LEADER+ led to LAG applications that were not in accordance with funding rules. The managing authority denied this.

In Finland there were regional differences in the extent of information provision, which was due to differences in the financial resources available to individual Employment and Economic Development Centres and the amount of staff dealing with LEADER+.

Many respondents and interviewees argued that the situation at the end of the funding period was much better than at the beginning.

## Networking

LAGs from all over Europe created and increasingly create networks. Networking under LEADER+ took place both internationally and nationally. Most LAGs had established contacts with other LAGs within their own country or Europe-wide. Many respondents stated that networking was very important for them. German LAG members were more satisfied with their LAGs' networking strategy than their Finnish counterparts. There were also differences in Germany and Finland as concerns the use of the national network unit and the European database for cooperation to help finding partners. Some German interviewees criticised the fact that that managing authorities formulated strict rules that prevented full and unrestricted cooperation.

## Local Action Groups and the Public

LAGs were generally open to new members, but membership was partially restricted in Germany. Obstacles for potential members to join were economic in nature.

Finnish and German LAGs had utilised a number of different strategies to inform the public about its activities, such as Internet platforms, information events and newsletters. In spite of their information policies, Finnish and German respondents argued that there was neither much interest in the work of the LAGs nor in membership. However, the situation was said to have improved over time. Half of the Finnish respondents thought that the work of their LAG had brought the EU closer to the local residents. German respondents were less optimistic. Only 20% of them shared the view of the Finnish respondents.

As far as cooperation with other local or regional actors that were not part of the LEADER+ administration is concerned, more than half of the German respondents argued that cooperation with municipalities was good or very good. Forty per cent of the Finnish respondents shared this view.

## The Core Critique and Solutions: Complexity, Efficiency and Decentralisation

Most Finnish and German respondents criticised the inefficiency of the decision-making structures in LEADER+. Only one-fifth of the German respondents were convinced that these structures were efficient. In the Finnish case only 8% of the respondents shared this view. Table 11.1 below is to summarise the main points of criticism raised by respondents and interviewees participating in the empirical research.

**Table 11.1    Main Points of Criticism Raised in Finland and Germany**

| Nature of the Problem | Country | |
|---|---|---|
| | *Finland* | *Germany* |
| Administration and Governance Structures | Lack of financial resources and personnel in decision-making authorities and LAGs<br>Too much/unnecessary bureaucracy | Complexity of structures/too many administrative levels involved<br>Lack of staff<br>Too much/unnecessary bureaucracy |
| Financial | Too much money available for projects/not leading to the selection of just the best projects | Pre-financing of projects<br>Co-financing by local authorities |
| Procedural | Application forms not made for 'ordinary members' of the LAGs, language and concepts used caused problems of comprehension<br>Incomplete applications/rather poor standard of applications at times<br>Monitoring reports only sent to Employment and Economic Development Centres<br>Language used in monitoring reports hardly comprehensible<br>Dialogue between the LAG and Employment and Economic Development Centres did not work properly sometimes | Duration of the application process<br>Favouritism<br>Selection of LAGs at the beginning of the programmatic period |

German respondents were less satisfied with the duration of the application process than the Finnish respondents. While almost half of the Finnish respondents said that they were satisfied or very satisfied, only 38% of German LAG members said the same. Thirty-six per cent of the German respondents and 32% of the Finnish respondents were dissatisfied or totally dissatisfied. In the Finnish case, according to several sources, the average time it took to process applications was 2–3 months. In Germany, the processing time of applications was, according to some interviewees, considerably longer.

German decision-making authorities received an overall positive evaluation from LAG members that took part in the survey as to their impact on the time it took to process applications. A large number of Finnish respondents had a positive perception of the impact of their decision-making authorities on the time it took for applications to be handled. In the German case, respondents and interviewees from some *Länder* provided a positive evaluation, whilst others criticised the duplication and triplication of functions. In addition, the inappropriate number of administrative levels involved was said to lead to unnecessary complications and delays in processing applications. However, in some German *Länder*, such as Schleswig-Holstein and Sachsen, the decision-making structures were very lean.

In Germany LAG management and decision-making authorities regularly cooperated before the applications were filed. Concerted interaction was an important part of interaction between decision-making authorities and LAG managers. Decision-making authorities reported to clarify issues internally and in advance as they saw this as a very important preliminary step. LAG managers were also invited to send draft applications to decision-making authorities.

There were a number of additional ideas in both countries voiced to speed up application procedures and increase efficiency. In Finland, the following reforms were favoured:

- Better and easier to understand instructions;
- Better application papers (improved language);
- Technical adjustments, for instance if the LAGs entered their data themselves electronically and the decision-making authorities cross-checked and adjusted it;
- More resources for administering the application/more staff in some of the decision-making authorities;
- Improved cooperation between decision-making authorities, for instance as far as international projects and the exchange of ideas on best-practices and potential sources of problems are concerned.

In Germany, suggestions to improve the administration of LEADER were among others:

- More resources for decision-making authorities;
- Decentralisation.

In Germany, due to the high number of levels involved in the administration of LEADER+ in some *Länder*, the accountabilities and responsibilities were not easy to locate. While decision-making structures in Germany were fairly decentralised in some of the *Länder*, for instance in Sachsen or Schleswig-Holstein, in other *Länder*, such as Baden-Württemberg, Niedersachsen or Sachsen-Anhalt, decision-making structures were highly complex. In addition, managing authorities had the potential to restructure administration and had empowered themselves and caused structural changes during the programming period. Therefore, there was a strong call for the reduction of administrative levels. Most respondents from both countries favoured a stronger LAG to increase efficiency in connection with a 'thinning out' of administrative levels.

While further empowering LAGs was favoured by many respondents participating in the survey, a number of reasons were discussed for preserving the structures in Finland. Above all, giving full decision-making power to the

LAGs would endanger the idea of local action groups which are public-private-partnerships and not public authorities. A LAG which also acts as decision-making authority would be a new public authority. Some interviewees pointed to technical problems, while others had doubts regarding political accountability. The Irish model was referred to as a very interesting example of decentralised decision-making but remained an exception under LEADER+.

Regarding decentralisation, the principle of tri-partition applied in Finland (*kolmikantaperiaatte*) in organising the executive committees of LEADER+ LAGs was very noticeable, too. In comparison to Germany, for instance, the representation of public administration in the steering committee was much more limited due to this principle. Most of the decision-makers in Germany that took part in this study considered tri-partition as the proper realisation of the LEADER principle. But heads of LAGs and decision-makers also reported that it proved difficult to motivate local residents and entrepreneurs to participate in the LAGs and fill even the 50% of places reserved for economic and social partners.

The mobilisation of local residents and the 'bringing together' of actors from the local area with different social and institutional backgrounds to become an active part of the EU's rural-development policy LEADER+ was more successful in Finland than in Germany. In Germany local residents were often only poorly involved, while many interviewees and other informants from Helsinki to Lapland and from Österbotten to Karelia regarded them as the core actors in Finnish LAGs. This is a key difference between the two countries in this study. Attracting and involving more local residents to construct a community of space, not of elites, should also be a top priority in Germany. The data this study generated leads to the conclusion that the situation has improved in Germany since 2000, when Bruckmeier published his analysis of LEADER and LEADER II. Nonetheless, after interviewing different actors, the impression is that in some German *Länder*, such as Niedersachsen and Baden-Württemberg, actors in managing authorities continued to perceive LEADER+ as 'government-dependent policy (that is, small and cheap regional "innovation centres" to stimulate economic growth in the region)' and not as a new governance model 'for autonomous regional and local development' (Bruckmeier 2000: 225). The habitus of some actors in managing authorities had similar consequences for LEADER+ in Germany as the habitus Kauppi observed for powerful groups in the EU in more general terms. According to Kauppi (2002: 21) within the EU 'certain interest groups have succeeded in stacking the cards, regularizing interactions favourable to them and delegitimizing others, while maintaining unequal resource distribution'.

Returning to LEADER+, the private sector, both according to the findings in this study as well as in the perception of the Commission, had some influence in the design of local development strategies and contributed to adapting it to local realities. However, it should be more prominently involved in the future, for instance by providing co-funding and thus assuming more responsibility.

The public sector continues, perhaps more than ever, to play an important role in steering and monitoring networks of public-private partnerships in modern governance. Therefore, people in responsible institutions, above all in the managing authorities, should have a clear conception of local needs and reality. Trust and partnership were crucial pre-conditions for the successful implementation of LEADER+ and were not, as demonstrated in the analysis, something that can be simply assumed to exist throughout the EU. Not trusting the subordinate levels and constructing strict and sometimes seemingly unnecessary control mechanisms (for instance in the form of new institutions) is part of a struggle for influence and (symbolic) capital. This struggle seems to follow a certain logic. Actors try to 'keep up with and identify with the immediately above' and at the same time seek 'to distinguish' themselves 'from the group immediately below' (Bourdieu 2006: 136).

For the future, a lot continues to depend on how much staff in administrations at the top of the 'bottom-up stream' is willing to empower subordinate units. LEADER+ did empower local actors to some degree but central state actors/ *Länder* ministries still had the strings in their hands and often found it hard to make space for those who, on paper, should have been empowered. This habitus needs to change. The interviewee from the Commission (Interview 16) was slightly positive on that note. According to him, endogenous development and governance are top priorities in all member states, at least on paper. He was also convinced that LEADER practitioners in the member states perceive LEADER as a tool to solve conflicts of interest in rural development because it helps to create partnerships and people get used to working together.

The future of rural-development policies and their institutional configuration will depend on reforms put in place at all levels of governance. Those actors contributing to this book by providing their views on the various shortcomings and ways to overcome them paint a fascinating picture of the state of rural-development policies in the current EU. Among the variety of ideas discussed, it remains to be seen which ones will prevail in the future and as part of a reformed CAP after 2013.

# Conclusions

In order to fully understand the process of European integration it is of paramount importance to consider developments at the sub-national and local levels of the EU. Yet, the rural has been largely absent from scholarly debates in the context of European integration and in EU Studies. As far as the local level is concerned in general, EU integration scholars shifted their attention to those areas only at the beginning of the 1990s with the concept of multi-level governance. This was a crucial step. The EU has constantly expanded its activities to cover an increasing number of areas and policy fields. It is not just member states and their meso-levels[1] that are affected. Local administrations in implementing EU regulations and guidelines, for instance, are increasingly operating under the influence of the EU and Europeanisation. In addition, new functional units, such as LEADER local action groups, have been set up to deal with particular policy-tasks and offer new options to participate in EU policies and to receive additional resources. It is not just public administrations that are involved in these units, but representatives from the private sector, economic and social partners as well as local residents.

Neglecting the inclusion of the local level, as some of the mainstream or 'grand theories' of European integration do, leads to the exclusion of the most important level of governance within the EU. As a consequence, these mainstream theories need to be replaced with a new approach – a combination of multi-level governance and structural constructivism – which is better equipped for the study of the impact of European integration on the local level and in rural contexts. This replacement is necessary because the local level is vital for the EU for several reasons. And not just because local public administrations implement EU legislation and policies. Being the lowest functional level of the EU, it is the closest to the people and has the potential to make the EU visible to the people. It is at the local level that local residents have access to and participate in policy-making.

In combination, both multi-level governance and structural constructivism contribute to a better understanding of how policy-making functions and how, where and why problems and dysfunctions arise. They can contribute to a realistic and more nuanced picture of local and sub-national levels in rural governance structures and in the multi-levelled EU. This concerns not only the negative impacts of integration but also the empowerment of local and sub-national actors in new modes of governance constructed in the process of European integration. This combination is also a reaction to Simon Bulmer's argument that 'the lack

---

1   On the different forms of meso-level tiers of government in the EU, see, for instance, Larsson (2000).

of interdisciplinary dialogue' has 'risked confining European integration to an intellectual "ghetto" within the social sciences.'[2]

This book concludes with three sets of arguments regarding rural policy and multi-level governance in the making. The following pages will reflect upon these arguments.

1.   Local-level actors – both public and private – have become important actors in EU policy-making and take part in new inter-institutional relations. However, in rural governance, LEADER+ local action groups, for instance, are demanding further decentralisation. Respondents to the survey (Chapters 5 to 11) stated that in Germany as far as LEADER+ is concerned, public administration has more weight in local action groups. In Finland, local residents have most weight. Local-level public administration in both countries seeks the involvement of private and social partners in policy-making and implementation. The prime example discussed in this context is the principle of tri-partition. However, local residents are interested in EU-sponsored rural-development policies only to a very limited extent. Finnish LAG members were more optimistic that they had succeeded in bringing the EU closer to the people than their German counterparts.

2.   In various EU policies, such as Regional Policy, rural-development policy or LEADER+, horizontal cooperation between the public and private sectors and the inclusion of social partners has been fostered due to, for instance, the partnership principle. However, the findings of the empirical analysis outlined in this book reveal that the higher levels of government within new systems of governance (MLG type II) also have reservations about delegating functions and empowering subordinate levels. If they do, or have to do this, they tend to control and restrict the local level. This was particularly the case in Germany, where LEADER+ was much more centrally controlled than was the case in Finland.

3.   The Finnish central state level, in the case of LEADER+ the Ministry of Agriculture and Forestry, and the *Länder* level of government in Germany as the managing authorities occupied the most influential positions. They were the 'national decision-making centers', to borrow Kauppi's term (2003, 19) and occupied this position for several reasons. They selected the LAGs, set the rules for actor involvement, and negotiated the overall financial framework with the EU Commission. They control implementation processes and, in the case of the second pillar of the Common Agricultural Policy, also the financial equipment of the different axes and thus, ultimately, also policy priority. Indeed its control is greater than the underlying legislation actually demands or expects. They also, in the case of some German *Länder*, re-structured administrative channels and recentralised power. While the institutional structures of each member state determine the degree of involvement of non-public actors, the farsightedness of

---

2   S. Bulmer cf. V. Guiraudon and A. Favell (2007: 10).

people in key positions at higher levels is also an important factor in how far the local level is empowered (Chapter 5). Individuals in key positions play a decisive role in deciding on how and indeed if resources are to be distributed and who is to become part of the game. In Germany, as far as LEADER+ is concerned, practices that did not correspond to the underlying principle of a bottom-up policy were identified. In Finland, different actors from the local area have been included more carefully in local action groups, since the principle of tri-partition has been chosen as the underlying principle for structuring the groups' executive committees. As a result, LEADER is much more decentralised in Finland than is the case in some parts of the Federal Republic of Germany and in other EU member states.

To formulate the points made above slightly differently, EU integration changed the formal and informal inter-institutional relations, linking the different levels of government. In addition, the private sector, including non-governmental institutions and interest groups, gained access to policy-making processes and increasingly interacts with government institutions at all levels of public administration. These developments do not necessarily result in the empowering of the local level as one might have expected from reading the initial and underlying programmes and treaty amendments. Actors at the top-end of the bottom-up stream defend their positions and prevent this from happening, as LEADER+ in Germany shows. On the other hand, using LEADER as an example, Finland is a prime example of multi-actor inclusion in policy-making.

### How to Study the Status of Local Actors and Decision-making Structures in the EU's Multi-levelled Polity?

The concept of multi-level governance paved the way for analysing the position of the sub-national level in EU governance. However, Jordan has convincingly argued that the multi-level governance approach has its weaknesses as concerns the sub-national level. Referring to research by Pollack and Bache, Jordan (2001: 201) claimed that multi-level governance 'greatly overstates the autonomy of sub national actors even in policy areas where one would expect it to perform quite well'. The findings of this book support this argument. In order to develop the concept further, some of its assumptions need to be rethought. This concerns for instance the power of national actors (in the case of Germany the *Länder*-level) or national hierarchy. At the very least, more consistent definitions of what scholars mean by these concepts are needed. It might be of great value if scholars of multi-level governance more intensively debated with protagonists of other concepts. Therefore, a basic comprehension of other theories of EU integration is fundamental. They can give access to developments taking place where these policies are shaped.

Furthermore, to interconnect multi-level governance with other approaches, such as structural constructivism, is appropriate in order to develop a proper theoretical framework for empirical reality. This concerns, above all, the problems observed in the multi-level polity. In this respect, structural constructivist methodology and empirical research carried out by structural constructivists was of considerable help and inspiration to the empirical research design of this book.

In order to draw a more realistic picture of the trends in rural Europe, one also has to depart from the perception that theory and empiricism are in contradiction, since, as Bourdieu and Wacquant (1992: 160) remind us, theory without research is empty and research without theory is blind. Empirical studies of individuals in institutions that are part of multi-level governance are one important direction to go. To paraphrase Mérand (2011: 181), this is because it is not the state and public institutions who think and who are socialised but individuals in these multi-level governance structures. Thus, moving the focus onto individuals engaged in rural policy – as this book does – contributes to our understanding of the differences in the implementation of EU public policies across member states.

In order to link problem-solving and the selection of solutions to the findings related to the multi-level and multi-actor governance structures of rural-development policies, it is important to highlight the issue of context specificity once again. Whilst, in general terms, the reform of EU rural-development policy concerns and involves the empowerment of different actors by ensuring their access to different policy-making phases, there are still differences among the member states as to how this empowerment is realised. In Finland, for instance, the grassroots level is an essential part of the national rural-development structures, whilst in the new member states, the project class constitutes a new powerful element in those structures.

## Linking the Empirical Findings to European Integration Theory

The conclusion is that a grand theory is ill-suited as far as a theoretical framework for studying local phenomena in a multi-levelled polity is concerned. Given that the EU polity is or resembles Burgess's (2004: 40) 'political, economic, social, and legal hybrid that is characterised by a combination of federal, confederal, supranational, and intergovernmental features', no single and general theory of European integration can be established. Being aware of developments in the 'other' camp, i.e. the ontology of other approaches, not only enables one to discuss and test one's own assumptions but also helps to complement one's own approach. The result is not necessarily a new 'grand theory' but, as Diez and Wiener (2004: 16) argued, one's findings and contribution to conceptualising this approach is a stone in an 'always-incomplete mosaic' and contributes to the construction of a 'multi-faceted picture of integration'. Wiener and Diez (2004: 19) see 'each approach as a stone that adds to the picture that we gain from the EU', and 'new stones' change the picture which means that it is 'likely to remain unfinished'.

The empirical findings of this book also support Checkel's view (2001b: 241) regarding theorising on integration, in that 'general theories of integration should be put aside in favour of partial frameworks with clearly specified micro-foundations – be they economic or sociological'. When it comes to the functioning and integration of rural policy-making structures in the EU, it is fruitful to apply two mid-range approaches that complement each other – as suggested in this book, multi-level governance and structural constructivism. Checkel would probably agree with this step in so far as he argued that a more intense interaction of theory and empirics 'helps scholars delimit the scope of their claims, thus creating space for analytical competitors. The point is not to make all schools happy; rather it is to bring our models closer to the empirical reality we observe on a daily basis' (2001b: 243).

If it comes to multi-level governance, this approach was very useful in mapping and analysing the general structures of LEADER+ in Finland and Germany. Yet, the ontology of multi-level governance forces one to look for other approaches and their methodologies if it is to study particularly 'the rural' in multi-level governance. Both multi-level governance and structural constructivism are suitable approaches for analysing multi-level, multi-actor interaction in the implementation of EU structural funds and rural policy. While the former has been helpful in mapping the overarching institutional structures, it has been criticised for being too descriptive and uncritical. This is where structural constructivism proves to be very helpful. It has the potential to solve one dilemma of the multi-level governance approach which provides a suitable image of institutions and levels, and how they are linked, but fails to provide clear answers to the question whether interaction is hierarchical or not or why there are regional differences as to the distribution and monopolising of power. Structural constructivism is appropriate for studying redistributive policies, such as LEADER+ since one of its assumptions is that redistribution has a decisive role in establishing political authority. As Bourdieu (2006: 123) has argued and shown, 'the conversion of economic capital into symbolic capital' is the 'central operation of this process' and 'produces relations of dependence that have an economic basis but are disguised under a veil of moral relations'. Structural constructivism as applied in this book helped in 'revealing the hidden power mechanisms' and served to demonstrate 'through what mechanisms political agents reproduce and transform the European political order' (Kauppi 2005: 39).

## Actors, Institutions and Power Structures in Rural Governance

In line with previous structural constructivist research, this book shifted the focus on the actors embedded in rural governance structures, on their perceptions, their behaviour, their social characteristics and their economic, social, cultural and symbolic capitals. Zooming in on the agents helps to better understand how policy-making structures are constructed, and by whom, and where power is situated and specifically with whom.

The German case shows that most of the power and influence remains with the public sector. One explanation for the reluctance of some managing authorities to trust subordinate levels is their wish to accumulate (symbolic) capital. Staff from the ministry need to control the decisions of those below them, since they are on top and part of the prestigious ministry. The struggle for various capitals is somewhat mitigated in Finland with the inclusion of tri-partition but, as the discussion in the empirical chapters show, still a feature of rural-development policies in the EU. Shucksmith (2000: 215) came to a similar conclusion in analysing LEADER in England. He argued that there is 'a tendency for endogenous development initiatives to favour those who are already powerful and articulate, and who already enjoy a greater capacity to act and to engage with the initiative. This may even lead to a capturing of the initiative by elites or sectional interests, in extreme cases. More marginalized groups are less able to participate or engage with the programme, and are less likely to be empowered unless explicit attention is given to their inclusion'.

Another argument brought forward by some scholars of 'new governance' in the EU is that the multi-levelled EU is non-hierarchical.[3] However, the empirical analysis made in this book suggests that especially as far as relations at the local level and in the governance of rural-development policy are concerned, relations between actors are based on persuasion as debate rather than on persuasion as manipulation.[4] Yet, some groups, so the respondents to the survey (Chapter 5) argued, have more weight. Some interviewees thought this was necessary. Whether it is perceived as domination depends on how actors in higher positions communicate their influence. In this context the results of the analysis also reveal that 'good relations' with higher-level authorities – that is informal contacts – are very important, too. [5] One problem is that such relations can also lead to the exclusion of potential actors. Thus, further integration can also lead to disintegration. Hirst, too, found that it often proved difficult for newcomers to gain entry. The problem with 'local-level social governance' is its exclusivity (Hirst 2000: 13). Members have exclusive benefits. Furthermore, even if more actors are able to participate, not all of them are necessarily included in the decision-making process itself. The number of these actors 'is kept small' (Benz 1998: 564). In that sense, the unequal distribution of capital including access to information, which can determine the structure of the entire field, forms, according to Bourdieu (2005d: 58), the basis for the specific

---

3   Hix (1998: 54), for instance, who intensively analysed studies of EU politics and policy concluded that 'new governance' as the more popular perspective, perceives the EU transforming 'politics and government at the European and national levels into a system of multi-level, non-hierarchical, deliberative and apolitical governance, via a complex web of public/private networks and quasi-autonomous executive agencies'. For others, hierarchy and the way government institutions and the state can steer or influence decisions and processes in governance are the most important issues for future research on governance. See Börzel (1997).

4   On the differences, see Checkel (2001a: 220–223).

5   Kiviniemi, Mustakangas and Vihinen (2003) found that in Finland, the power of the public, private and voluntary sectors is changing. Corresponding to what I found in my study on the German local level, much depends on the activity of individuals, not only in building networks locally but in trying to find partners region-wide.

effects of capital, namely the ability of acquiring profits and the enforcement of rules which are as advantageous as possible for capital and its reproduction.

One important question to be elaborated in this context is the diffusion of the member states' authority and the motivation in doing so. Is it to enhance efficiency or to tackle the democratic deficit by closer involving those that are affected by policy-making? The further involvement of local-level actors was intended to enhance both democracy and effectiveness but, as this book shows, with the emphasis more on effectiveness. At the end of the day governmental institutions have the final say. In some German *Länder*, LEADER+ was more 'government-dependent policy' than a new governance model 'for autonomous regional and local development' (Bruckmeier 2000: 225). Another impression surveys and interviews gave was the higher authorities' lack of trust in sub-ordinate levels. In Germany, local residents were often only poorly involved, while many interviewees and other informants in Finland perceived them as the core actors in Finnish LAGs.

If Finland – a central state – is compared to the Federal Republic of Germany, the implementation of LEADER+ projects in Finland was much more decentralised. This argument is based on the analysis of various aspects, such as the principle of tri-partition, which made the involvement of local residents in addition to public administration and local enterprises in Finnish local-action-group steering committees obligatory. The claim that the situation in Finland was different was shared by an interviewee from the EU Commission's LEADER+ Observatory (Interview 16), who summarised his experience with Finnish authorities and their pragmatism as follows:

> they trust people, the human dimension of development. They focus on people and not on systems or organisation of institutions. The Finns are very practical. They are really oriented towards finding solutions. Rules do not have an absolute value; Finns always find ways to solve problems pragmatically. This is what I like in Finland.

In Finland, the overall context in which rural policies are implemented can be characterised as a tradition of openness at all levels of public administration and – as shown in previous chapters of this book – by the will to cooperate across scales and sectors.

This identification of differences in the design and implementation of LEADER+, including the distinct capacities individuals had in various locations was only possible by focussing on those individuals in the multi-levelled structures of this policy. LEADER may be treated simply as a political programme, a community initiative or an 'Axis' of the Second Pillar of the Common Agricultural Policy. Yet, by doing this, one tends to ignore the essence of this policy; its noteworthy practices but also its malfunctions. In that sense, this book shows that LEADER is not a monolithic institution but it 'embodies diverse, contested and possibly competing webs of belief informed by different traditions' (Bevir 2010: 266).

## Considerations for Future Research and Practice – Moving towards Meta-governance?

One important issue for future study concerns local residents and strategies to improve their awareness of and their mobilisation for EU-sponsored rural-development policies. Here the most fundamental practical questions are if and how a more thorough decentralisation might be realised. Is it possible, as the majority of the survey respondents were demanding, to empower the LAGs further, and if so, how? Despite problems mentioned by interviewees and respondents and discussed in this book, tri-partition as applied in Finland should serve as a model for similar policies in other EU member states.[6]

This requires a careful deliberation, selection and fusion of different forms of governance, that is a sophisticated system of meta-governance (Jessop 2003, 2005[7]; Whitehead 2003; Meuleman 2010; Engberg and Larsen 2010; Glasbergen 2011; Christopoulos, Horvath and Kull 2012[8]). Scholars of meta-governance – and as opposed to some accounts of multi-level governance – assume that the State or political authority at different scales is needed to render self- or co-governance possible because such participatory approaches need a framework in the form of ground rules. According to Kooiman and Jentoft, meta-governance 'is needed to guide the institutional and problem-solving choices, *ex ante* in underpinning future oriented activities, and *ex post* in appraising governance activities by serving as criteria for evaluation'. (Kooiman and Jentoft 2009: 823). Importantly, ideas, norms and governance principles leading to reforming a policy have to be deliberated upon by all relevant actors in the policy community irrespective of the functional background of the actor and in order to come to appropriate choices.

In conclusion, the future of rural policy in general and LEADER-type activities in particular must continue to be built with responsible people who have the know-how and the (local) knowledge to implement development projects, people that already made LEADER a success in the past. In spite of the challenges identified in this book, Finland continues to serve as a role model within the EU.

---

6   The Finnish model was elevated even beyond the EU and is implemented as a development project in South Africa and Latin America.

7   Jessop (2005) used the concept of meta-governance to describe the changed functions of national governments and other political authorities in governance. Those authorities are setting the conditions in which governance takes place, the 'ground rules' and the 'regulatory order'.

8   Christopoulus et al. (2012) defined meta-governance as the 'reflexive coordination and organization of the framework conditions under which governance can take place through joint identification of potentials or counterbalancing of observed failures in traditional modes of governance, such as in relation to decision-making, steering or coordination of collective action' (in Kull and Kettunen 2013).

# Appendix

## Conducted Interviews

| Interview number | Interviewed Person | Date |
|---|---|---|
| 1 | Manager of a LAG from Sachsen-Anhalt | 30.12.2003 |
| 2 | Head of a LAG from Sachsen-Anhalt | 30.12.2003 |
| 3 | Senior civil servant from a *Verwaltungsgemeinschaft* in Sachsen-Anhalt | 19.05.2004 |
| 4 | Head of a LAG from Eastern Germany | 22.02.2005 |
| 5 | Manager of a LAG from Northern Germany | 04.05.2005 |
| 6 | Senior civil servant from the Finnish Ministry of Agriculture and Forestry (managing authority) | 23.08.2005 |
| 7 | Corporate analyst from a TE Keskus in Southern Finland (decision-making authority) | 12.01.2006 |
| 8 | Senior inspector from a TE Keskus in Central Finland (decision-making authority) | 20.01.2006 |
| 9 | Area manager from a regional development agency in Eastern Germany | 16.02.2006 |
| 10 | Corporate analyst from a TE Keskus in Eastern Finland (decision-making authority) | 24.02.2006 |
| 11 | Head of department from a TE Keskus in Western Finland (decision-making authority) | 14.03.2006 |
| 12 | Civil servant from a decision-making authority in Baden-Württemberg | 08.05.2006 |
| 13 | Civil servant of decision-making authority in Sachsen | 09.05.2006 |
| 14 | Civil servant from the *Ministerium ländlichen Raum, Ernährung, Landwirtschaft und Verbraucherschutz Niedersachsen* (managing authority) | 10.05.2006 |
| 15 | Civil servant from a decision-making authority in Niedersachsen | 10.05.2006 |
| 16 | Civil servant of the DG Agriculture, LEADER+ Observatory, European Commission | 09.06.2006 |
| 17 | Civil servant from a decision-making authority in Schleswig-Holstein (decision-making authority) | 20.06.2006 |

## The Amount of Leader+ LAGs per Lan

| Land | Number of LAGs |
|---|---|
| Baden-Württemberg | 5 |
| Bayern | 45 |
| Brandenburg | 13 |
| Hessen | 8 |
| Mecklenburg-Vorpommern | 12 |
| Niedersachsen | 17 |
| Nordrhein-Westfalen | 3 |
| Rheinland-Pfalz | 7 |
| Saarland | 1 |
| Sachsen | 9 |
| Sachsen-Anhalt | 10 |
| Schleswig-Holstein | 6 |
| Thüringen | 12 |
| Total amount of LAGs | 148 |

## Statements and Questions for the National Workshops

ETUDE/WP6
Hilkka Vihinen & Michael Kull /13.11.2008

### STATEMENTS AND QUESTIONS FOR THE NATIONAL WORKSHOPS

*REGIONAL LEVEL*
Accessibility of rural policy budgets is currently uneven and a block in unfolding the rural web. Co-financing capacities should be improved, or co-financing should be abolished.

Participatory rural development approaches should be reformed and opened genuinely for the wide array of actors in the rural web.

The distribution of public funds for RD should be decided trough a participatory process involving all the stakeholders (actors in the rural web). A multi-stakeholder arena should be established and institutionalised at the regional level to articulate the needs to the regional administration.

Different policies affect the rural web. These policies should be monitored from the point of view of the functioning of the web. Rural proofing is needed: require all public bodies at all levels to demonstrate that they have taken rural interests into account in framing and implementing policy and to identify the extent to which their strategies will benefit rural areas.

A mediating institution at regional level to coordinate and network local and regional stakeholders – Multi-stakeholder platforms should be established at all levels (local, regional, national, EU)

Propelling the unfolding of the web – Which administrative level should intensify territory based cooperation in your country? Which level could or should "stimulate the construction of new alliances that underlie the rural web idea?

### NATIONAL LEVEL

Tools for local development have to be increased and strengthened.

From Narrow to Broad Policy perspectives?

From Rural to Rural-Urban policies?

From individual beneficiaries to network oriented support systems?

Networking needs: above all trust and networking skills should be supported.

Promote farms as the sites of multiple rural activities, e.g. diversified agriculture.

The importance of market governance in the reconstruction and revalorisation of agriculture and rural areas: Market governance as a key intended *outcome* of RD initiatives?

Create space for novelty production: e.g. funds for farm modernisation could be directed to innovative new starts; offer also some funds for experiments that may be risky.

### EU LEVEL

CAP reforms and strengthening of the RD pillar – or moving RD issues to cohesion policy?

There is a bias in favor of one branch in the EU rural development program: agricultural – non-agricultural aspects.

Health Check of the CAP – too little focus on the whole of the rural web, in particular on the human aspect?

EU 'state-support proof' checks – is this a major obstacle for the endogenous development of rural areas?

### GENERAL STATEMENT

Facilities and role of civil society should to be strengthened at all levels of activity.

Is something essential missing from your point of view?

## Participants in the EEF Meeting 19 December 2008, Rome

| | |
|---|---|
| Hanne Tanvig | Senior research adviser, University of Copenhagen |
| Imre Kovach | Head, Institute of Political Science, Hungarian Academy of Sciences and President of the European Society for Rural Sociology |
| Laurent van Depoele | Professor, Institute of International and European Policy, Catholic University of Leuven and former director of rural development at DG Agri |
| Ika Darnhofer | Senior researcher, Institute of Agricultural and Forestry Economics, University of Natural Resources and Applied Life Sciences Vienna |
| Ernest Reig | Professor of Economics, Valencia University |
| Elena Saraceno | Adviser, Bureau of European Policy Advisers, European Commission |
| Anamarija Slabe | Director, Institute for Sustainable Development, Ljubljana |
| Ralfs Spade | Director, State Regional Development Agency, Riga |

# References

Aarrevaara, T. 2003. Municipalities and Europeanized Networks. *Kunnallistieteellinen aikakauskirja*, 4, 298–306.

Aarrevaara, T. and Seppälä, T. 2001. Paikallishallinnon osallistumisesta Eurooppalaiseen päätöksentekoon. *Kunnallistieteellinen aikakauskirja*, 4, 389–395.

Allen, D. 2000. Cohesion and the Structural Funds, in *Policy-Making in the European Union*, edited by H. Wallace and W. Wallace. Oxford and New York: Oxford University Press.

Armstrong, H.W. 1995. The Role and Evolution of European Community Regional Policy, in *The European Union and the Regions* edited by B. Jones and M. Keating. Oxford: Clarendon Press.

Armstrong, H.W. 1996. *Crisis or Opportunity? Regional Policy and Structural Aid*. Hull: Centre for European Union Studies.

Aunapuu-Lents, V. 2013. Rural Policy in Estonia: The LEADER Approach and the Concentration of Power. *Administrative Culture*, 14 (1), 125–144.

Bache, I. 1998. *The Politics of EU Regional Policy: Multi-level Governance or Flexible Gatekeeping?* Sheffield: UACES/Sheffield Academic Press.

Bache, I. 1999. The Extended Gatekeeper: Central Government and the Implementation of EC Regional Policy in the UK. *Journal of European Public Policy*, 6(1), 28–45.

Bache, I. 2001. Regional and Structural Policies, in *Politics in the European Union*, edited by S. George and I. Bache. Oxford: Oxford University Press.

Bache, I. 2010. Partnership as an EU Policy Instrument: A Political History. *West European Politics* 33(1): 58–74.

Bache, I. and Flinders, M. 2005. *Multi-level Governance*. Oxford: Oxford University Press.

Bache, I., Bartle, I. and Flinders, M. 2012. *Unravelling Multi-level Governance: Beyond the Binary Divide*. Paper prepared for delivery at the Governance and Participation Research Workshop, Department of Politics, University of Sheffield, 6 June 2012.

Baldersheim, H. 2002. Subsidiarity at Work: Modes of Multi-Level Governance in European Countries, in *Local Government at the Millennium*, edited by J. Caulfield and H.O. Larsen. Opladen: Leske + Budrich.

Banchoff, T. and Smith, M.P. 1999. Introduction: Conceptualizing Legitimacy in a Contested Policy, in *Legitimacy and the European Union – the contested policy*, edited by T. Banchoff and M.P. Smith. London and New York: Routledge.

Beauvallet, W. and Michon, S. 2006. 'From notables to specialists: European Parliamentarians and the Construction of New Political Roles', reworked version of a paper presented at the General Conference of the *3rd European Consortium for Political Research (ECPR)*, Budapest, September 10, 2005 available at http://www.cees-europe.fr/fr/etudes/revue9/r9a6.pdf#search=%22beauvallet%2C%20w%22. (1.3.2008).

Bell, C. and Newby, H. 1971. *Community Studies*. London: Allen and Unwin.

Benz, A. 1998. Politikverflechtung ohne Politikverflechtungsfalle – Koordination und Strukturdynamik im europäischen Mehrebenensystem. *Politische Vierteljahresschrift*, 39(3), 558–589.

Benz, A. 2003. Mehrebenenverflechtung in der Europäischen Union, in *Europäische Integration*, edited by M. Jachtenfuchs and B. Kohler-Koch. Opladen: Leske+ Budrich.

Benz, A. and Eberlein, B. 1999. The Europeanization of Regional Policies: Patterns of Multi-level Governance. *Journal of European Public Policy*, 6(2), 329–48.

Bevir, M. 2010. *Democratic Governance*. Princeton: Princeton University Press.

Blank, K., Marks, G. and Hooghe, L. 1996. European Integration since the 1980s. State-centric Versus Multi-Level Governance. *Journal of Common Market Studies*, 34(3), 343–378.

Böcher, M. 2008. Regional Governance and Rural Development in Germany: the Implementation of LEADER+. *Sociologia Ruralis*, 48(4), 372–388.

Börzel, T. 1997. What's So Special About Networks? – An Exploration of the Concept and its Usefulness in Studying European Governance. *European Integration online papers*, 1(16), available online at http://eiop.or.at/eiop/pdf/1997-016.pdf.

Börzel, T. and Risse, T. 2000. *Who is Afraid of a European Federation? How to Constitutionalise a Multi-Level Governance System*, Harvard Law School: Jean Monnet Working Paper No. 7/00, Symposium: Responses to Joschka Fischer also published in Christian Joerges, Yves Mény and Joseph H.H. Weiler (eds) *What kind of Constitution for What Kind of Polity? – Responses to Joschka Fischer.* Florence: Robert Schuman Centre for Advanced Studies at the EUI.

Börzel, T. and Risse, T. 2010. Governance without a State: Can it Work? *Regulation & Governance*, 4(2), 113–134.

Bourdieu, P. 2005a. *Die verborgenen Mechanismen der Macht.* Hamburg: VSA-Verlag.

Bourdieu, P. 2005b. Politik, Bildung und Sprache, in *Die verborgenen Mechanismen der Macht*, by P. Bourdieu. Hamburg: VSA-Verlag.

Bourdieu, P. 2005c. Die Könige sind nackt, in *Die verborgenen Mechanismen der Macht*, by P. Bourdieu. Hamburg: VSA-Verlag.

Bourdieu, P. 2005d. Ökonomisches Kapital – Kulturelles Kapital – Soziales Kapital, in *Die verborgenen Mechanismen der Macht*, by P. Bourdieu. Hamburg: VSA-Verlag.

Bourdieu, P. 2006. *The Logic of Praxis*. Stanford: Stanford University Press.

Bourdieu, P. and Wacquant, L. 1992. *An Invitation to Reflexive Sociology.* Chicago and London: University of Chicago Press.

Bruckmeier, K. 2000. LEADER in Germany and the Discourse of Autonomous Regional Development. *Sociologia Ruralis*, 40(2), 219–227.

Brugmans, H. 1948. *Fundamentals of European Federalism.* London: British Section of the European Union of Federalists.

Brugmans, H. 1969. *La Pensée Politique du Fédéralisme.* Leyde: Sijthoff.

Brunori, G., Jiggins, J., Gallardo, R. and Schmidt, O. 2008. *The 2nd SCAR Foresight Exercise – New challenges for agricultural research: climate change, food security, rural development, agricultural knowledge systems*, available online at http://ec.europa.eu/research/agriculture/scar/pdf/scar_2nd_ foresight_exercise_en.pdf (16.6.2009).

Buller, H. 2000. Re-creating rural territories: LEADER in France. *Sociologia Ruralis*, 40(2), 190–199.

Burgess, M. 2004. Federalism, in *European Integration Theory*, edited by A. Wiener and T. Diez. Oxford: Oxford University Press.

Bursig, B. 1990. *Die Regionalpolitik der Europäischen Gemeinschaft.* Frankfurt am Main: Peter Lang.

Carter, C. and Smith, A. 2008. Revitalizing Public Policy Approaches to the EU: 'Territorial Institutionalism', Fisheries and Wine. *Journal of European Public Policy*, 15(2), 263–281.

Checkel, J. 1998. The Constructivist Turn in International Relations Theory. *World Politics*, 50(2), 324–348.

Checkel, J. 2001a. From Meta- to Substantive Theory? Social Constructivism and the Study of Europe. *European Union Politics*, 2(2), 219–226.

Checkel, J. 2001b. Constructivism and Integration Theory: Crash Landing or Safe Arrival? *European Union Politics*, 2(2), 240–249.

Checkel, J. 2006. Constructivist Approaches to European Integration. *Arena Working Paper No. 6, 2006.* Available online at www.arena.uio.no (7.3.2013).

Christiansen, T., Jørgensen, K.E. and Wiener, A. 1999. The Social Construction of Europe. *Journal of European Public Policy*, 6(4), 528–544.

Christopoulos, S., Horvath, B and Kull, M. 2012. Advancing the Governance of Cross-Sectoral Policies for Sustainable Development: A Metagovernance Perspective. *Public Administration and Development*, 32(2), 305–323.

Chryssochoou, D.N. 2001. *Theorizing European Integration.* London: Sage.

Csurgó, B., Kovách, I. and Kučerová, E. 2008. Knowledge, Power and Sustainability in Contemporary Rural Europe. *Sociologia Ruralis*, 48(3), 292–312.

Curtin, C., Haase, T. and Tovey, T. 1997. *Poverty in Rural Ireland.* Dublin: Oak Tree Press.

Deutsch, K.W. 1953. *Nationalism and Social Communication an Inquiry into the Foundations of Nationality.* Cambridge: MIT Press.

Deutsch, Karl W. 1972. Attaining and Maintaining Integration, in *European Integration*, edited by M. Hodges. Harmondsworth: Penguin Books.

Diez, T. and Wiener, A. 2004. Introducing the Mosaic of Integration Theory, in *European Integration Theory*, edited by A. Wiener and T. Diez. Oxford: Oxford University Press.

Drechsler, W. 2004. Governance, Good Governance, and Government: The Case for Estonian Administrative Capacity. *TRAMES*, 8(4), 388–396.

Drechsler, W. 2013. Coercive Municipal Amalgamation Today – With Illustrations from Estonia. *Administrative Culture*, 14(1), 158–165.

Eberlein, B. and Grande, E. 2005. Beyond Delegation: Transnational Regulatory Regimes and the EU Regulatory State. *Journal of European Public Policy*, 12(1), 89–112.

Enderlein, H., Wälti, S. and Zürn, M. (eds) 2010. *Handbook on Multi-Level Governance*. Cheltenham: Edward Elgar.

Engberg, L. and Larsen, J. 2010. Context-Oriented Meta-Governance in Danish Urban Regeneration. *Planning Theory & Practice*, 11(4), 549–571.

Fairbrass, J. and Jordan, A. 2005. Multi-level Governance and Environmental Policy, in *Multi-level Governance*, edited by I. Bache and M. Flinders. Oxford: Oxford University Press.

Fischer, F. 2007. Policy Analysis in Critical Perspective: The Epistemics of Discursive Practices. *Critical Policy Analysis*, 1(1), 97–109.

Friedrich, C.J. 1964. Preface, in *Politica methodice digesta, atque exemplis sacris et profanis illustrate*, by J. Althusius. Boston: Beacon Press. Also available at www.constitution.org/alth/alth_pr0.htm.

Georgakakis, D. and de Lassalle, M. 2008. *La "nouvelle gouvernance européenne": Genèses et usages politiques d'un livre blanc*. Strasbourg: Presses Universitaires de Strasbourg.

George, S. and Bache, I. (eds) 2001. *Politics in the European Union*. Oxford and New York: Oxford University Press.

Giddens, A. 1991. *Modernity and Self-Identity*. Cambridge: Polity Press.

Glasbergen P. 2011. Mechanisms of Private Meta-governance: An Analysis of Global Private Governance for Sustainable Development. *International Journal of Strategic Business Alliances*, 2(3), 189–206.

Grande, E. 2000. Multi-Level Governance: Institutionelle Besonderheiten und Funktionsbedingungen des europäischen Mehrebenensystems, in *Wie problemlösungsfähig ist die EU?*, edited by E. Grande and M. Jachtenfuchs. Baden-Baden: Nomos.

Grande, E. and Jachtenfuchs, M. (eds) 2000. *Wie problemlösungsfähig ist die EU?* Baden-Baden: Nomos.

Grande, E. and Pauly, L.W. (eds) 2005. *Complex Sovereignty: Reconstituting Political Authority in the Twenty-First Century*. Toronto: University of Toronto Press.

Guiraudon, V. and Favell, A. 2007. The Sociology of European Integration, paper presented at the EUSA Tenth Biennial International Conference, Montreal, 17–19 May, 2007 available at http://www.unc.edu/euce/eusa2007/papers/guiraudon-v-09a.pdf (1.11.2011).

Guiraudon, V. and Favell, A. (eds) 2011a. *Sociology of the European Union.* Basingstoke: Palgrave.

Guiraudon, V. and Favell, A. 2011b. Sociology of the European Union: An Introduction, in *Sociology of the European Union*, edited by V. Guiraudon and A. Favell. Basingstoke: Palgrave.

Guzzini, S. 2005. The Concept of Power: a Constructivist Analysis. *Millennium: Journal of International Studies*, 33(3), 495–521.

Haas, E.B. 1964. *Beyond the Nation State – Functionalism and International Organization.* Stanford: Stanford University Press.

Haas, E.B. 1966. International Integration: The European and the Universal Process, in *European Integration*, edited by M. Hodges. Harmondsworth: Penguin Books.

Haas, E.B. 2004. *The Uniting of Europe – Political, Social, and Economic Forces 1950–1957.* Notre Dame: University of Notre Dame Press.

Habermas, J. 1989. Towards a Communication-Concept of Rational Collective Will-Formation. A Thought-Experiment. *Ratio Juris*, 2(2), 144–154.

Haveri, A. 2005. Monitasohallinnankaan ei tarvitsisi olla kaaosta. *Kunnallistieteellinen aikakauskirja* 1, 5–7.

Heinelt, H. 1998. Regionale Strukturpolitik im europäischen Mehrebenensystem, in *Gestaltung regionaler Politik*, edited by A. Benz and E. Holtmann. Opladen: Leske + Budrich.

Héraud, G. 1968. *Les Principes du Fédéralisme et la Fédération Européenne.* Paris: Presses d'Europe.

Héritier, A. 1999. Elements of Democratic Legitimation in Europe: An Alternative Perspective. *Journal of European Public Policy*, 6(2), 269–282.

High, C. and Nemes, G. 2007. Social Learning in LEADER: Exogenous, Endogenous and Hybrid Evaluation in Rural Development. *Sociologia Ruralis*, 47(2), 103–119.

Hirst, P. 2000. Democracy and Governance, in *Debating Governance*, edited by J. Pierre. Oxford: Oxford University Press.

Hix, S. 1998. The Study of the European Union II: The 'New Governance' agenda and its Rival. *Journal of European Public Policy*, 5(1), 38–65.

Hoffmann, S. 1966. Obstinate or Obsolete? The Fate of the Nation-State and the Case of Western Europe. *Daedalus*, 95(3), 862–915.

Hooghe, L. and Marks, G. 2001. *Multi-Level Governance and European Integration.* Oxford: Rowman & Littlefield Publishers.

Hooghe, L. and Marks, G. 2003. Unraveling the Central State, But How? – Types of Multi-Level Governance. *American Political Science Review*, 97(2), 233–243.

Hurrelmann, A. 2006. The Policy Framework of Agricultural Sustainability in the EU. European Commission, DG for Agriculture and Rural Development. Presentation available online at http://www.forescene.net/Resources/Florence/ Forescene_Florence_Hurrelmann_19Oct06.pdf (3.6.2013).

Jachtenfuchs, M. 2000. Die Problemlösungsfähigkeit der EU: Begriffe, Befunde, Erklärungen, in *Wie problemlösungsfähig ist die EU?*, edited by E. Grande and M.Jachtenfuchs. Baden-Baden: Nomos.

Jachtenfuchs, M. and Kohler-Koch, B. (eds) 1996a. *Europäische Integration.* Opladen: Leske + Budrich.

Jachtenfuchs, M. and Kohler-Koch, B. 1996b. Regieren in der Europäischen Union – Fragestellungen für eine interdisziplinäre Europaforschung. *Politische Vierteljahresschrift*, 37(3), 537–556.

Jachtenfuchs, M. and Kohler-Koch, B. (eds) 2003a. *Europäische Integration.* Opladen: Leske + Budrich.

Jachtenfuchs, M. and Kohler-Koch, B. 2003b. Regieren und Institutionenbildung, in *Europäische Integration*, edited by M. Jachtenfuchs and B. Kohler-Koch. Opladen: Leske+ Budrich.

Jessop, B. 2003. *Governance, Governance Failure, and Metagovernance*, paper presented at an international seminar held at the Università della Calabria, 21–23 Nov. 2003.

Jessop, B. 2005. Multi-level Governance and Multi-level Metagovernance, in *Multi-level Governance*, edited by I. Bache and M. Flinders. Oxford: Oxford University Press.

Joerges, C., Mény, Y. and Weiler, J. 2000. *What kind of Constitution for What Kind of Polity? – Responses to Joschka Fischer.* Florence: Robert Schuman Centre for Advanced Studies at the EUI.

John, P. 2001. *Local Governance in Western Europe.* London: Sage Publications.

Jordan, A. 2001. The European Union: An Evolving System of Multi-level Governance … or Government. *Policy & Politics*, 29(23), 193–208.

Jordan, A. 2008. Environmental Policy, in *The Europeanization of British Politics*, edited by I. Bache and A. Jordan. Basingstoke: Palgrave.

Kauppi, N. 2002. Elements for a Structural Constructivist Theory of Politics and of European Integration. *Center for European Studies Working Paper Series #104*, Center for European Studies at Harvard University. Available at http://www.people.fas.harvard.edu/~ces/publications/docs/pdfs/Kauppi104.pdf.

Kauppi, N. 2003. Bourdieu's Political Sociology and the Politics of European Integration. *Theory and Society*, 32, 775–789.

Kauppi, N. 2005. *Democracy, Social Resources and Political Power in the European Union.* Manchester: Manchester University Press.

Kauppi, N. 2011. EU Politics, in *Sociology of the European Union*, edited by A. Favell and V. Guiraudon. Basingstoke: Palgrave.

Keating, M.1995. Europeanism and Regionalism, in *The European Union and the Regions*, edited by B. Jones and M. Keating. Oxford: Clarendon Press.

Kettunen, P. and Kull, M. 2009. Governing Europe: The Status and Networking Strategies of Finnish, Estonian and German Subnational Offices in Brussels. *Regional and Federal Studies*, 19(1), 117 – 142.

Kiviniemi, M., Mustakangas, E. and Vihinen, H. 2003. *Partnership at municipal level in rural policy implementation.* Available online at http://www.mtt.fi/met/pdf/met29.pdf (1.2.2008).

Kohler-Koch, B. (ed.) 2003. *Linking EU and National Governance.* Oxford: Oxford University Press.

Kohler-Koch, B. and Rittberger, B. 2006. Review Article: The 'Governance Turn' in EU Studies. *Journal of Common Market Studies*, 44, 27–49.

Kooiman, J. 1993. *Modern Governance*. London: Sage Publications.

Kooiman, J. and Jentoft, S. 2009. Meta-Governance: Values, Norms and Principles, and the Making of Hard Choices. *Public Administration*, 87 (4), 816–836.

Koslowski, R. 1999. A Constructivist Approach to Understanding the European Union as a Federal Polity. *Journal of European Public Policy*, 6(4), 561–578.

Kovách, I. 2000. LEADER, a New Social Order, and the Central- and East-European Countries. *Sociologia Ruralis*, 40(2), 181–189.

Kovách, I. and Kučerová, E. 2006. The Project Class in Central Europe: The Czech and Hungarian Cases. *Sociologia Ruralis*, 46(1), 3–21.

Kovách, I. and Kučerová, E. 2009. The Social Context of Project Proliferation – The Rise of a Project Class. *Journal of Environmental Policy & Planning*, 11(3), 203–221.

Kull, M. 2008. EU Multi-Level Governance in the Making: The Community Initiative Leader+ in Finland and Germany. *Acta Politica*, 32, Department of Political Science, University of Helsinki.

Kull, M. 2009. Local and Regional Governance in Finland. A Study on Institutionalisation, Transformation and Europeanization. *Administrative Culture*, 10, 22–39.

Kull, M. and Kettunen, P. 2013. Local Governance, Decentralization and Participation: Meta-Governance Perspectives. *Administrative Culture*, 14(1), 4–10.

Lang, S. 2010. *Transformations in European R&D and Regional Policies within the Multi-Level Governance Framework: The Changing Nature of the European Union Ten Years after the Launch of the Lisbon Strategy*. Tallinn University of Technology Doctoral Theses Series I: Social Sciences, No. 13. Tallinn: TUT Press.

Larsson, T. 2000. The Internal Enlargement of the European Union and the Surplus of the Intermediate Level of Government. *Eipascope*, 2, 1–9.

Lenschow, A. 2005. Europeanization of Public Policy, in *European Union. Power and Policy-making*, edited by J. Richardson. London: Routledge.

Lorvi, K. 2013. Unpacking Administrative Capacity for the Management of the Structural Funds in Small and Large Municipalities: The Estonian Case. *Administrative Culture*, 14(1), 98–124.

Majone, G. 1994. The Rise of the Regulatory State in Europe. *West European Politics*, 17(3), 77–101.

Majone, G. 1996. The European Community as a Regulatory State. *Collected courses of the Academy of European Law*. Dordrecht: Nijhoff.

Majone, G. 1998. Europe's 'Democratic Deficit': The Question of Standards. *European Law Journal*, 4, 5–28.

March, J.G. and Olson, J.P. 1995. *Democratic Governance*. New York: Free Press.

Marks, G. 1993. Structural Policy and Multilevel Governance in the EC, in *The State of the European Community*, edited by A. Cafruny and G. Rosenthal. Boulder: Lynne Rienner.

Marks, G. 1996. Politikmuster und Einflußlogik in der Strukturpolitik, in *Europäische Integration*, edited by B. Kohler-Koch and M. Jachtenfuchs. Opladen: Leske + Budrich.

Mérand, F. 2011. EU Policies, in *Sociology of the European Union*, edited by A. Favell and V. Guiraudon. Basingstoke: Palgrave.

Meuleman L. 2010. The Cultural Dimension of Metagovernance: Why Governance Doctrines May Fail. *Public Organization Review*, 10(1), 49–70.

Meuleman, L. 2013. Metagovernance as catalyst for sustainable change in rural areas. *Rural resilience and vulnerability: the rural as locus of solidarity and conflict in times of crisis*, XXV Congress of the European Society for Rural Sociology, eProceedings, 381–382.

Milone, P. and Ventura, F. (eds.) 2010. *Networking the Rural – The future of green regions in Europe*. Assen: Van Gorcum Press.

Milward, A.S. and Sørensen, V. 1994. Interdependence or Integration? A National Choice, in *The Frontier of National Sovereignty – History and Theory 1945–1992*, edited by A. Milward, F.M.B. Lynch, F. Romero, R. Ranieri and V. Sørensen. London and New York: Routledge.

Mitrany, D. 1975. The Prospect of Integration: Federal or Functional, in *Functionalism – Theory and Practice in International Relations*, edited by A. Groom and P. Taylor. London: University of London Press.

Moravcsik, A. 1991. Negotiating the Single European Act: National Interests and Conventional Statecraft in the European Community. *International Organization*, 45(1), 19–56.

Moravcsik, A. 1993. Preferences and Power in the European Community: A Liberal Intergovernmentalist Approach. *Journal of Common Market Studies*, 31(4), 473–524.

Moravcsik, A. 1998. *The Choice for Europe: Social Purpose and State Power from Messina to Maastricht*. Ithaca: Cornell University Press.

OECD. 2006. *The New Rural Paradigm – Policies and Governance*. Paris: OECD Rural Policy Reviews.

OECD. 2010. *Finland – Working Together to Sustain Success*. Paris: OECD Public Governance Reviews.

Peters, B.G. 1997. Escaping the Joint-Decision Trap: Repetition and Sectoral Politics in the European Union. *West European Politics*, 20(2), 22–36.

Peters, B.G. 2000. Governance and Comparative Politics, in *Debating Governance*, edited by J. Pierre. Oxford: Oxford University Press.

Peters, B.G. and Pierre J. 1998. Governance without Government? Rethinking Public Administration. *Journal of Public Administration Research and Theory*, 8(2), 223–243.

Peters, B.G. and Pierre, J. 2001. Developments in intergovernmental Relations: Towards Multi-Level Governance. *Policy and Politics*, 29(2), 131–135.

Piattoni, S. 2009. Multi-level Governance: A Historical and Conceptual Analysis. *Journal of European Integration*, 11(2), 163–80.

Pierre, J. (ed.) 2000a. *Debating Governance*. Oxford: Oxford University Press.

Pierre, J. 2000b. Conclusions: Governance beyond State Strength, in *Debating Governance*, edited by J. Pierre. Oxford: Oxford University Press.

Pitschas, R. 1994. *Europäische Integration als Netzwerkkoordination komplexer Staatsaufgaben*. Baden-Baden: Nomos.

Ploeg, J.D. van der, Broekhuizen, R. van, Brunori, G., Sonnino, R., Knickel, K., Tisenkopfs, T. and Oostindie, H. 2008. Towards a Framework for Understanding Regional Rural Development, in *Unfolding Webs – The dynamics of regional rural development* edited by J.D. van der Ploeg and T. Marsden. Assen: Royal van Gorcum.

Pollitt, C. and Bouckaert, G. 2000. *Public Management Reform: A Comparative Analysis*. Oxford: Oxford University Press.

Pollitt, C. and Bouckaert, G. 2004. *Public Management Reform: A Comparative Analysis* (2nd edition). Oxford: Oxford University Press.

Pollitt, C. and Bouckaert, G. 2011. *Public Management Reform: A Comparative Analysis – New Public Management, Governance, and the Neo-Weberian State* (3rd edition). Oxford: Oxford University Press.

Remmers, G. 1996. Hitting a Moving Target: Endogenous development in marginal European areas. *Gatekeeper Series No. 63*. Available online at http://pubs.iied.org/pdfs/6111IIED.pdf (5.6.2013).

Rhodes, R. 1996. The New Governance: Governing without Government. *Political Studies*, 44, 652–667.

Rhodes, R. 2000. Governance and Public Administration, in *Debating Governance*, edited by J. Pierre. Oxford: Oxford University Press.

Risse, T. 2009. Social Constructivism and European Integration, in *European Integration Theory*, edited by A. Wiener and T. Diez. Oxford: Oxford University Press.

Rosamond, B. 2000. *Theories of European Integration*. Basingstoke: Palgrave.

Rosenau, J. 1992. Governance, Order, and Change in World Politics, in *Governance without Government: Order and Change in World Politics*, edited by J. Rosenau and E.-O. Czempiel. Cambridge: Cambridge University Press.

Rosenau, J. and Czempiel, E.-O. (eds) 1992. *Governance without Government: Order and Change in World Politics*. Cambridge: Cambridge University Press.

Rural Policy Committee. 2007. *A Viable Countryside – Ministries' Responsibilities and Regional Development – Special Rural Policy Programme 2007–2010*. Available online at http://www.maaseutupolitiikka.fi/index.phtml?s=211 (4.6.2013).

Ryynänen, A. 2003. Modification of Finnish Local Government – Between Continuity and Change. *Finnish Local Government Studies*, 4, 255–266.

Sbragia, A. 2000. The European Union as Coxswain: Governance by Steering, in *Debating Governance*, edited by J. Pierre. Oxford: Oxford University Press.

Scharpf, F.W. 1995. Mehrebenenpolitik im vollendeten Binnenmarkt, in *Jahrbuch zur Staats- und Verwaltungswissenschaft Band 8*, edited by T. Ellwein, D. Grimme, J. Hesse and G. Schuppert. Baden-Baden: Nomos.

Scharpf, F.W. 1997. *Games Real Actors Play. Actor – Centred Institutionalism.* Boulder, Oxford: Westview Press.

Scharpf, F., Reissert, B. and Schnabel, F. 1976. *Politikverflechtung. Theorie und Empirie des kooperativen Föderalismus in der Bundesrepublik.* Kronberg: Scriptor.

Schmid, J. 1987. Wo schnappt die Politikverflechtungsfalle eigentlich zu? *Politische Vierteljahresschrift*, 28(4), 446–452.

Schmidt, V. 2008. Discursive Institutionalism: The Explanatory Power of Ideas and Discourse. *Annual Review of Political Science*, 11, 303–326.

Schmitter, P.C. 2004. Neo-Neofunctionalism, in *European Integration Theory*, edited by A. Wiener and T. Diez. Oxford: Oxford University Press.

Schneider, V. 2004. State Theory, Governance and the Logic of Regulation and Administrative Control, in *Governance in Europe*, edited by A. Warntjen and A. Wonka. Baden-Baden: Nomos.

Shucksmith, M. 2000. Endogenous Development, Social Capital and Social Inclusion: Perspectives from LEADER in the UK. *Sociologia Ruralis*, 40(2), 208–218.

Smith, S. 1999. Social Constructivisms and European Studies: A Reflectivist Critique. *Journal of European Public Policy*, 6(4), 682–691.

Spinelli, A., Rossi, E. and Colorni, E. 1941. *Towards a free and united Europe – a draft manifesto.* Available at http://www.federalunion.org.uk/archives/ventotene.shtml 1.2.2008).

Spinelli, A. 1957. The Growth of the European Movement since the Second World War, in *European Integration*, edited by M. Hodges. Harmondsworth: Penguin Books.

Ståhlberg, K. 1999. Changing Finnish Local Government. *Finnish Local Government Studies*, 3, 203–204.

Taylor, M. 1996. Good Government: On Hierarchy, Social Capital and the Limitations of Rational Choice Theory. *Journal of Political Philosophy*, 4(1), 1–28.

Thuesen, A. A. 2010. Is LEADER Elitist or Inclusive? Composition of Danish LAG Boards in the 2007–2013 Rural Development and Fisheries Programmes. *Sociologia Ruralis*, 50(1), 31–45.

Tömmel, I. 1992. System-Entwicklung und Politikgestaltung in der Europäischen Gemeinschaft am Beispiel der Regionalpolitik. *Politische Vierteljahresschrift, Sonderheft 1992*, 185–208.

Uusitalo, E. 2004. Future Perspectives for Finnish National Rural Policy. *Finnish Journal of Rural Research and Policy, English Supplement*, 5–13.

Uusitalo, E. 2009. *Maaseutu – väliinputoajasta vastuunkantajaksi. Maaseutupolitiikan itsenäistyminen alue- ja maatalouspolitiikan puristuksessa.* Helsingin Yliopisto, Ruralia-instituutin julkaisuja 17.

Voutilainen O. 2012. Relationship between Agricultural and Rural Development within the Context of the European Union's Common Agricultural Policy: the Case of Finland. Doctoral dissertation. *MTT Agrifood Research Finland, MTT Science 19.* Available online at http://www.mtt.fi/mtttiede/pdf/mtttiede19.pdf. (1.3.2013).

Wæver, O. 2009. Discursive Approaches, in *European Integration Theory*, edited by A. Wiener and T. Diez. Oxford: Oxford University Press.

Wallace, H., Caporaso, J.A., Scharpf, F.W. and Moravscik, A. 1999. Review section symposium: The choice for Europe: Social purpose and state power from Messina to Maastricht. *Journal of European Public Policy*, 6(1), 155–177.

Wallace, H., Wallace, W. and Pollack, M. (eds) 2005. *Policy-Making in the European Union*, Oxford: Oxford University Press.

Whitehead, M. 2003. 'In the shadow of hierarchy': Meta-governance, Policy Reform and Urban Regeneration in the West Midlands. *Area*, 35(1): 6–14.

Wiener, A. and Diez, T. (eds) 2004. *European Integration Theory.* Oxford: Oxford University Press.

Wiener, A. and Diez, T. (eds) 2009. *European Integration Theory* (2nd edition). Oxford: Oxford University Press.

*Official Documents*

Commission of the European Communities 2005. Commission Staff Working Document – Annex to the Proposal for a Council Decision on Community strategic guidelines for Rural Development, COM(2005) 304 final}, SEC(2005) 914, available at http://europa.eu.int/comm/agriculture/capreform/rdguidelines/impact_en.pdf (1.2.2008).

Committee of the Regions 2009. The Committee of the Regions' White Paper on Multilevel Governance. CdR 89/2009 fin FR/EXT/RS/GW/ym/ms (1.11.2009).

Council of the European Union 2005. Press release 9991/05 (Presse 143) on the 2669th Council meeting 'Agriculture and Fisheries'.

Council Regulation (E.E.C.) No 4255/88.

European Commission 1988. *The future of rural society – (COM (88) 501 final.* Available at http://ec.europa.eu/agriculture/cap-history/crisis-years-1980s/com88–501_en.pdf. (15.1.2014).

European Commission 1996. *Structural Funds and Cohesion Fund 1994–99.* Luxembourg: Office for Official Publication of the European Communities.

European Commission 1997. *The Impact of Structural Policies on Economic and Social Cohesion in the Union*", Luxembourg: Office for Official Publications of the European Communities.

European Commission 2001. European Governance – A White Paper, available at http://europa.eu.int/eur-lex/en/com/cnc/2001/com2001_0428en01.pdf (1.2.2008).

European Commission 2003. Report from the Commission on European governance, available at http://europa.eu.int/comm/governance/docs/comm_rapport_en.pdf (1.2.2008).

European Commission/Leader+ Observatory Contact Point 2005a. Country data sheet Finland, available at http://ec.europa.eu/agriculture/rur/leaderplus/pdf/country_sheets/FN.pdf (1.2.2008).

European Commission/Leader+ Observatory Contact Point 2005b. Country data sheet Germany, available at http://ec.europa.eu/agriculture/rur/leaderplus/pdf/country_sheets/GER.pdf (1.2.2008).

Finnish Regional Development Act (602/2002), published under http://www.finlex.fi/pdf/saadkaan/E0020602.PDF.

KOM 2001. Eurooppalainen Hallintotapa-Valkoinen Kirja, available at http://europa.eu.int/eur-lex/fi/com/cnc/2001/com2001_0428fi01.pdf (1.2.2008).

Land Sachsen-Anhalt. Programm zur Gemeinschaftsinitiative LEADER+, available at http://www.sachsen-anhalt.de/pdf/pdf25375.pdf (8.2.2006).

Land Sachsen-Anhalt 1999. Leitlinie für eine Umsetzung gebietsspezifischer Projekte von lokaler Dimension orientierte Landesinitiative LOCALE" available at http://www1.europa.sachsen-anhalt.de/vademecum/Entscheidungen_Durchfuehrungsregeln/LI/L_LI_Locale.pdf. (8.2.2006)

LEADER+ Programme for Finland, available at http://www.mmm.fi/english/agriculture/Leader_Englanti_korj.pdf (1.2.2008).

Leader+ in Niedersachsen, available at http://www1.ml.niedersachsen.de/leaderplus/leader-plus.pdf (1.2.2008).

Ministry of Agriculture and Forestry Finland 2002. Regional Rural Development Programme
for areas outside Objective 1 for 2000 – 2006. Available online at http://www.mmm.fi/julkaisut/julkaisusarja/MMMjulkaisu2001_11b.pdf (16.3.06).

The Rural Policy Committee 2009. *Countryside for Vigorous Finland – Government Report to Parliament on Rural Policy, Publications of the Rural Policy Committee 10/2009.*

Special LEADER Symposium Towards a new Initiative for rural development: 800 leaders give their views, available at http://europa.eu.int/comm/archives/leader2/rural-en/biblio/coll/art04.htm (1.2.2008).

Suomen LEADER+ Ohjelman Väliarviointoraportti 2003 (Mid-term evaluation of the Finnish LEADER+ Programme 2003), available at http://wwwb.mmm.fi/julkaisut/julkaisusarja/MMMjulkaisu2004_2.pdf#search=%22Suomen%20LEADER%2B%22 (13.2.2008).

*Treaty establishing a Constitution for Europe*, available online at http://europa.eu.int/constitution/download/part_I_EN.pdf (1.2.2008).

'Report of the Finnish government on the Commission's White Paper', adopted in the Cabinet Committee for EU Affairs on 22 March 2002.

*Position Papers, Press Reports and Press Releases*

Association of Finnish Local and Regional Authorities: 'The Position of the Association of Finnish Local and Regional Authorities on the Reform of European Governance', available at http://europa.eu.int/comm/governance/contrib_aflra_en.pdf (1.2.2008).

Eurocities: 'Eurocities Response to the Commission's White Paper on European Governance', available at http://europa.eu.int/comm/governance/contrib_eurocities_en.pdf (1.2.2008).

German Association of Cities and Towns: 'Statement on the White Paper on *"European Governance"* by the German Association of Cities and Towns', available at http://europa.eu.int/comm/governance/contrib_dstellungnahme_en.pdf (1.2.2008).

German Association of Towns and Municipalities (DStGB): 'Position paper of the German Association of Towns and Municipalities (DStGB) on the European Commission's White Paper on *"European Governance"'*, available at http://www.dstgb.de/index_inhalt/homepage/positionspapiere/new_governance/english/positiongovernance_en1.pdf (1.2.2008).

Jahresbericht 2004 der LAG Entwicklungsgruppe Burgwald.

Unpublished draft position paper *'Die Gemeinsame Agrarpolitik der europäischen Union'* by a work group consisting of actors from several *Landkreise, Bezierksregierungen* and regional chambers of agriculture in North-Western Niedersachsen written in 2004.

*Press Articles*

'LEADER-Macher suchen neuen Schwung', published on 30.5.05 in *Ostee-Zeitung*. The article is available at www.leaderplus-ruegen.de/artikel/article.php?article_file=111744160.txt&printview=1 (7.6.05).

*Other Internet Sources*

Homepage of the European Commission's DG Agriculture and Rural Development, available at http://ec.europa.eu/agriculture/rur/leaderplus/intro_en.htm.

Homepage of the European Commission's DG Regio, available at http://ec.europa.eu/regional_policy/reg_prog/po/prog_396.htm.

Homepage of the European Commission's DG Regio, available at http://ec.europa.eu/regional_policy/archive/atlas/factsheets/pdf/fact_eu25_en.pdf.

Homepage of the European Union's Summaries of Legislation, available at http://europa.eu/legislation_summaries/regional_policy/provisions_and_instruments/l60014_en.htm.

Homepage of the EQUAL community initiative available at http://ec.europa.eu/employment_social/equal/index_en.cfm.

Homepage of the Government Offices of the British Regions, available at http://www.gos.gov.uk/european/?a=42496.

Le Grand Dictionnaire, available at http://www.granddictionnaire.com.

*Oxford English Dictionary*, available online at http://www.oed.com/.

# Index

For Product Safety Concerns and Information please contact our EU
representative GPSR@taylorandfrancis.com Taylor & Francis Verlag GmbH,
Kaufingerstraße 24, 80331 München, Germany


Printed and bound by CPI Group (UK) Ltd, Croydon, CR0 4YY
08/05/2025
01864345-0001